Building Effective Employment Programs
for Unemployed Youth in the
Middle East and North Africa

DIRECTIONS IN DEVELOPMENT
Human Development

Building Effective Employment Programs for Unemployed Youth in the Middle East and North Africa

Diego F. Angel-Urdinola, Arvo Kuddo, and Amina Semlali, Editors

In collaboration with
Saad Belghazi, Anne Hilger, Rene Leon-Solano, May Wazzan, and Diane Zovighian

THE WORLD BANK
Washington, D.C.

ISBN (paper): 978-0-8213-9904-0
ISBN (electronic): 978-0-8213-9905-7
DOI: 10.1596/978-0-8213-9904-0

Cover photos: Arne Hoel / World Bank. Used by permission. Further permission required for reuse.

Cover design: Naylor Design.

Library of Congress Cataloging-in-Publication Data

Angel-Urdinola, Diego F.
    Building effective employment programs for unemployed youth in the Middle East and North Africa / Diego F. Angel-Urdinola, Arvo Kuddo and Amina Semlali; in collaboration with Rene Leon-Solano, Anne Hilger, May Wazzan, Diane Zovighian, and Saad Belghazi.
        pages cm. — (Directions in development)
    Includes bibliographical references.
    ISBN 978-0-8213-9904-0 (alk. paper) — ISBN 978-0-8213-9905-7
    1. Employment agencies—Middle East. 2. Employment agencies—Africa, North. 3. Unemployed youth—Middle East. 4. Unemployed youth—Africa, North. I. Kuddo, Arvo, 1954- II. Semlali, Amina. III. World Bank. IV. Title.
    HD5961.9.A6A54 2013
    362.71—dc23   2013009648

Contents

Figures

Map

Tables

Foreword

There is considerable movement in labor markets in developing countries. People of working age transit continuously from school to work, into and out of the labor force, between jobs, or into and out of unemployment or disability. These critical transitions largely determine individuals' income flows and labor productivity during their lives. Unfortunately, market and government failures can negatively affect these transitions, hindering workers' ability to improve their employment outcomes. Lack of information about job opportunities, for instance, can affect transitions into wage employment, as can inadequate skills. Barriers to entry, a lack of contacts, and insufficient credit can preclude transitions into self-employment or small-scale entrepreneurship.

Active Labor Market Programs (ALMPs) can be an effective tool to facilitate labor market transitions and improve social welfare and productivity growth. The problem is that in developing countries, these programs have generally had a dismal performance. This does not mean that these services are not needed or are a bad idea, but simply that there have been significant problems in terms of design and implementation. These problems begin with inappropriate governance and accountability arrangements that reduce incentives to respond to the needs of job seekers and employers.

In the wake of the Arab Spring, countries of the Middle East and North Africa face the urgent need to address joblessness among youth and other labor market challenges. ALMPs are already widely used in the region, but much needs to be done to overcome obstacles to their effectiveness.

For the first time, this book offers a comprehensive look at the problems facing publicly provided ALMPs in the Middle East and North Africa and proposes a series of reforms that could improve their performance. These reforms are likely to be relevant for countries in other regions as well. They are very welcome at a time when governments throughout the developing world are compelled to improve labor market opportunities for their populations, particularly for youth.

David Robalino
Lead Economist, Human Development Network, The World Bank
Leader of the Labor and Youth Team at the World Bank and Co-director of the Employment and Development program at the Institute for the Study of Labor (IZA), Bonn

Preface

Coping with high unemployment is among the main challenges that countries in the Middle East and North Africa (MENA) region will face in the years to come. In the aftermath of the Arab Spring, attaining more and better jobs in the region has become a cornerstone not only for economic development but also for social cohesion.

Although unemployment rates in MENA are high and rising, employers in the region are still struggling to fill vacancies due to a shortage of candidates with the relevant qualifications and skills. A combination of inadequate skills and lack of information about existing vacancies is contributing to critical labor market failures that restrain employment mobility. This is confirmed by available data from employment agencies throughout the region suggesting that thousands of vacancies are not being filled, despite the existence of many thousands of individuals who are both willing and able to work. In this context, effective Active Labor Market Programs (ALMPs) could be a relevant policy instrument to enhance labor mobility and to match job seekers with available vacancies. Surely, employment programs cannot substitute for private-led employment creation nor address the structural constraints of the region's labor market, such as stagnant labor demand, low productivity, low competitiveness, and high informality. But these programs, if well designed and effectively delivered, could be a mechanism for relieving high unemployment rates while providing the population with some immediate and visible results.

With high unemployment among youth, ALMPs in the region have been widely used to target high-skilled unemployed individuals and, notably, university graduates who are first-time job seekers. However, employment agencies in the region face many constraints that undermine their capacity to provide effective programs and services, namely weak administrative capacity, system fragmentation, lack of governance and accountability, regulation bottlenecks, and flaws in program design.

Against this backdrop, this study has two main objectives. First, it surveys international best practices for the delivery of employment programs and reviews the provision of these services in a select group of countries in the MENA region, with a focus on public provision through existing public employment agencies. Second, it proposes a road map for reform based on the development of solid partnerships between public agencies, public providers, and employers for the design and implementation of flexible employment programs that respond to the needs of the labor market.

This study makes valuable contributions in many directions. First, it is based on a newly compiled dataset that takes stock of the main characteristics of national employment agencies in seven countries—the Arab Republic of Egypt, Jordan, Lebanon, Morocco, the Syrian Arab Republic, Tunisia, and the Republic of Yemen. These data provide information about the institutional setup of the public employment agencies (number of staff, number of offices, and types of services provided), their budgets, and the characteristics of registered job seekers in recent years. The study also provides specific details on the beneficiaries, targeting, and expenditures of ALMPs during this same period. These data, gathered and assembled in one place for the first time, allow for country comparisons on the delivery of employment programs and services in the region and for benchmarking MENA in relation to the wider, international context.

Second, the study proposes a series of reforms that could improve the performance of ALMPs in the region and that are likely to be relevant for countries in other regions as well. In particular, the study reveals an urgent need to involve the private sector in the design and implementation of employment programs in MENA. Many such programs are currently designed and delivered solely by public agencies and do not necessarily provide job seekers with the tools and skills they need to access available vacancies. Public-private partnerships for the delivery of ALMPs will, therefore, be pivotal as a means to develop employment programs that better prepare beneficiaries to respond to the needs of the private sector. These partnerships should include strong governance mechanisms to ensure that they deliver concrete results. Providers of employment programs should, for example, be assessed (and remunerated) based on their demonstrated capacity to connect beneficiaries to available internships and jobs.

This study was conducted as background for the World Bank's 2013 regional flagship report on employment, *Jobs for Shared Prosperity: Time for Action in the Middle East and North Africa*. It is part of a compendium of analytical work undertaken by the Human Development Department of the World Bank's MENA region in an effort to respond to regional priorities within the context of the Arab World Initiative (AWI).

The analysis and policy directives highlighted in this study are welcome at a time when countries in the region are struggling to find innovative ways to improve labor market prospects for their citizens.

Roberta Gatti
Sector Manager and Lead Economist
Human Development Group, Europe and Central Asia Region
The World Bank

Acknowledgments

This report is the collaborative product of a core team led by Diego F. Angel-Urdinola and comprising Arvo Kuddo and Amina Semlali, with important contributions from Saad Belghazi, Anne Hilger, Rene Leon-Solano, May Wazzan, and Diane Zovighian. Amina Semlali, Anne Hilger, and Ines Rodriguez supported coordination of the project at different stages. The work was conducted under the strategic guidance of Steen Jorgensen, Roberta Gatti, Hana Polackova Brixi, and Yasser El-Gammal and was overseen and supported by Caroline Freund.

Background papers for the report were written by Diego F. Angel-Urdinola and Rene Leon-Solano (Policy Framework), Arvo Kuddo (International Best Practices of Public Employment Services), Amina Semlali and Diego F. Angel-Urdinola (the Arab Republic of Egypt), May Wazzan and Diane Zovighian (Jordan, Lebanon, and the Syrian Arab Republic), Saad Belghazi (Morocco), Diego F. Angel-Urdinola, Anne Hilger, and Rene Leon-Solano (Tunisia), and Diane Zovighian (the Republic of Yemen). Other useful material was provided by Haneen Sayed (Jordan, Lebanon, and Syria), Mira Hong (the Republic of Yemen), and Nadine T. Poupart (Morocco).

We thank our peer reviewers, David Robalino and Maria Laura Sanchez-Puerta, for their valuable guidance, and our colleagues Andras Bodor, Stefanie Brodmann, Theresa Jones, Hana Polackova Brixi, and Haneen Sayed for their insightful feedback. The report also benefited greatly from feedback received from representatives of academia, civil society, governments, and international organizations during several workshops and dissemination events. These included the 7th Institute for the Study of Labor (IZA)/World Bank Conference on Employment and Development held in Delhi, India, in November 2012; the Middle East and North Africa (MENA) chief economist's brown-bag lunch series at the World Bank in December 2012; the launch forum for the MENA Community of Practice on Employment and Social Safety Nets in Istanbul, Turkey, in January 2013; and the Social Protection and Labor brown-bag lunch series organized by the Human Development Network at the World Bank in February 2013.

We also thank the Center of Mediterranean Integration for hosting a workshop on international best practices for the design and implementation of employment services in Marseille, France, in May 2010. This workshop identified important information gaps related to existing employment programs in the region, and constituted an important first step that triggered the production of this study.

We are grateful to the governments of Egypt, Jordan, Lebanon, Morocco, Syria, Tunisia, and the Republic of Yemen for facilitating the team's access to valuable administrative data on social and employment services, and to all counterparts in these governments who participated in the process of data collection. Their support was indispensable for the completion of this study.

The World Bank's Office of the Publisher coordinated production of the report, which was edited by Cathy Sunshine. Our thanks to all.

Editors and Contributors

Diego F. Angel-Urdinola is a senior economist in the Human Development Department of the Middle East and North Africa Region of the World Bank, where he conducts applied research on poverty, inequality, labor markets, international migration, and human development. He has contributed to operational research for various developing countries, especially in Latin America, Europe and Central Asia, Sub-Saharan Africa, and North Africa. He has published articles in various academic and nonacademic publications, including the *Journal of Economic Inequality*, *Journal of International Development*, *Economics Bulletin*, and *Labour*, as well as several working paper series. He holds a PhD in economics from Georgetown University.

Saad Belghazi is an international consultant on labor and social protection policy. He has been a professor at the National Institute of Statistics and Applied Economics in Rabat, Morocco. He has worked in several line ministries in Morocco, including the Ministry of Industry and Commerce. In 2009–10 he served at the International Labour Organization, where he led several research projects on economic growth, employment, poverty, and international labor migration. He has conducted research for the preparation of free trade agreements in Morocco and for various sectoral studies. He holds a PhD in economics from the University of Grenoble.

Anne Hilger is a research analyst in the Human Development Department of the Middle East and North Africa Region of the World Bank, where she focuses on labor markets and social safety nets. Before joining the World Bank, she worked at the German Development Institute (DIE) in Bonn. She holds a master's degree in public policy and human development from the Maastricht Graduate School of Governance.

Arvo Kuddo is a senior labor economist on the Labor and Youth Team in the Human Development Anchor of the World Bank. He has specialized in labor market institutions, including labor regulations, employment services, and active labor market programs. He is author or coauthor of about 160 research papers, books, reports, and articles, and has contributed to 38 World Bank lending operations and over 70 nonlending operations. Before joining the World Bank, he was minister of labor and social affairs of Estonia (1990–92). He holds a PhD in economics and demography from Lomonosov Moscow State University.

Rene Leon-Solano is a social protection economist in the Human Development Department of the Middle East and North Africa Region of the World Bank. He works on labor market issues and youth employment in Tunisia and Morocco and has provided operational, technical, and analytical support to those governments following the Arab Spring. Before joining the World Bank, he worked for the Inter-American Development Bank and the Organization of American States, where he designed, implemented, and supervised loans and grants in 18 countries in Latin America and the Caribbean. He holds a master's degree in public policy from the John F. Kennedy School of Government at Harvard University.

Amina Semlali specializes in skills development and works on issues related to employment, labor market integration, and active labor market policies in the Human Development Department of the Middle East and North Africa Region of the World Bank. She is also the focal point for the unit's outreach and external relations work. She previously worked for the World Bank's Children and Youth Unit, focusing on youth entrepreneurship and early childhood development. She has published numerous articles and also writes for the Huffington Post and Al Jazeera. She holds a master's degree in international relations and political science from Uppsala University.

May Wazzan is a junior associate at McKinsey & Company. She previously worked as a research analyst in the Lebanon Country Office of the World Bank and as a junior professional associate in the Social Protection Department of the World Bank's Middle East and North Africa Region. She has worked on operational and analytical projects in countries including Jordan, Lebanon, Syria, and the Gulf states, and on regional projects in the areas of employment and labor markets. She holds a master's degree from the London School of Economics and Political Science.

Diane Zovighian is a consultant to the World Bank in the areas of social protection, labor policy, governance, and gender. She has worked in the Human Development Department of the Middle East and North Africa Region and at the Fragile States, Conflict and Social Development Unit of the Africa Region at the World Bank. She previously worked at the United Nations Economic and Social Commission for Western Asia. She holds a master's degree in comparative politics with a specialization in the Middle East from the Paris Institute of Political Studies (Sciences Po).

Abbreviations

ALMP	active labor market program
AMAL	Programme de Recherche Active d'Emploi au Profit des Diplômés de l'Enseignement Supérieur (Active Employment Search Program for Higher Education Graduates), Tunisia
ANAPEC	Agence Nationale de Promotion de l'Emploi et des Compétences (National Agency for Employment and Skills Promotion), Morocco
ANETI	Agence Nationale pour l'Emploi et le Travail Indépendant (National Agency for Employment and Independent Work), Tunisia
BEST	Building and Extending Skills Training Systems
BTS	Banque Tunisienne de Solidarité (Tunisian Solidarity Bank)
CAIP	Contrat d'Adaptation et d'Insertion Professionnelle, Tunisia
CDP	Community Development Program, the Arab Republic of Egypt
CEFE	Création d'Entreprises et Formation d'Entrepreneurs, Tunisia
CES	Contrat Emploi-Solidarité (Employment Solidarity Contract), Tunisia
CIDA	Canadian International Development Agency
CIDES	Contrat d'Insertion des Diplômés de l'Enseignement Supérieur, Tunisia
CRVA	Contrat de Réinsertion dans la Vie Active, Tunisia
CV	curriculum vitae
DET	Department of Employment and Training, Jordan
DGVET	Directorate General of Vocational Education and Training, Lebanon
DH	Moroccan dirhams
ELAS	Egyptian Labor Adjustment Services
ELE	electronic labor exchange
ELMSR	Egyptian Labor Market Service Reform Project
E-TVET	Employment—Technical and Vocational Education and Training, Jordan

EU	European Union
GCC	Gulf Cooperation Council
GDP	gross domestic product
GIZ	German Agency for International Cooperation
HRDP	Human Resource Development Program, Egypt
ICT	information and communication technologies
IDSC	Information and Decision Support Center, Egypt
IFC	International Finance Corporation
ILO	International Labour Organization
ISSP	Integrated SME Support Program, Lebanon
JD	Jordanian dinars
KfW	Kreditanstalt für Wiederaufbau
LE	Egyptian pounds
LIWP	Labor-Intensive Work Program, the Republic of Yemen
LL	Lebanese pounds
LMIS	labor market information system
M&E	monitoring and evaluation
MENA	Middle East and North Africa
MEHE	Ministry of Education and Higher Education, Lebanon
MoET	Ministry of Economy and Trade, Lebanon
MoL	Ministry of Labor, Jordan and Lebanon
MoMM	Ministry of Manpower and Migration, Egypt
MORAINE	Méthode Originale de Recherche Active d'Idées Nouvelles pour Entreprendre
MoSA	Ministry of Social Affairs, Lebanon
MoSAL	Ministry of Social Affairs and Labor, the Syrian Arab Republic and the Republic of Yemen
MoTVET	Ministry of Technical and Vocational Education and Training, the Republic of Yemen
MSEs	micro and small enterprises
MSMEs	micro, small, and medium enterprises
MVTE	Ministry of Vocational Training and Employment, Tunisia
NCHRD	National Center for Human Resources Development, Jordan
NEC	National Employment Center, Jordan
NEO	National Employment Office, Lebanon
NETC	National Employment and Training Company, Jordan
NGO	nongovernmental organization
NOW	New Work Opportunities for Women
NTEP	National Training and Employment Project, Jordan

OECD	Organisation for Economic Co-operation and Development
OFPPT	Office de la Formation Professionnelle et de la Promotion du Travail (Office of Vocational Training and Labor Promotion), Morocco
OJT	on-the-job training
ONEQ	Observatoire National de l'Emploi et des Qualification
OPEC	Organization of Petroleum Exporting Countries
ORDEV	Organization for Reconstruction and Development of the Egyptian Village
PAPPE	Programme d'Accompagnement des Promoteurs des Petites Entreprises, Tunisia
PCEED	Public Commission for Employment and Enterprise Development, Syria
PEA	public employment agency
PES	public employment services
PPP	public-private partnership
PRD	Programme Régional de Développement
PWP	Public Works Program, Egypt
SCHRD	Supreme Council for Human Resources Development, Egypt
SCV	Service Civil Volontaire, Tunisia
SDC	Social Development Center, Lebanon
SEDO	Small Enterprise Development Organization, Egypt
SFD	Social Fund for Development, Egypt and the Republic of Yemen
SIVP	Stage d'Initiation à la Vie Professionnelle, Tunisia
SMEs	small and medium enterprises
SMED	Small and Micro Enterprises Development Program, the Republic of Yemen
SMEPS	Small and Micro Enterprise Promotion Services, the Republic of Yemen
SPL	social protection and labor
SWOT	strengths, weaknesses, opportunities, and threats
TD	Tunisian dinars
TVET	technical and vocational education and training
USAID	United States Agency for International Development
VTC	Vocational Training Center, Egypt and Jordan
VTD	Vocational Training Department, Lebanon
YEP	National Youth Employment Program, Egypt
YRl	Yemeni rial

All dollar amounts are U.S. dollars.

Overview

Diego F. Angel-Urdinola and Rene Leon-Solano

Rationale and Relevance

This study surveys active labor market programs (ALMPs) in selected countries of the Middle East and North Africa (MENA) region, identifies key challenges to their effective and efficient delivery, and proposes a policy framework for reforming public service provision. This study draws on data collected through surveys administered to public social, employment, and education agencies in selected MENA countries to identify key constraints and options for reforming publicly provided employment programs.

Recent political transitions arising from the Arab Spring have contributed to the deterioration of labor market outcomes in the MENA region. In this context, ALMPs could become an important policy lever to address some of the challenges facing labor markets. These include:

- *Joblessness.* MENA has a large share of untapped human resources. Joblessness in the region, defined as the share of the working-age population in either unemployment or economic inactivity, is more prevalent in MENA than in any other middle-income region, including Europe and Central Asia and Latin America and the Caribbean (figure O.1). Female labor force participation, at 25.4 percent in the Middle East and 28.1 percent in North Africa, is significantly lower than the world average of 51.6 percent. Youth unemployment is higher in the Middle East (19 percent) and North Africa (25 percent) than in any other developing region. At the same time, population growth in MENA is also among the highest in the world, with a demographic transition in which the youth bulge (ages 15–24) accounts for about 30 percent of the overall population, compared to 18 percent worldwide (World Bank 2013).

- *Skills mismatches.* About 40 percent of the employers in selected MENA countries identify skills mismatches as a major constraint to doing business and to firm growth (World Bank 2013). This percentage is the highest among developing regions (figure O.2, panel a). Skills shortages seem more severe for large

Figure O.1 Composition of the Working-Age Population by Employment Status, MENA and Other Regions, 2010

percent

a. Non-GCC Middle East and North Africa

Formal workers, 19

Inactive, 48

Unemployed, 6

Informal workers, 27

b. Latin America and the Caribbean

Inactive, 31

Formal workers, 27

Unemployed, 5

Informal workers, 37

c. Europe and Central Asia

Inactive, 38

Formal workers, 40

Unemployed, 6

Informal workers, 16

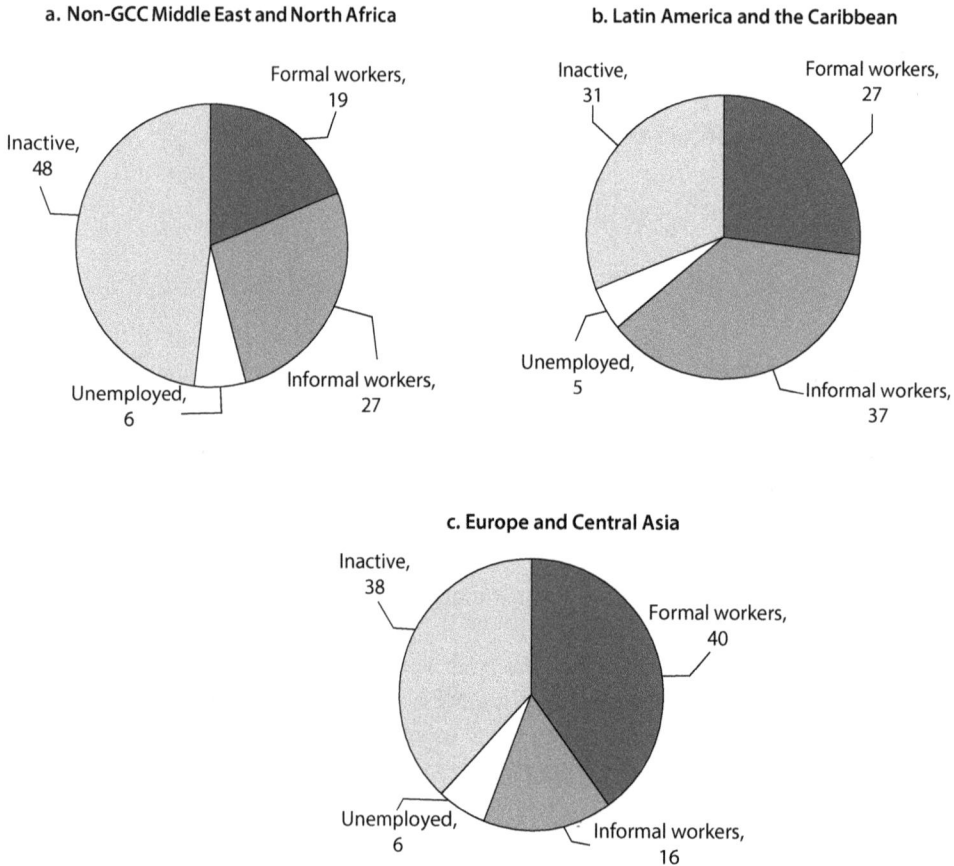

Source: World Bank 2013, based on data from International Labour Organization, Key Indicators of the Labour Market 2010.
Note: MENA figures exclude the countries of the Gulf Cooperation Council (GCC).

firms than for small firms in the Syrian Arab Republic, Morocco, and the Republic of Yemen, whereas the reverse is true in Algeria, Jordan, and West Bank and Gaza (figure O.2, panel b).

- *Lack of labor market mobility.* Available evidence indicates important constraints to labor market transitions in MENA (World Bank 2013). This is particularly true for the school-to-work transition, as well as for short-run transitions from unemployment or inactivity into employment. Recent work indicates that while the school-to-work transition in developed countries generally takes less than two years (measured as the difference between the age at which 50 percent of the population has left education and the age at which 50 percent has found employment), in many MENA countries it takes over five years (Angel-Urdinola and Semlali 2010; World Bank 2013). Mobility constraints at

Figure O.2 Percentage of Firms that Identify Inadequately Educated Workforce as a Major Constraint for Business Operation and Growth, by Region and Firm Size

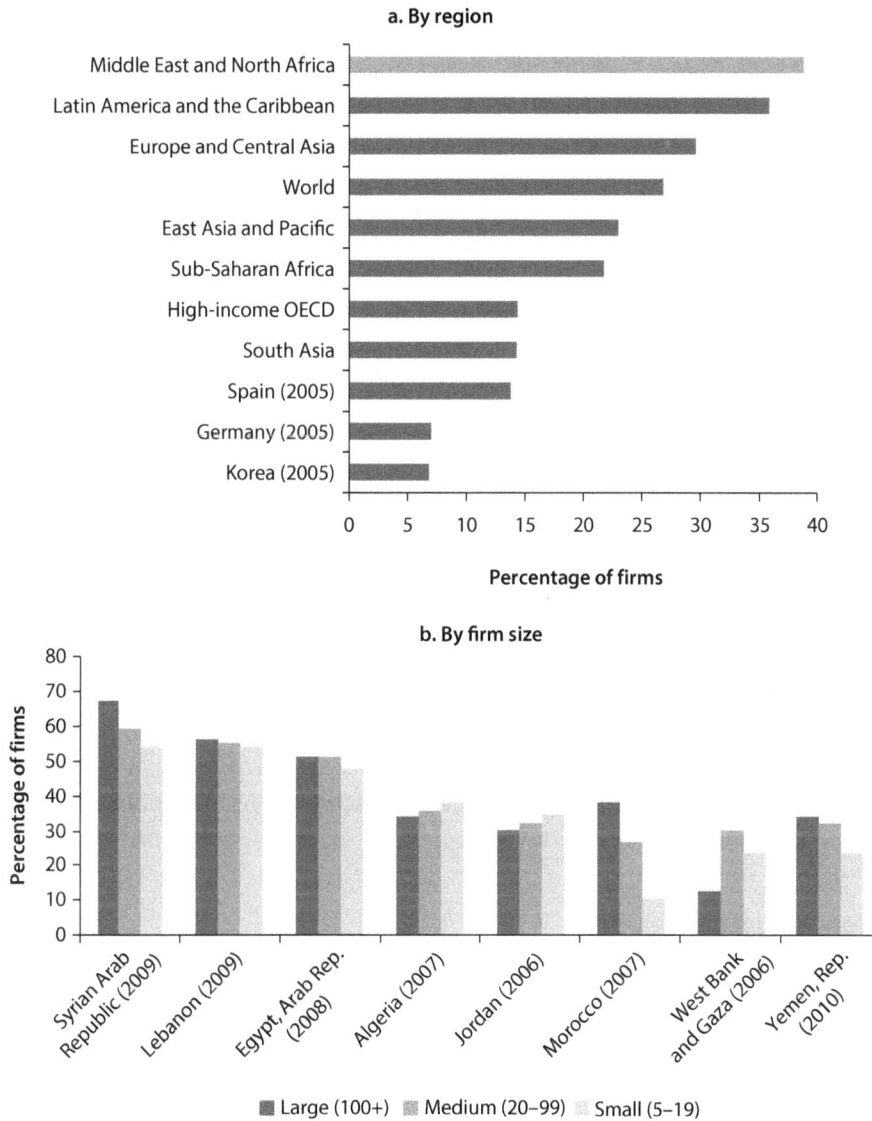

a. By region

b. By firm size

■ Large (100+) ▨ Medium (20–99) ▨ Small (5–19)

Source: World Bank 2013, based on data from Enterprise Surveys.

all levels may be due to lack of suitable vacancies, lack of information about available vacancies, or skills mismatches.

- *A large and expanding informal sector.* The share of the labor force not contributing to social security in MENA ranges from 45 percent in the Arab Republic of Egypt to 90 percent in the Republic of Yemen. Unfortunately, informal employment in the region is often associated with low-quality, low-paying jobs, more so than in any other developing region (Angel-Urdinola and

Tanabe 2012). In a context of low growth and insufficient job creation, many people, especially those with tertiary education, will have no option but to settle for an informal job and/or self-employment. Unfortunately, self-employment in MENA has not achieved its full potential, so job seekers who become entrepreneurs will also face significant challenges in terms of stability and earnings (World Bank 2013).

• *Lack of formal employment networks.* The large majority of workers in MENA report that they found their jobs through personal connections (Gatti et al. 2012). This is particularly the case for informal workers. For example, 85 and 74 percent of informal workers in Lebanon and Syria, respectively, report finding jobs through personal contacts. In other words, private and public formal employment networks play a limited role in labor intermediation.

In light of these labor market challenges, ALMPs could play an important role addressing some of these constraints. This study reviews the provision of ALMPs in a selected group of countries in the MENA region, with a focus on public provision through existing public employment agencies. For each country, the study identifies key challenges in the delivery of publicly provided ALMPs and proposes a reform agenda based on international best practices. Surely, employment programs cannot substitute for private-led employment creation nor address the structural constraints of the region's labor market, such as stagnant labor demand, low productivity, low competitiveness, and high informality. But these services, if well designed and effectively delivered, could be a mechanism for relieving high unemployment rates while providing the population with some immediate and visible results.

Conceptual Framework

Active Labor Market Programs

The two overarching objectives of ALMPs are to enhance employability and promote job creation. ALMPs are considered "active" programs because beneficiaries are required to engage in a job-search activity ("activation") in exchange for obtaining particular benefits or services. In this respect, ALMPs differ from "passive" measures such as unemployment insurance/assistance, which are designed to mitigate the financial hardship of unemployment.

ALMPs can help correct employment barriers that can arise from the existence of skills mismatches, insufficient labor demand, and information asymmetries (table O.1). For example, skills mismatches may lead to unfilled vacancies, which can be addressed through training or retraining of the labor force. Lack of information about available vacancies along with job seekers' inability to signal their competences and skills may slow or prevent the filling of vacancies, thus causing frictional unemployment. Lack of information can be addressed through

Table O.1 Selection of ALMP Type by Objective and Employment Barrier

Barrier to employment	Type of ALMP	Program objective
Skills mismatches	Training (on the job, in class)	Enhance employability
Information asymmetries	Intermediation services	Enhance employability/promote job creation
Insufficient labor demand	Wage subsidies, public works programs, self-employment	Promote job creation

Source: Angel-Urdinola, Semlali, and Brodmann 2010.

intermediation and counseling. Finally, in times of stagnant labor demand, ALMPs can stimulate job creation through programs such as public works, wage subsidies, and self-employment.

ALMPs have been widely used by governments around the world to mitigate the impacts of economic downturns by providing both employers and employees with incentives to participate in the labor market (see Kuddo 2009). There are five main types of ALMPs:

- *Training and retraining.* Training, the most widely used ALMP, seeks to enhance beneficiaries' employability and thus increase their chances of employment. Training can be provided in the classroom or in the workplace, and it can be supplemented with other services such as life skills training and counseling. International evidence suggests that training programs are most effective when they are comprehensive (combining classroom and workplace training with other services), when they are designed taking into account labor demand, and when they are delivered by private providers through performance-based contracting (World Bank 2013).

- *Intermediation services.* Information asymmetries are another barrier affecting the insertion of the unemployed in the labor market. Intermediation services address this market failure by providing job seekers with information on job vacancies as well as counseling and placement assistance. Such services are the least expensive ALMPs, but their effectiveness depends on the capacity of employment agencies, the legal framework regulating the provision of employment services, and, ultimately, the availability of jobs.

- *Wage subsidies.* Subsidizing workers' wages or the contributions to social security that employers need to make on a worker's behalf, can lead to increased demand for labor and thus job creation. These types of ALMPs are often used to support the insertion of vulnerable groups, such as youth, in the labor market. International evidence suggests that wage subsidy programs are most efficient when they are targeted at these groups (World Bank 2013).

- *Public works programs.* These programs can also promote job creation, albeit in the short term. Public works programs provide beneficiaries with income support and are most effective when used as a safety net, especially when targeted at the most marginalized. International evidence suggests that, when compared to other ALMPs, public works programs have the lowest placement rates and the highest per-placement costs (World Bank 2013). As a result, some countries are now including training modules (technical, life skills, literacy, numeracy) in their public works programs to improve the employability of program beneficiaries.

- *Self-employment.* Technical and financial support can be provided to unemployed persons who wish to set up their own businesses, particularly in times of limited economic growth and insufficient labor demand.

International experience shows that the impact of ALMPs on labor market outcomes is positive, but modest. While many ALMPs have effectively addressed market failures in countries with very different labor market challenges, many others have not succeeded in improving beneficiaries' livelihoods. Using meta-analysis, Card, Kluve, and Weber (2010) reviewed a set of impact evaluations of ALMPs for a sample containing 199 separate "program estimates" (i.e., estimates of the impact of a particular program on a specific subgroup of participants). The estimates were drawn from 97 studies conducted between 1995 and 2007. The authors found that (a) job search assistance programs are likely to yield positive impacts on employment outcomes, that is, employment levels and wages; (b) training programs yield relatively positive impacts on beneficiaries' employment outcomes in the medium term, but often have insignificant or negative impacts in the short term; and (c) the impact of public works programs on employment outcomes is limited. Indeed, the efficiency of ALMPs depends largely on their design, as well as on the country's institutional capacity to provide services continuously on a national scale (Angel-Urdinola, Semlali, and Brodmann 2010; World Bank 2013).

Program costs for ALMPs vary widely, and some ALMPs are more cost-effective than others. ALMPs that seek to encourage labor demand in times of economic downturn generally involve providing subsidies to either firms or workers. The amount of the transfer (and thus total program cost) depends largely on the country's economic and political context as well as on its labor market institutions and wage levels. The cost of training programs also varies, as it depends on the training's length, content, and necessary equipment. As a result, policy makers need to pay special attention to the cost-effectiveness of ALMPs. For example, results from Romania show that training programs are more cost-effective than employment services and public works programs (Rodriguez-Planas and Benus 2010). The authors found that training programs have, on average, high placement rates after program completion (above 40 percent) and low per-capita placement costs (about $2,000 per beneficiary). In contrast, public works programs have, on average, low insertion rates after program completion (approximately 12 percent) and are more costly on a per-capita basis than training programs.

Public Employment Services

Public employment agencies are the institutions responsible for delivering public employment services (PES). These agencies deliver employment services free of charge to job seekers (both the unemployed and job changers) as well as some services to employers and the inactive population. Services provided by public employment agencies include (a) information services, ranging from ad hoc information and referrals for job seekers to job brokerage services for employers; (b) individual case management services, such as intensive counseling and guidance, job search assistance, and personalized action plans; and (c) active and passive programs, including opportunities for work, training, and other forms of assistance such as unemployment insurance.

In developed countries, PES have been instrumental in helping unemployed workers find jobs. This is the finding of most experimental studies carried out in Canada, the Nordic countries, the United Kingdom, and the United States. For example, a study in Denmark found that workers who received personalized job search assistance, career counseling, and regular check-up meetings at the local public employment agency (PEA) had a 30 percent higher rate of employment than a control group that did not receive these services (Graverson and Van Ours 2007). An evaluation of a similar package of services in four regions of Sweden also found that participants had a 30 percent higher employment rate than a control group and, moreover, that the effects were most positive for job seekers aged 45 years or older (Hägglund 2009). When targeted at specific groups, PES seem to work best for women on welfare (in the United States) and for the long-term unemployed (in the Netherlands, New Zealand, and the United Kingdom). In contrast, they are ineffective for young workers (in Canada and the Netherlands) and in cases of mass layoffs (in Canada) (Rodriguez-Planas 2007). In Romania, evidence suggests that both intermediation services and small-business assistance programs can help the unemployed go back to work, but that of these two types of PES, intermediation services have higher placement rates (Rodriguez-Planas 2007).

In developing countries, the effects of PES on labor market outcomes have been found to be less positive. Many developing countries have large informal sectors and face low economic growth, conditions under which PES can play only a limited role, as these programs are geared primarily toward wage employment (Betcherman, Olivas, and Dar 2004). In general, the success of PES depends largely on program design and implementation as well as on institutional capacity. Indeed, successful PES are characterized by a combination of good design, implementation, and governance features that include coordination with the private sector, quality assurance and accreditation mechanisms, and solid monitoring and evaluation (M&E). Unfortunately, these features are often lacking in PES offered by developing countries (Angel-Urdinola, Semlali, and Brodmann 2010).

Modern PES play an important activation role. The functions of PES have changed over the years, partly because of the gradual disappearance of lifelong jobs and an increasing need for job mobility. In the past, the role of PES was confined to job intermediation and unemployment insurance. Today, many PES are helping individuals take ownership of their own job search and human capital development—the so-called activation agenda. Activation policies encourage job seekers and other vulnerable groups to become more active in finding work and improving their employability, including investing in their own skills (see, for example, OECD 2007).[1] In many countries, activation increasingly is based on the principle of "mutual obligations." That is, in return for receiving support, such as unemployment benefits or social assistance, individuals must comply with a set of eligibility requirements, which can range from active job search behavior to participation in training or other (re)employment programs. Good activation policies seek to improve beneficiaries' personal, social, and vocational skills and/or help them plan, design, and implement individual employment and career plans.[2]

Private sector involvement in the provision of PES has been a key feature of successful PES reform. The importance of including the private sector in the delivery of these services was confirmed by the Private Employment Agencies Convention adopted by the International Labour Organization (ILO) in 1997 (Convention 181 supported by Recommendation 188). It encouraged "cooperation between public and private employment agencies in relation to the implementation of a national policy on organizing the labor market." For Public Employment Agencies, one of the main advantages of cooperating with or subcontracting private agencies is that they offer more specialized services, which are needed in light of the increasing complexity of the labor market. Private agencies are often more efficient and effective than the public sector in the provision of PES, as they can provide services to smaller, targeted segments of the labor market and are better positioned to reach out to the private sector. In general, public employment agencies serve individuals with lower skills and limited education, while private employment agencies serve the better-skilled and better-educated.[3]

Public and Private Provision of ALMPs in the Middle East and North Africa Region

In recent years, ALMPs have been widely used in the MENA region. While some MENA countries (Tunisia and to some extent Morocco) still provide ALMPs primarily through the public sector, others (such as Lebanon, Egypt, and Jordan) actively involve the private sector in the provision of training, job brokerage, and other labor market services. For instance, according to a recent World Bank study, there are 45 licensed private employment agencies in Jordan and 54 in Egypt. ALMPs are also subcontracted to external providers in Lebanon (Angel-Urdinola, Kuddo, and Semlali 2013).

Private Provision

ALMPs delivered by the private sector are common in the MENA region. The work of Angel-Urdinola, Semlali, and Brodmann (2010) is a first attempt to gather information on privately provided ALMPs in MENA, with a focus on

North Africa. Based on data collection in 2009–10, the authors compiled an inventory of privately provided ALMPs across nine economies in the region: Algeria, Egypt, Jordan, Lebanon, Morocco, Syria, Tunisia, West Bank and Gaza, and the Republic of Yemen. Information about 17 programs was collected in Egypt, where private provision of ALMPs is very common, followed by Morocco (14 programs), West Bank and Gaza (13 programs), Lebanon (10 programs), and Jordan (8 programs).

Training is the most common ALMP offered by private providers in MENA. According to Angel-Urdinola, Semlali, and Brodmann (2010), private providers in the region offer primarily traditional in-class training, which accounted for about 91 percent of all interventions included in the inventory (figure O.3). Other employment services, such as entrepreneurship training, intermediation, and self-employment promotion, together constituted less than 9 percent of all privately provided ALMPs. According to the authors, most of the training programs in the inventory focus solely on the provision of hard skills (64 percent) and are conducted in classrooms (71 percent). Very few privately provided training programs surveyed as part of this study provide on-the-job training (OJT), soft-skills training, or intermediation services, even though international best practices show that all of these are critical to improve the employability and employment chances of unemployed individuals.

University graduates in urban areas are the main beneficiaries of privately provided ALMPs in MENA (figure O.4). For the most part, privately provided ALMPs require their beneficiaries to have a minimum set of skills. Therefore, low-income people, most of whom have low levels of education and live in rural areas, often cannot benefit from these programs. In fact, only 5 percent of all

Figure O.3 Distribution by Program Type of Privately Provided ALMPs in MENA, 2010
percent

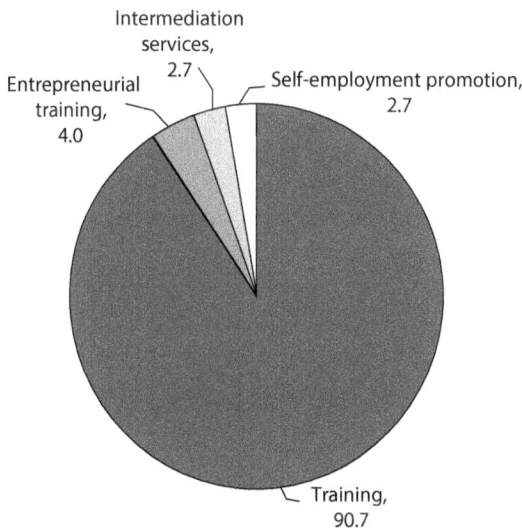

Source: Angel-Urdinola, Semlali, and Brodmann 2010.

Figure O.4 Target Groups of Privately Provided ALMPs in MENA, 2010

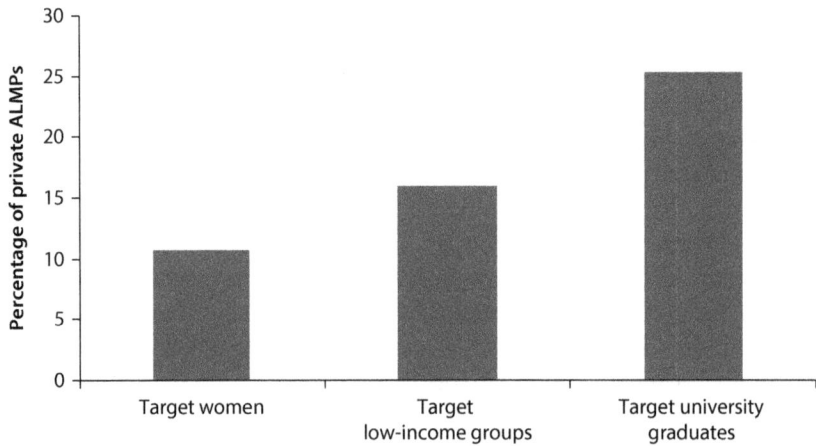

Source: Angel-Urdinola, Semlali, and Brodmann 2010.

programs in the MENA inventory were found to target rural areas (Angel-Urdinola, Semlali, and Brodmann 2010).

Public Provision

While publicly provided ALMPs are more diverse than those provided by the private sector in terms of types of programs, training remains the most popular ALMP provided by the public sector in MENA. Angel-Urdinola, Kuddo, and Semlali (2013) conducted the first survey of publicly provided ALMPs in MENA. The authors surveyed a total of 33 ALMPs that were implemented in 2010 by the national public employment agencies of seven countries in the region: Egypt, Jordan, Lebanon, Morocco, Syria, Tunisia, and the Republic of Yemen.

The study found that the majority of these ALMPs focused on enhancing the employability of program participants, with training being the most widely used intervention (figure O.5). In fact, 30 percent of the ALMPs surveyed for the study focused on vocational training. Morocco and the Republic of Yemen did offer packages that combined in-class training with other services such as wage subsides and start-up incentives. In the Republic of Yemen, only one ALMP was implemented by the PEA in 2010, but this program included several components such as training, labor intermediation, direct job creation, and out-of-work income support. Other ALMPs that were implemented by participating public employment agencies included direct job creation through public works (15 percent of all programs in the inventory), start-up incentives (9 percent), and programs targeted at persons with disabilities (3 percent).

Employment-incentive programs, mainly wage subsidies, have a more prominent role in Jordan, Morocco, and Tunisia than in the other four countries in this study. These programs encourage potential employers to hire labor. For example, a program in Jordan subsidizes 100 percent of the employee's contribution and 50 percent of the employer's contribution to social security for a period of two

Figure O.5 Distribution by Program Type of Publicly Provided ALMPs, Selected MENA Countries, 2008 and 2010

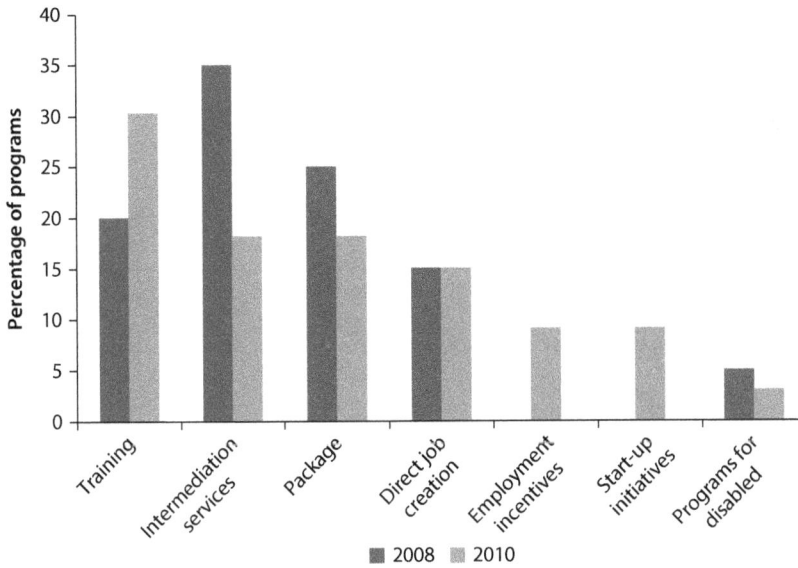

Source: Angel-Urdinola, Kuddo, and Semlali 2013.
Note: Countries included are Egypt, Jordan, Lebanon, Morocco, Syria, Tunisia, and the Republic of Yemen.

years. In Tunisia, OJT programs targeting primarily first-time job seekers subsidize part of social security contributions and wages for a period of one year (renewable), thus decreasing labor costs and promoting job creation.

Almost half of ALMPs delivered by public employment agencies in MENA (47 percent) target high-skilled unemployed individuals, notably university graduates who are first-time job seekers. Considering that high-skilled youth face higher than average, and increasing, rates of unemployment, it is no surprise that publicly provided ALMPs target this segment of the population (World Bank 2013).[4] Nevertheless, there are some publicly provided ALMPs that mainly benefit individuals living in rural areas and target the low-skilled unemployed, women, and other vulnerable groups (figure O.6). While most publicly provided ALMPs are open to both men and women, women are radically underrepresented, except in Tunisia. This could be explained by many factors, including lack of schedule flexibility and child care constraints.

Most public employment agencies in MENA offer intermediation services. Many countries in the region have developed job banks that can be accessed electronically, using computers at home or in local employment offices or other public premises. Employers can enter their vacancies, and the job seeker can upload a curriculum vitae (CV) to the database with the help of a placement officer or independently. The intermediation services for job seekers and employers provided by public employment agencies in the countries surveyed by Angel-Urdinola, Kuddo, and Semlali (2013) are presented in tables O.2 and O.3.

Figure O.6 Targeting of Publicly Provided ALMPs, Selected MENA Countries, 2010

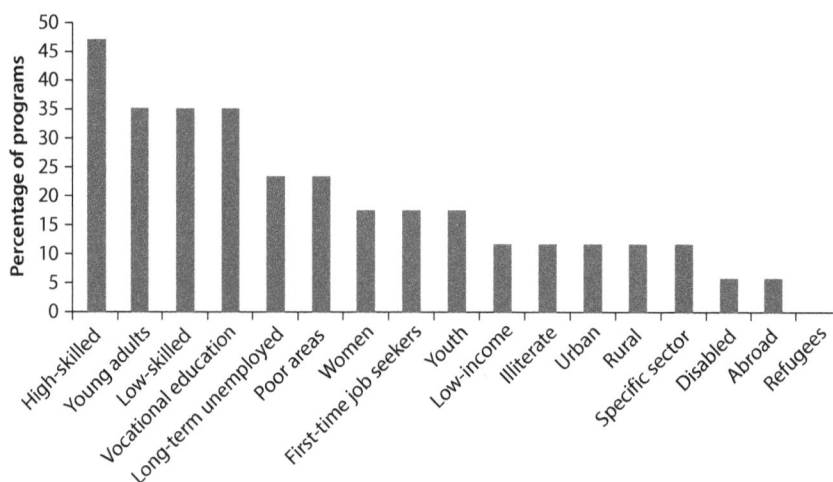

Source: Angel-Urdinola, Kuddo, and Semlali 2013.
Note: Countries included are Egypt, Jordan, Lebanon, Morocco, Syria, Tunisia, and the Republic of Yemen. Youth are ages 15–24; young adults are ages 25–34.

Table O.2 Public Intermediation Services for Registered Job Seekers, Selected MENA Countries, 2010

Country	Walk-in centers	Database search for job offers	Posting of job profiles	Posting of CVs	Alerts for matches
Egypt, Arab Rep.	Yes	Yes	No	Yes	No
Jordan	Yes	Yes	Yes	Yes	Yes
Lebanon	Yes	No	No	No	No
Morocco	Yes	Yes	No	Yes	No
Syrian Arab Republic	Yes	Yes	Yes	Yes	Yes
Tunisia	Yes	Yes	Yes	Yes	No

Source: Angel-Urdinola, Kuddo, and Semlali 2013.

Table O.3 Public Intermediation Services for Employers, Selected MENA Countries, 2010

Country	Posting of job vacancies	Database search for job profiles	Matching	Alerts for matches	Automated collection and forwarding of applications	Prescreening
Egypt, Arab Rep.	Yes	Yes	Yes	Yes	No	Yes
Jordan	Yes	Yes	Yes	Yes	Yes	No
Lebanon	Yes	Yes	Yes	No	No	No
Morocco	Yes	Yes	No	No	No	Yes
Syrian Arab Republic	No	No	No	No	No	Yes
Tunisia	Yes	Yes	Yes	No	Yes	Yes

Source: Angel-Urdinola, Kuddo, and Semlali 2013.

Despite their availability, intermediation services are not widely used by either employers or employees. This is partly because most firms in MENA do not believe that public employment agencies have the capacity to do effective matching. This is true to a large extent, as PEAs generally do not have a systematic way (or staff dedicated) to match registered unemployed to available vacancies.

Challenges to the Effective and Efficient Delivery of Publicly Provided ALMPs in the Middle East and North Africa Region

This section briefly describes the main obstacles to the effective and efficient delivery of publicly provided ALMPs in MENA, based on data collected by Angel-Urdinola, Kuddo, and Semlali (2013). The analysis focuses on institutional and operational challenges, namely system fragmentation, limited administrative capacity, lack of governance and accountability, and flawed program design. Other challenges affecting the labor market, such as stagnant labor demand, skills mismatches, and demographics, are beyond the scope of this section.

System Fragmentation

Countries in the region have different institutional arrangements for administering publicly provided ALMPs. For example, in Egypt, Jordan, and the Republic of Yemen these programs are administered directly by the Ministry of Labor (MoL), sometimes by a specialized department within the ministry. On the other hand, in Lebanon, Morocco, Syria, and Tunisia these programs are administered by independent and autonomous public employment agencies that are supervised by the MoL.

The delivery of publicly provided ALMPs, and especially of training services, is typically fragmented. Many government entities other than national public employment agencies are involved in the provision of publicly provided ALMPs. For example, Egypt has 1,237 vocational training centers that are affiliated with 27 different ministries and that operate somewhat independently throughout the country's 19 governorates.

The fragmentation in the delivery of ALMPs leads to duplication and inefficiencies. In Tunisia, publicly provided ALMPs, notably public works and employment programs targeted at vulnerable groups such as disabled people, are often delivered by different ministries, namely Vocational Training and Employment, Regional Development, and Social Affairs. Due to poor interministerial coordination and lack of a single registration mechanism, many of these programs are redundant and provide incentives for individuals to participate in several programs, even concurrently, thereby promoting welfare dependency (Belghazi 2012). Furthermore, there is little coordination between training programs and the needs of the labor market. Curricula are outdated and are not reviewed frequently, and many training centers provide predesigned training courses that do not necessarily meet the needs of the private sector (Angel-Urdinola and Semlali 2010).

Limited Administrative Capacity

An important factor contributing to the success of publicly provided ALMPs is the institutional capacity of the national employment agencies. This includes the number and qualifications of their staff at both national and regional levels, their geographic coverage, the legal framework in which they operate, and their budget allocations. Indeed, the efficiency of a country's employment policy is, to a large extent, related to the amount of resources available for financing ALMPs. There is wide variation in spending on publicly provided ALMPs across MENA countries. According to available data, in 2010–11, Tunisia spent 0.8 percent of gross domestic product (GDP) on ALMPs, Morocco 0.1 percent, and Lebanon 0.04 percent. As a reference, across the European Union (EU), a total of 64 billion euros, or 0.5 percent of EU-27 GDP, was spent on ALMPs in 2009—a year of economic downturn (Kuddo 2012).

Public employment agencies in MENA are generally understaffed. The workload of personnel in direct contact with clients, that is, caseworkers, is critical for the effective and efficient provision of publicly provided ALMPs. Available data from 2010 show wide variations in levels of staffing among the seven MENA countries that participated in the study (Angel-Urdinola, Kuddo, and Semlali 2013). The highest staff caseload was reported in Syria, with more than 14,000 registered job seekers per staff person in the PEA. Next was Morocco, with over 1,500 job seekers per caseworker, followed by Lebanon, with over 1,200 (table O.4). Of the total PEA staff in Syria, Lebanon, and Jordan, fewer than half are frontline employment counselors. Within the EU, the average staff caseload is around 1:150, while the ratio recommended by the ILO is even lower, at 1:100.[5] Therefore, in many countries in the MENA region, the number of PEA staff, in particular frontline counselors, is inadequate for the provision of effective and personalized intermediation services.[6]

Table O.4 Numbers of Unemployed, Registered Job Seekers, and Public Employment Agency Staff, Selected MENA Countries, 2010

Country	Number of registered job seekers (thousands)	Total number of PEA staff	Number of PEA staff in contact with job seekers and employers	Staff caseload[a]	Ratio of frontline counselors to total PEA staff (%)
Egypt, Arab Rep.	895.1	1,600	1,550	577	97
Jordan	28.0	133	63	444	47
Lebanon[b]	12.2	32	10	1,220	31
Morocco	517.0	547	343	1,507	63
Syrian Arab Republic	1,703.8[c]	397	120	14,199	30
Tunisia	281	1,271	1,052	267	82

Source: Angel-Urdinola, Kuddo, and Semlali 2012.
Note: Data for Tunisia are for the year 2011.
a. Average number of registered unemployed per PEA staff person in contact with job seekers.
b. Beirut only.
c. Public sector only, including individuals queuing for civil service and other public sector jobs.

Table O.5 Job-Seekers-to-Vacancy Ratio and Number of Job Placements per 1,000 Registered Job Seekers, Selected MENA Countries, 2010

Country	Number of registered job seekers (thousands)	Number of registered job vacancies (thousands)	Number of job seekers per one registered vacancy	Average placements per year (thousands)	Job placements per 1,000 job seekers per month
Egypt, Arab Rep.	895.1	222.9	4.0	40.1	45
Jordan	28.0	2.6	10.8	0.7	25
Lebanon[a]	12.2	3.6	3.4	—	—
Morocco	517.0	27.7	18.7	4.4	9
Tunisia	281	100.4	2.8	45.6	4.7

Source: Angel-Urdinola, Kuddo, and Semlali 2013.
Note: — = not available.
a. Beirut only.

With few exceptions, public employment agencies in MENA play a limited role in job matching. In Egypt and Lebanon (Beirut only), public employment agencies are quite active in registering job vacancies. While this drives the ratio of registered job seekers per vacancy down, this ratio remains modest by international standards (table O.5). On the other hand, the job-seekers-to-vacancy ratio is relatively high in both Jordan and Morocco. However, although this ratio gives important information on institutional capacity to do intermediation, it is the job placement rate that is critical for evaluating public employment agencies' efficiency. In Egypt, less than 5 percent of registered job seekers are employed every month, in Jordan less than 3 percent, and in Morocco only about 1 percent.

Lack of Governance and Accountability

Most publicly provided ALMPs in MENA do not have proper governance and accountability frameworks. User feedback is largely absent, as is information about the impacts and cost-effectiveness of programs. Most of the ALMPs surveyed by Angel-Urdinola, Kuddo, and Semlali (2013) have output-based monitoring systems, but they lack results-based systems and rigorous program evaluations. Indeed, data on program outcomes, such as insertion rates and wages after program completion, were not available for most of the programs included in the study. Only a small minority (15 percent) conducted an impact evaluation, and a mere handful (7 percent) carried out a cost-effectiveness analysis (figure O.7). Most of the evaluations that were done lacked scientific rigor, rarely using control groups that would have allowed for an estimation of the programs' net impact. Morocco conducted qualitative evaluations for three of its four ALMPs to assess their effect on labor market outcomes. In Tunisia, there have been some attempts to use impact evaluations to assess employment programs delivered by the PEA, National Agency for Employment and Independent Work (ANETI), but results are outdated, sporadic, donor-driven, and lacking in scientific credibility (Belghazi 2012).

Public employment agencies rarely accredit or assess the performance of the private operators they work with to deliver ALMPs. Most private contractors are

Figure O.7 Percentage of Publicly Provided ALMPs that Have Conducted an Impact Evaluation or Cost-Benefit Comparison, Selected MENA Countries, 2010
percent

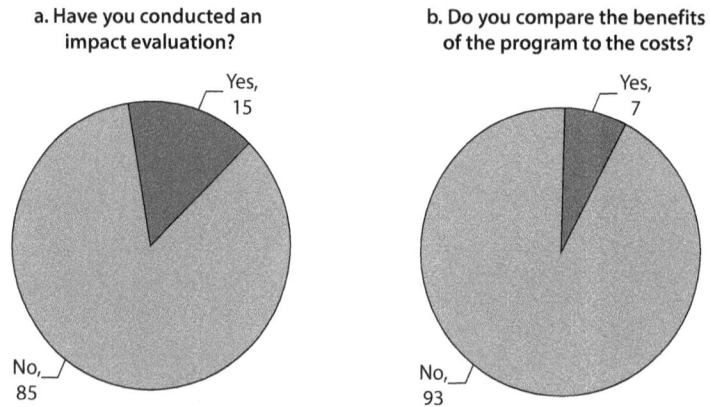

Source: Angel-Urdinola, Kuddo, and Semlali 2013.
Note: Countries included are Egypt, Jordan, Lebanon, Morocco, Syria, Tunisia, and the Republic of Yemen.

paid based on outputs, usually the number of people trained, rather than based on the quality of the service delivered. Consequently, many training programs offered by private providers are supply-driven and of poor quality. Accreditation practices vary from country to country. For example, Syria and the Republic of Yemen lack standard accreditation systems, while Jordan and Lebanon have more developed accreditation systems that help improve quality standards and overall service delivery. Nevertheless, according to the data collected in this study, only 50 percent of all private providers working with public employment agencies in the region are properly accredited (Angel-Urdinola, Kuddo, and Semlali 2013).

Flawed Program Design

The success of ALMPs depends largely on program design and implementation. To effectively address a given failure in the labor market, it is critical to choose the right type of ALMP. Equally important is identifying the specific design features that will increase the likelihood of program success, independently of the program type. This section describes the main design challenges found among the publicly provided ALMPs in MENA that were surveyed by Angel-Urdinola, Kuddo, and Semlali (2013).

Poor Targeting Practices

Most employment programs in MENA do not use a consistent targeting methodology. While some define a target group and eligibility criteria, weak institutional capacity, limited access to data, and lack of information diffusion mechanisms lead to poor targeting practices. For instance, while some programs target first-time job seekers, few programs identify who among them will be hard to place. Therefore, the programs end up benefiting individuals who would have obtained jobs without any intervention, leading to deadweight losses.

Program Fragmentation

Many publicly provided ALMPs in MENA lack coherence and are fragmented and duplicative. For instance, in 2011 Tunisia had six wage subsidy programs (paid internships and OJT), some of which were largely redundant. Many individuals who completed one program simply moved to another, and some enrolled in more than one program simultaneously (Belghazi 2012). Reducing fragmentation across programs can decrease inefficiencies, enhance coverage, and improve responsiveness to risks.

Supply-Driven and In-Class Training Programs

The majority of training programs in the region are supply-driven, and only a few are designed in close collaboration with the private sector. Most are conducted in classrooms and focus largely on the provision of hard skills. Available programs rarely focus on the provision of soft skills and/or practical experience through OJT.[7] Both hard and soft skills, as well as practical experience, are essential to increase the employability and insertion of program beneficiaries. According to the World Bank (2012), comprehensive programs—those combining in-class training with practical experience, or combining in-class training and practical experience with other services such as life skills training and counseling—have higher rates of success, with success defined as improving the probability of obtaining employment and/or higher earnings. In contrast, programs offering only in-class training or only practical experience were less successful. The "Jóvenes" programs in Latin America are examples of comprehensive programs that have successfully improved the employability and insertion of program beneficiaries (World Bank 2012).

Entrepreneurship Programs That Are Limited in Scope

Entrepreneurship programs have traditionally been at the core of employment policy in many MENA countries. Most of these programs target the low-skilled unemployed and are delivered by social funds (Egypt and the Republic of Yemen), microcredit institutions (Tunisia), or donors (Egypt and Lebanon) (Angel-Urdinola, Semlali, and Brodmann 2010). National employment agencies in Egypt, Lebanon, Morocco, Syria, and Tunisia are now offering training programs for those registered unemployed who want to establish their own business (Angel-Urdinola, Kuddo, and Semlali 2013). However, entrepreneurship programs in MENA, whether delivered by social funds or by national employment agencies, typically benefit relatively few people and do not address some of the other key constraints facing potential entrepreneurs, such as access to credit and the need for personalized coaching and incubator services.

Lack of Graduation/Exit Strategies

Many employment programs in the MENA region lack a clear graduation/exit strategy, allowing program beneficiaries to become dependent on government support. Program benefits are often too high and continue for too long, which creates distortions in the labor market and discourages the unemployed from actively searching for a job. Transfers at such levels are also fiscally unsustainable. While some programs provide referrals to employment services and require beneficiaries to comply with certain conditions to continue receiving transfers, these conditions for the most part are not enforceable, given the lack of monitoring systems and other capacity constraints. For instance, following the Jasmine Revolution, Tunisia introduced the AMAL ("hope" in Arabic) active search program, which provides first-time job seekers with at least an associate's degree from an accredited institution a monthly stipend conditional on their participation in training, counseling, and/or internships. However, because of weak institutional capacity, fewer than 20,000 beneficiaries out of the 145,000 who registered for the program in 2011 participated in any of the program activities. In other words, more than 85 percent of the beneficiaries benefited only from a cash transfer. This had negative repercussions on the nation's budget and on the employment outcomes of beneficiaries, as the stipend allowed many to remain idle while waiting for public sector jobs to become available (Belghazi 2012).

Lack of Signaling

Although its performance is far from ideal, the public sector is doing better than the private sector in terms of program certification. In the MENA region, as in most regions of the world, a diploma signals that its bearer has achieved a particular level of knowledge and competence, allowing access to higher levels of instruction. Angel-Urdinola, Semlali, and Brodmann (2010) found that less than 10 percent of training programs delivered by private providers in MENA provide beneficiaries with some type of recognized credential upon program completion. In comparison, about 50 percent of publicly provided training programs in the region do so. However, certification practices vary from country to country. For example, Syria and the Republic of Yemen largely lack standard certification systems and national qualifications networks, while Jordan and Lebanon have accreditation systems that are better developed (Angel-Urdinola, Kuddo, and Semlali 2013).

Poor Relevance

ALMPs in the MENA region are, for the most part, conceived at the national level without taking into account regional and local realities. Other important stakeholders, notably the private sector, are not consulted at the design stage, which makes ALMPs irrelevant for addressing the needs of the labor market. In the case of ALMPs that seek to encourage labor demand through wage subsidies, lack of ownership discourages companies from implementing program components and from investing in program beneficiaries. This translates into high levels of turnover among program beneficiaries and overall low insertion levels. In Tunisia, administrative data indicate that less than 25 percent of all beneficiaries who benefit from ALMPs find employment after program completion.

Policy Framework to Improve the Performance of Publicly Provided ALMPs in the Middle East and North Africa Region

This study proposes a policy framework for improving the delivery of publicly provided ALMPs in the MENA region. It identifies four main policy directives that address the challenges discussed above:

- Develop results-based public-private partnerships (PPPs)
- Develop results-based M&E frameworks
- Promote entrepreneurship, OJT, and life skills training among job seekers
- Promote systems and program integration

Table O.6 shows the institutional constraints to which these policy directives respond, and table O.7 outlines several policy instruments that can be used to implement each directive. The policy directives included in the framework are based on available information on what works and does not work in MENA, as well as on documented experiences and lessons learned from throughout the world (see Angel-Urdinola and Leon-Solano 2013).

Develop Results-Based Public-Private Partnerships

PPPs can improve the delivery of publicly provided ALMPs if incentives are designed to provide high-quality services and if the performance of private

Table O.6 Policy Framework for Improving the Delivery of Publicly Provided ALMPs in MENA

Institutional constraint		Policy directive
Limited administrative capacity	Insufficient ratio of counselors to registered unemployed	Develop results-based PPPs
	Insufficient national coverage	
	Inadequate skills of counselors	
	Lack of performance incentives	
	Weak intermediation capacity (prospection)	
	Poor data quality of registries (nomenclature, qualifications)	
System and program fragmentation	Too many public players in the provision of ALMPs	Promote systems and program integration
	Lack of integration of ALMPs with safety net systems	
	Lack of interinstitutional coordination	
	Program fragmentation (too many small programs and lack of coherence across programs)	
Lack of governance and accountability	Lack of results-based M&E systems and frameworks	Develop results-based M&E frameworks
	Lack of systems to promote user feedback	
	Lack of accreditation of private providers	
	Lack of information about quality of private providers	
	Poor insertion rates	
	Poor targeting	
	Lack of graduation/exit strategies	Promote systems and program integration
Flawed program design	Lack of involvement by the private sector in program design	Promote entrepreneurship, on-the-job-training, and life skills training among job seekers
	Failure to focus on provision of soft skills and/or on-the-job-training	
	Entrepreneurship programs that are limited in focus and scope	

Source: Angel-Urdinola and Leon-Solano 2013.

Table O.7 Main Policy Instruments for Improving the Delivery of Publicly Provided ALMPs in MENA

Develop results-based PPPs	Develop results-based M&E frameworks	Promote entrepreneurship, OJT, and life skills training among job seekers	Promote systems and program integration
Subcontract with private providers using performance-based contracts (based on placement rates) for provision of training and intermediation services	Adopt proper results-based M&E systems and ensure proper financing for periodic program evaluation	Develop training on entrepreneurship awareness	Promote one-stop shops for ALMPs, unified registry, program consolidation
Use information and communication technologies to foster intermediation	Pilot and evaluate programs before scaling up nationally	Facilitate access to finance	Use ALMPs as graduation/exit strategies for existing safety net programs
Develop training programs in close coordination with the private sector (focus on soft skills)	Conduct periodic social audits and user satisfaction surveys	Develop programs to enhance the productivity of potential self-employed workers (e-lancing, provision of market information, etc.)	Establish interministerial committees/task forces on employment programs (centrally and regionally) and involve the private sector
Liberalize and ease regulation bottlenecks for the provision of private intermediation services (e.g., in Tunisia)		Broaden the focus of existing training programs to include both OJT and life skills training	
Develop national qualification frameworks and proper and periodic accreditation systems for providers			

Source: Angel-Urdinola and Leon-Solano 2013.

partners is monitored and evaluated against specific, predetermined results. In most high-income countries, public employment agencies, while large and important players in service provision, do not have a monopoly on the delivery of employment services. In fact, in Australia all job seekers are referred to external service providers, with public authorities serving primarily as gatekeepers of a private quasi-market. However, public authorities are generally still responsible for processing payments. Private providers can be employment agencies, including temporary employment, recruitment, and guidance/counseling agencies; they may also be training and educational institutions, community-based organizations, and employers themselves. Partnering with private service providers can ensure that programs respond to market conditions, thus improving labor market outcomes among program beneficiaries.

Contracting out is key to ensuring more effective and efficient partnerships with private providers. Service contracts with private providers are typically performance-based, covering a provider's base costs while providing an incentive for placement through a bonus tied to outcomes.[8]

Results-based contracting has become an international best practice. Countries like Australia and the United Kingdom have successfully introduced performance-based systems in which payments to private providers depend upon insertion and placement duration. Australia has been outsourcing services to private agencies and nongovernmental organizations since the 1990s. Under Job Services Australia (formerly the Job Network), hundreds of licensed job placement organizations in more than 2,700 locations across Australia offer placement services to the unemployed. In 2003, the Australian government introduced an active participation model for job seekers, adopting a more intensive and individualized approach to placement. Service providers are offered incentives through payment for placing job seekers in work, with higher payments for difficult-to-place clients than for short-term unemployed clients (Tergeist and Grubb 2006). This is also the case in Germany, where a placement voucher entitles the job seeker to use a private agency. If the voucher leads to employment, the agency receives a predetermined percentage of the payment at insertion and the remainder six months after placement (Schneider 2008). This model is also used by the United Kingdom's Jobcentre Plus, which provides payments to contractors depending on job outcome (off-flow from benefit into employment) and sustainability of jobs (placed beneficiary still in job after 13 and 26 weeks).

Results-based contracting requires a well-developed network of private employment providers that may be lacking in most MENA countries. However, developing the capacity of private employment providers (and NGOs) as well as putting in place systems and procedures to help governments in MENA manage this kind of system seems a plausible option to improve the delivery of public employment services in the short run, especially given the region's political economy and the weak administrative capacity of its public employment agencies. Of course, in the long run, a comprehensive public sector reform will be required.

As public agencies in the region begin to work in partnership with the private sector, it will be necessary to develop instruments that assist relevant stakeholders to promote quality assurance and recognition of training programs delivered by the public and private sectors. For example, the development of a Qualifications Framework (QF), defined as "an instrument for the development, classification and recognition of skills, knowledge and competencies along a continuum of agreed levels" (ILO 2007), can serve as the basis for improving the quality and relevance of education, thus addressing the skills mismatches that are so prevalent in MENA.

Finally, in order to improve the effectiveness of labor intermediation services, it is recommended that public employment agencies partner with the private sector to use information and telecommunication technologies (ICTs) to better disseminate market information. Souktel provides a concrete example of how the use of technology can improve labor intermediation services in MENA. Souktel is a private enterprise (established in 2006) that promotes the use of mobile phones to link people with jobs. In the West Bank and Gaza, Souktel serves 10,000 job-seekers and 200 employers daily. A recent qualitative evaluation of this initiative shows that 84 percent of those job-seekers surveyed in the West Bank and Gaza experienced a reduction in job-search time from 12 weeks to less than 1 week, and 64 percent report higher monthly incomes as a result of jobs sourced through the service.

Develop Results-Based M&E Frameworks

MENA countries need to establish a clear governance structure, quality assurance mechanisms, and an M&E strategy based on results, not merely outputs, to increase program efficiency and effectiveness and improve the use of public resources. Rigorous, independent impact evaluations are needed to demonstrate what works, encourage sharing of best practices, enhance capacity in the region, and improve overall policy making. Australia offers perhaps the best example of how countries can effectively mainstream M&E practices into the policy-making process. Its M&E system requires that every program be evaluated every three to five years. Each ministry has to prepare an M&E plan to evaluate its programs, identifying resource and policy implications, and all completed M&E activities must be recorded and published. Australia's M&E systems have improved service delivery, strengthened program governance and accountability, and promoted a culture of evidence-based policy making. While resources and capacity in many developing countries are not aligned to those in countries like Australia and Sweden, more and more employment programs, even in the developing world, have started to include monitoring systems and to be evaluated. In developing countries, however, these evaluations are generally donor driven. In order to develop and improve this culture of M&E it is recommended that (a) monitoring focus on outcomes and not on outputs, and (b) program evaluation financing be part of the program's budget and/or proper budget allocations be made for monitoring and evaluation. While impact evaluations could be regarded as costly and methodologically challenging (often requiring the identification of control groups that are deprived of a certain service at some point of time), the costs of impact evaluation are often small when compared to total program allocations.

Setting up performance targets that can be monitored is also a way to improve the delivery of publicly provided ALMPs. Key quantitative indicators may include the numbers of visitors to local employment offices, registered job seekers, participants in ALMPs, placements, and job vacancies filled within a certain time. Targets might include an increase in the PEA's market share of notified vacancies and a reduction in the prevalence of unemployment that is long-term (over one year) or very long-term (two years or more). A key qualitative indicator is satisfaction on the part of job seekers and employers with the PEA's services. A results-based monitoring system enables the oversight entities to intervene early when needed with corrective or countering action.

At minimum, every PEA should periodically collect data on the following core indicators (Betcherman et al. 2010):

- *Job placement rate.* The number of registered unemployed in quarter t who are employed in quarter $t+1$.

- *Placement cost*. Number of beneficiaries who obtained a job in year t divided by program budget in year t.
- *Job retention rate*. The number of registered unemployed in quarter t who are employed in both quarters $t+2$ and $t+3$.
- *Average earnings*. Average earnings in quarters $t+2$ and $t+3$ for those registered unemployed in quarter t who retained employment in these quarters.
- *Filled vacancy rate*. The number of registered job vacancies in quarter t that are filled by registered job seekers in quarter $t+1$.

Promote Entrepreneurship, On-the-Job Training, and Life Skills Training among Job Seekers

Much of the private sector in the MENA region is made up of small firms that lack incentives to diversify, innovate, and invest, which undermines their ability to grow and create quality employment. Obstacles include burdensome business regulations and discretionary enforcement, low skill levels among entrepreneurs, poor access to credit, and subsidies that distort energy prices (Gatti et al. 2012). Given the increasing number of university graduates and the limited absorption capacity of the public sector, it is no surprise that many MENA countries face deteriorating labor market outcomes. For this reason, promoting a culture of entrepreneurship that encourages experimentation and learning among youth, especially unemployed university graduates, can improve labor market outcomes.

Most MENA countries have developed entrepreneurship programs, and these have had, for the most part, a positive impact on youth employment. However, these efforts are limited in scale and scope. They target primarily the low-skilled, whose businesses tend to remain small and thus have a limited impact on job creation. Several studies show that educational levels among the owners of micro and small informal enterprises are an important determinant of innovation, rate of return on capital, and employment growth (World Bank 2012). Evidence from a World Bank entrepreneurship program in Tunisia, which allows university students to develop a business plan rather than a traditional thesis to meet graduation requirements, shows that provision of entrepreneurship training and personalized coaching is effective in increasing the rate of self-employment among university graduates. Of course, these types of initiatives need to be complemented with information, coaching, access to credit, and other instruments such as incubators and guarantee funds.

Training programs are widely used throughout MENA, but most are traditional and supply-driven. They are conducted in classrooms and focus largely on the provision of hard skills. International evidence suggests that such traditional programs have a negative impact on beneficiaries' chances of employment. However, the effectiveness of training programs as measured by their insertion rate increases when they include on-the-job or life skills training or both (World Bank 2012). A recent evaluation by the Inter-American Development Bank of the Juventud y Empleo (Youth and Employment) program in the Dominican Republic found that in the short run, the life skills package (work experience + life skills) was more

Building Effective Employment Programs for Unemployed Youth in the Middle East and North Africa • http://dx.doi.org/10.1596/978-0-8213-9904-0

cost-effective than the traditional vocational training package (work experience + vocational training + life skills) (Martinez 2013).

Promote Systems and Program Integration

Many MENA countries have developed a plethora of small and independent employment and social programs that target various groups and that are implemented at different geographic levels by different stakeholders. The few existing evaluations show that these efforts have had some impact on the livelihoods of program beneficiaries. However, these programs lack complementarity and coherence, thus leading to redundancy and inefficiencies. It is therefore critical to promote systems and program integration, as this will help countries improve the effectiveness, efficiency, and governance of their social protection and labor (SPL) programs. For example, between 2009 and 2012 Tunisia consolidated 41 employment programs into only four instruments.. It is hoped that this reform will pave the way for the development of an integrated SPL system, helping Tunisia improve coordination at all levels.

Building SPL systems requires collaboration and sustained, coordinated efforts by all stakeholders. It is a gradual process that depends on strong government support and close partnerships with the private sector. A possible way to start this process is by designing and piloting programs that introduce specific design and administrative features that help integrate employment and social programs. These features include beneficiary registries, cash delivery mechanisms, and unified targeting approaches. These pilots can then be evaluated and, if successful, replicated at the national level, where they can serve as the basis for SPL systems that are cost-effective and embedded into the country's broader policy environment (figure O.8).

To ensure the sustainability of SPL systems, it is critical to engage in capacity-building activities targeted to key stakeholders, to promote ownership,

Figure O.8 Social Protection and Labor Systems: Three Levels of Operation

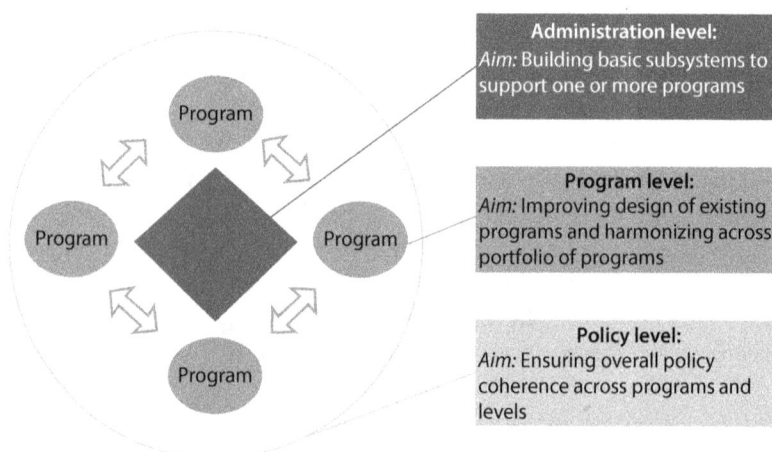

Administration level:
Aim: Building basic subsystems to support one or more programs

Program level:
Aim: Improving design of existing programs and harmonizing across portfolio of programs

Policy level:
Aim: Ensuring overall policy coherence across programs and levels

Source: Robalino, Rawlings, and Walker 2012.

and to involve nontraditional partners (especially the private sector) in the design and implementation of employment and social programs. Sharing of information and data access must be expanded and strengthened. A number of countries have successfully established effective SPL systems. For example, the United Kingdom established a one-stop shop known as Jobcentre Plus, where beneficiaries of employment and social programs can access a variety of services in a single place. Having a one-stop shop reduces transaction and administrative costs, improves service delivery, and facilitates program M&E.

Conclusion

The MENA region is facing a number of serious challenges affecting its labor markets. They include sluggish labor demand, high rates of joblessness among youth and women, prevalence of skills mismatches, stagnant labor mobility, high rates of informal employment, and lack of formal employment networks. ALMPs could play an important role in addressing market failures related to labor demand, labor supply, and information asymmetries, thus increasing the employability and employment chances of program beneficiaries. However, the efficiency and effectiveness of ALMPs depend largely on their design, as well as on the country's institutional capacity to implement them.

ALMPs have been widely used in the MENA region. While some MENA countries, namely Tunisia and to some extent Morocco, still provide ALMPs primarily through the public sector, others, such as Egypt, Jordan, and Lebanon, actively involve the private sector in the provision of training, job brokerage, and other labor market services. However, as noted in this study, publicly provided ALMPs in MENA face important institutional and operational challenges that hinder their efficiency and effectiveness. These include limited administrative capacity, system and program fragmentation, lack of governance and accountability, and flaws in program design.

This study proposes a policy framework to improve the delivery of publicly provided ALMPs in the MENA region. It identifies four main policy directives, each of which addresses the main challenges discussed throughout this paper. These policy directives are to (a) develop results-based PPPs; (b) develop results-based M&E frameworks; (c) promote entrepreneurship, OJT, and life skills training among job seekers; and (d) promote systems and program integration.

The effective application of the proposed reform agenda, however, requires that countries in MENA satisfy a minimum set of conditions. To begin with, political will is needed at all levels to facilitate the involvement of private entities in the delivery of publicly provided ALMPs. This means enabling private actors to engage in intermediation, as well as reforming national procurement rules and regulations to facilitate contracting and contract management with private providers. In addition, institutional capacity building is needed to ensure proper identification, selection, and monitoring of private providers of employment services as well as to engage in effective M&E of available employment programs. The establishment of SPL systems includes setting up administrative systems or improving existing ones, which in turn requires access to quality data as well as improved coordination and information sharing among stakeholders. Finally, in addition to providing technical support to potential entrepreneurs, countries need to promote their financial literacy and improved access to the banking system. Less emphasis on public sector hiring can also help promote entrepreneurship among job seekers.

Given these conditions, successfully implementing the proposed policy directives will require galvanizing support and buy-in from various stakeholders, including unions. However, for many MENA countries, there is currently a window for changing the status quo. Efforts to improve employment outcomes among the unemployed should be at the forefront of the policy agenda. ALMPs cannot substitute for private-led employment creation nor address the structural constraints of the region's labor market. However, these services, if well designed and effectively delivered, could be a mechanism for relieving high unemployment rates while providing the population with some immediate and visible results.

Notes

1. Employability refers to a person's ability to access a job. This concept is one element in the European Employment Strategy first adopted by the European Union member states in 1997.

2. The main target groups for activation programs are recipients (or claimants) of income replacement benefits that are conditional on availability for work. This includes most recipients of unemployment benefits. Unfortunately, only a few countries in the MENA region have unemployment insurance systems, namely Algeria, Bahrain, Egypt, the Islamic Republic of Iran, and Kuwait.

3. In the absence of public regulation, private placement agencies will tend to concentrate on (or "cream off") those unemployed persons who are most easily placed.

4. Results from the World Bank (2013) indicate that high-skilled unemployed individuals in MENA (proxied by those who attained a tertiary education degree) account for 20–30 percent of the stock of unemployed.

5. This EU average figure hides considerable variation: for example, Germany has a ratio of about 1:200 and the Netherlands 1:60.

6. High rates of registration often indicate that job seekers sign up with the national employment agency in hopes of securing public sector employment. Indeed, in some countries like Egypt, Syria, and Tunisia, registration with the national employment agency is a requirement for participation in the selection process for civil servants.

7. Hard skills are the technical, mechanical, administrative, or other skills needed to do a specific job. Soft skills are the cluster of personality traits and interpersonal skills that help a person function effectively in the workplace, including social graces, language and communication abilities, amenability to training, ability to get along with other people, and ability to think creatively and independently.

8. Prior to 2009, employment guarantees were included in some training contracts financed by the Turkish National Employment Office, ISKUR. In-class training programs with employment guarantees displayed much higher job placement rates (54 percent) than similar programs without guarantees (33 percent) (see Betcherman et al. 2010).

References

Angel-Urdinola, D., A. Kuddo, and A. Semlali. 2013. *Public Employment Agencies in the Middle East and North Africa*. Washington, DC: World Bank.

Angel-Urdinola, D., and R. Leon-Solano. 2013. *A Reform Agenda for Improving the Delivery of ALMPs in the MENA Region*. Washington, DC: World Bank.

Angel-Urdinola, D., and A. Semlali. 2010. "Labor Markets and School-to-Work Transition in Egypt: Diagnostics, Constraints, and Policy Framework." MPRA Paper 27674, Munich Personal RePEc Archive. http://mpra.ub.uni-muenchen.de/27674.

Angel-Urdinola, D., A. Semlali, and S. Brodmann. 2010. "Non-Public Provision of Active Labor Market Programs in Arab-Mediterranean Countries: An Inventory of Youth Programs." Social Protection Discussion Paper 1005, World Bank, Washington, DC.

Angel-Urdinola, D., and K. Tanabe. 2012. "Micro-Determinants of Informal Employment in the Middle East and North Africa Region." Social Protection Discussion Paper 66594, World Bank, Washington, DC.

Belghazi, S. 2012. "Evaluation Stratégique du Fonds National pour l'Emploi de la Tunisie." World Bank, Tunis.

Betcherman, G., R. Gussing, P. Jones, R. Can, and J. Benus. 2010. "Policy Note on Turkey's Active Labor Market Programs." World Bank, Washington, DC.

Betcherman, G., K. Olivas, and A. Dar. 2004. "Impacts of Active Labor Market Programs: New Evidence from Evaluations with Particular Attention to Developing and Transition Countries." Social Protection Discussion Paper 0402, World Bank, Washington, DC.

Card, D., J. Kluve, and A. Weber. 2010. "Active Labor Market Policy Evaluations: A Meta Analysis." NBER Working Paper 16173, National Bureau of Economic Research, Cambridge, MA.

Gatti, R., D. F. Angel-Urdinola, J. Silva, and A. Bodor. 2012. *Striving for Better Jobs: The Challenge of Informality in the Middle East and North Africa*. Washington, DC: World Bank.

Graverson, B. K., and J. C. van Ours. 2007. "How to Help Unemployed Find Jobs Quickly: Experimental Evidence from a Mandatory Activation Program." Discussion Paper 6057, Centre for Economic Policy Research, London.

Hägglund, P. 2009. *Effects of Intensified Employment Service Activities of the Swedish Public Employment Service: Experiences from Randomized Experiments*. Report 2009:15. Uppsala, Sweden: Institute for Labour Market Policy Evaluation.

Kuddo, A. 2009. "Employment Services and Active Labor Market Programs in Eastern European and Central Asian Countries." Social Protection Discussion Paper 0918, World Bank, Washington, DC.

———. 2012. "Public Employment Services, and Activation Policies." Social Protection Discussion Paper 1215, World Bank, Washington, DC.

Martinez, S. 2013. "Vocational and Life Skills in Youth Training: A Randomized Experiment in the Dominican Republic." PowerPoint presentation for Human Development Week 2013, Human Development Network, World Bank, Washington, DC.

OECD (Organisation for Economic Co-operation and Development). 2007. *Employment Outlook 2007*. Paris: OECD.

Robalino, D. A., L. Rawlings, and I. Walker. 2012. "Building Social Protection and Labor Systems: Concepts and Operational Implications." Background paper prepared for the Social Protection and Labor Strategy 2012–22, World Bank, Washington, DC.

Rodriguez-Planas, N. 2007. "What Works Best for Getting the Unemployed Back to Work: Employment Services or Small-Business Assistance Programmes? Evidence from Romania." Discussion Paper 3051, IZA, Bonn, Germany.

Rodriguez-Planas, N., and J. Benus. 2010. "Evaluating Active Labor Market Programs in Romania." *Empirical Economics* 38 (1): 65–84.

Schneider, H. 2008. "The Labour Market Reform in Germany and Its Impact on Employment Services." In *Paying for Success: How to Make Contracting Out Work in Employment Services*, edited by P. Lilley and O. M. Hartwich, 49–58. London: Policy Exchange.

Tergeist, P., and D. Grubb. 2006. "Activation Strategies and the Performance of Employment Services in Germany, the Netherlands and the United Kingdom." OECD Social, Employment and Migration Working Paper 42, OECD, Paris.

World Bank. 2012. *World Development Report 2013: Jobs*. Washington, DC: World Bank.

———. 2013. *Jobs for Shared Prosperity: Time for Action in the Middle East and North Africa*. Washington, DC: World Bank.

CHAPTER 1

Public Employment Agencies in the Middle East and North Africa Region

Diego F. Angel-Urdinola, Arvo Kuddo, and Amina Semlali

Introduction

Given the challenges facing the labor market in the Middle East and North Africa (MENA), employment services and active labor market programs (ALMPs) could constitute a useful policy instrument to address labor market frictions, help individuals find available jobs, and enhance the match between labor supply and demand through skills building (Angel-Urdinola and Kuddo 2010). Based on the latest available data, unemployment in MENA, excluding the countries of the Gulf Cooperation Council, is higher than in other regions of the world (World Bank 2013). Youth unemployment is higher in the Middle East (19 percent) and North Africa (25 percent) than in any other developing region. At the same time, population growth in MENA is also among the highest in the world, with a demographic transition in which the youth bulge (ages 15–24) accounts for about 30 percent of the population, compared to 18 percent worldwide. Skills mismatches are also more prevalent than in any other developing region, and formal employment networks are largely lacking (World Bank 2013).

International experience shows that the impact of ALMPs on labor market outcomes is positive, but modest. While many ALMPs have effectively addressed some market failures in countries with very different labor market challenges, many others have not succeeded in improving beneficiaries' livelihoods. Using meta-analysis, Card, Kluve, and Weber (2010) reviewed a set of impact evaluations of ALMPs for a sample containing 199 separate "program estimates" (i.e., estimates of the impact of a particular program on a specific subgroup of participants). The estimates were drawn from 97 studies conducted between 1995 and 2007. The authors found that (a) job search assistance programs are likely to yield positive impacts on employment levels and wages; (b) training programs yield relatively positive impacts on beneficiaries' employment outcomes in the medium term, but often have insignificant or negative impacts in the short term; and (c) the impact of public works programs on employment outcomes is generally limited. Indeed, the efficiency of ALMPs depends largely on their design, as well as on the country's institutional capacity to provide services continuously on a national scale (Angel-Urdinola, Semlali, and Brodmann 2010; World Bank 2012).

This study looks at the public provision of ALMPs, mainly those provided by the national public employment agencies, in a selected group of countries in the region. ALMPs can be delivered by public or private actors. While some MENA countries (namely Tunisia and to some extent Morocco) still provide ALMPs primarily through the public sector, others (such as the Arab Republic of Egypt, Jordan, and Lebanon) actively involve the private sector in the provision of training, job brokerage, and other labor market services (Angel-Urdinola, Semlali, and Brodmann 2010; Martín 2010). This chapter focuses on public delivery of ALMPs through the national public employment agency (PEA), which is the government body in each country responsible for the implementation of publicly delivered ALMPs and employment services. PEAs generally deliver services free of charge to job seekers (both the unemployed and job changers) as well as to employers.

Data included in this study were collected through face-to-face interviews with officers from the national PEA in a selected group of countries—Egypt, Jordan, Lebanon, Morocco, the Syrian Arab Republic, Tunisia, and the Republic of Yemen—between January 2010 and June 2011. The survey asked for information about the institutional setup of the PEA (number of staff, number of offices, and budget; characteristics of registered job seekers; and services provided) in 2008, 2009, and 2010. The questionnaire was based on instruments already developed for similar purposes in countries of the Organisation for Economic Co-operation and Development (OECD) and in Europe and Central Asia (see Lippoldt and Brodsky 2004; Kuddo 2009).

Several problems were encountered in conducting the survey. For example, many participating PEAs were reluctant to disclose financial data. Also, availability of data and procedures for collection and updating of data—for instance, on registered unemployment—differ from country to country, making it difficult to produce international and regional comparisons. Moreover, the survey collected information only from the delivery side; the report largely lacks data from the recipients' side, such as on users' perceptions of services. Only a few program evaluations are available to assess either the quality or impact of available interventions.

Notwithstanding these methodological challenges, the data point to some useful results. The PEA in a typical MENA country faces a number of severe problems: it lacks proper funding, is understaffed, delivers programs with important design flaws, does not interact proactively with the private sector, and is heavily constrained by a fragmented network of microcredit and training institutions. While most PEAs in the region provide a variety of programs, such as training, entrepreneurship promotion, direct job creation through public works, and employment incentives such as wage subsidies, the impact and cost-effectiveness of the interventions remain largely unassessed. Indeed, while most PEAs in the region do have some type of monitoring system that provides information about clients served, they lack results-based indicators to assess performance. Program evaluation practices are almost nonexistent.

In order to address these challenges, a comprehensive reform agenda could be developed based on four policy directives:

- Develop results-based public-private partnerships (PPPs)
- Develop results-based M&E frameworks
- Promote entrepreneurship, OJT, and life skills training among job seekers
- Promote systems and program integration

Administration and Financing of Public Employment Agencies in the Middle East and North Africa Region

The reviewed MENA countries offer different models for administration of the national PEA. The PEA often comes under the labor ministry or a department within the ministry, but it can also be an autonomous agency. In some countries the PEA provides most ALMPs; in others, private providers and nongovernmental organizations (NGOs) play a big role in program provision. For example, in the Republic of Yemen, 150 registered NGOs work with the PEA. Private employment agencies are allowed to function in some countries, while in others, private provision of employment services is not allowed (table 1.1).

In Egypt, the Ministry of Manpower and Migration (MoMM) is the primary public employment agency. Established in 1961, it has 307 branches throughout

Table 1.1 Public Employment Agencies, Selected MENA Countries, 2010

Country	Name of national PEA and/or ministry responsible for employment services	Year established	Number of regional offices	Number of NGOs providing services	Number of private employment agencies
Egypt, Arab Rep.	Ministry of Manpower and Migration	1961	307	3	54
Jordan	Department of Employment and Training, Ministry of Labor (MoL)	2006	14	—	45
Lebanon	National Employment Office, MoL	1977	3	4	0
Morocco	National Agency for Employment and Skills Promotion (ANAPEC), Ministry of Employment and Vocational Training	2001	74	—	—
Syrian Arab Republic	Central Nomination Unit, Directorate of Labor, Ministry of Social Affairs and Labor (MoSAL)	2001	28	4	Legalized in 2010
Tunisia	National Agency for Employment and Independent Work (ANETI), Ministry of Vocational Training and Employment	1993	91	2	Private agencies are illegal
Yemen, Rep.	MoSAL	1996	20	150	0

Source: Angel-Urdinola, Kuddo, and Semlali 2013.
Note: In Morocco, both NGOs and private employment agencies provide employment services, but exact numbers are not available.
— = data not available.

the country. Over the past 10 years the agency has seen its role change dramatically as the national employment strategy has shifted from public sector employment guarantees to private sector–led employment creation.

In Jordan, the Ministry of Labor (MoL) is the main provider of public employment services. The Department of Employment and Training runs the basic labor intermediation function and also licenses private employment agencies. In parallel, the National Training and Employment Project (NTEP), an autonomous agency under the MoL, also provides ALMPs to the unemployed. The Vocational Training Center is the main agency directly providing training programs and accrediting training providers. Finally, an independent agency called the National Employment and Training Company (NETC), managed by the Jordanian Armed Forces, runs a specialized training programs for the construction sector.

In Lebanon, the National Employment Office (NEO) is a financially and administratively independent agency under the authority of the minister of labor, who chairs its board of directors. The board includes both employer and worker representatives as well as representatives from the education sector. At the time of the survey in 2010, NEO had only three offices, in Beirut, Tripoli, and Sidon.

In Morocco, the National Agency for Employment and Skills Promotion (Agence Nationale de Promotion de l'Emploi et des Compétences, ANAPEC) is the primary provider of employment services. The agency currently has 74 branches nationally. These branches are located in large cities. For smaller cities where there is insufficient economic activity to justify the creation of a branch, ANAPEC instead partners with territorial authorities, local professional associations, and NGOs to provide offices equipped with self-service job terminals. Job seekers can use these to access the ANAPEC database on existing job offers.

In Syria, the Ministry of Social Affairs and Labor (MoSAL) is responsible for setting the labor policy agenda and providing employment services. The Central Nomination Unit at the Directorate of Labor is tasked with coordinating and supervising the operations of 15 regional employment offices, activated in 2001 and located in all governorates. Every unemployed person in Syria must register with the PEA in his or her governorate.

In Tunisia, the National Agency for Employment and Independent Work (Agence Nationale pour l'Emploi et le Travail Indépendant, ANETI) comprises a network of 91 employment offices. These can be either multiservice employment offices, sector-related employment offices, or specialized employment offices. Multiservice employment offices carry out complex operational tasks related to information provision and career counseling, job placement, and the promotion of microenterprises and self-employment. Sector-related employment offices facilitate operations related to a specific economic sector identified as highly important to the region where they operate.

The Republic of Yemen has three main public institutions involved in the delivery of employment services: the MoSAL, the Ministry of Technical and Vocational Education and Training (MoTVET), and the Social Fund for

Development (SFD). These institutions, however, work in silos, and there is little coordination among them.

The budget of the national PEA varies from country to country, influenced by unemployment rates and the differing generosity of the programs. Based on available data, in 2010–11 Tunisia spent 0.80 percent of gross domestic product (GDP), Morocco 0.1 percent of GDP, and Lebanon 0.04 percent of GDP on ALMPs provided by the national PEA. In Tunisia the financing for ALMPs comes mainly through the National Employment Fund, which is financed through a special account in the Treasury. Its budget comes from general tax revenues, private contributions, resources from its interventions, and a portion of privatization proceeds. The fund is responsible for (a) financing the ALMPs delivered by the PEA, ANETI; (b) funding microcredits through the Tunisian Solidarity Bank (TSB); and (c) providing financial support to governorates to implement regional employment programs, notably public works. In Morocco, employment services and ALMPs are financed by the Ministry of the Economy and Finances through special Treasury accounts. ANAPEC had a budget of 808 million Moroccan dirhams ($100 million) in 2009.

An important factor contributing to the success of public employment agencies is the institutional capacity of the national offices to deliver quality services to registered job seekers. The institutional capacity of PEAs is often proxied by the available network of offices, the agency's budget, and especially the number and professional level of the staff at local employment offices relative to the number of registered job seekers. Of course, this proxy has a lot of caveats as available resources may or may not be used effectively. Most of the reviewed countries have databases that include a significant number of registered unemployed (table 1.2).

However, the roster of registered job seekers may in some cases provides a misleading picture of the needs of the labor market, as data sets are rarely

Table 1.2 Numbers of Unemployed, Registered Job Seekers, and Public Employment Agency Staff, Selected MENA Countries, 2010

Country	Number of registered job seekers (thousands)	Total number of PEA staff	Number of PEA staff in contact with job seekers and employers	Staff caseload[a]	Ratio of frontline counselors to total PEA staff (%)
Egypt, Arab Rep.	895.1	1,600	1,550	577	97
Jordan	28.0	133	63	444	47
Lebanon[b]	12.2	32	10	1,220	31
Morocco	517.0	547	343	1,507	63
Syrian Arab Republic	1,703.8[c]	397	120	14,199	30
Tunisia	281	1,271	1,052	267	82

Source: Angel-Urdinola, Kuddo, and Semlali 2013.
Note: Data for Tunisia are for the year 2011.
a. Average number of registered unemployed per PEA staff person in contact with job seekers.
b. Beirut only.
c. Public sector only, including individuals queuing for civil service and other public sector jobs.

updated. This occurs in part because registered individuals remain on the rolls, waiting to get scarce public sector jobs (PEAs in countries like Egypt, Syria, and Tunisia also oversee public sector hiring). In Syria, for example, the PEA had around 1.7 million people on the roster in 2009 (table 1.2), although fewer than 12,000 were appointed to government jobs during that year. A key aspect to consider in such contexts is the establishment of clear rules to maintain an accurate roster of job seekers. In emerging market economies, a common strategy is to remove "passive" job seekers from the roster. Typical reasons for removal include unexcused failure to report to the PEA, refusal to accept a suitable job offer, failure to meet the conditions of actively seeking employment and maintaining availability for work, or working informally while registered as unemployed. For example, in Belarus, removal from the registry occurs 36 calendar months from the date of registration as unemployed. In MENA, by contrast, many individuals remain on the PEA roster indefinitely.

In many MENA countries the number of available staff is inadequate to provide effective and personalized employment services. What really matters for the delivery of services to the unemployed is the proportion of staff in direct contact with clients—that is, caseworkers—and their workload. Of the total PEA staff in Jordon, Lebanon, and Syria, fewer than half are frontline employment counselors/advisers. High staff caseload does not allow the PEA to deliver personalized job intermediation services. In 2010, among the reviewed countries, the highest caseload was reported in Syria, with more than 14,000 registered job seekers per PEA staff person. Next were Morocco, with over 1,500 job seekers per staff person, and Lebanon, with over 1,200. Within the European Union (EU), the average staff caseload is around 1:150, while the figure recommended by the International Labour Organization (ILO) is even lower, at 1:100.[1]

First-time job seekers typically account for a great majority of those who register with employment agencies. In other respects, registered job seekers are a heterogeneous set of individuals, often with multiple employment barriers, including difficulties related to skills, health, and home lives (for example, lack of transportation or child care).

Table 1.3 shows the main characteristics of registered job seekers in five MENA countries. In several countries, a significant portion are women and/or have attained higher education. Job seekers with tertiary education account for one-third to one-half in Lebanon, Morocco, and Tunisia.

In Lebanon, Morocco, and Tunisia, long-term unemployment is the predominant form of joblessness. Employers highly value recent work experience when recruiting. Individuals with a large gap in their work history, who have lost touch with the labor market, and those without any work experience, such as youth and other labor market entrants, have little chance of being hired. Moreover, unemployment early in a person's working life has been shown to increase the probability of joblessness and of low wages in the future (Kuddo 2009). High rates of long-term unemployment in MENA may also indicate that some individuals, especially young university graduates, wait to get jobs in the public

Table 1.3 Characteristics of Registered Job Seekers, Selected MENA Countries, 2010
percent

Country	Women	Disabled	Long-term unemployed	Vocational education	Tertiary education
Egypt, Arab Rep.	22.3	1.0	10.1	26.2	11.2
Lebanon[a]	38.5	3.0	93.7	22.3	44.8
Morocco	40.6	0.1	82.0	33.4	33.2
Syrian Arab Republic	31.9	1.9	—	49.6	8.2
Tunisia	60.0	—	66.3	—	73

Source: Angel-Urdinola, Kuddo, and Semlali 2013.
Note: — = not available. Data for Tunisia are for the year 2011.
a. Beirut only.

sector, where wages and benefits are sometimes more competitive than in the private sector.

Women constitute a significant share of all registered job seekers. In Tunisia, more than half of registered job seekers are females. This is explained in part by an increase in educational levels among women and in the labor force participation of women with tertiary education. In other countries in the region, such as Egypt, Lebanon, Morocco, and Syria, women account for 22–41 percent of all registered job seekers.

Programs Provided by National PEAs

Training and intermediation services are the most common type of intervention. The inventory collected a total of 33 employment interventions implemented by the national PEA in the seven countries included in the review: Egypt, Jordan, Lebanon, Morocco, Syria, Tunisia, and the Republic of Yemen. Of this total, in 2010, 30 percent were training programs and 18 percent were intermediation services (figure 1.1). Tunisia implemented four on-the-job training programs. Lebanon and Syria carried out two in-class training programs each, and Egypt and Jordan one each. Morocco and the Republic of Yemen offered program packages generally composed of in-class training combined with other employment services, such as wage subsides and start-up incentives. The Republic of Yemen implemented just one program in 2010, but it included several components such as training, labor intermediation, direct job creation, and out-of-work income support. To a lesser extent, programs provided by the PEAs included direct job creation through public works (15 percent of all programs in the inventory), start-up incentives (9 percent), and programs targeted at persons with disabilities (3 percent).

Entrepreneurship promotion for first-time job seekers is increasingly offered by PEAs in the region. While entrepreneurship promotion programs have long been implemented in MENA, these programs have not traditionally been delivered by the national PEA. Most such programs have been provided

Figure 1.1 Distribution by Program Type of Publicly Provided ALMPs, Selected MENA Countries, 2008 and 2010

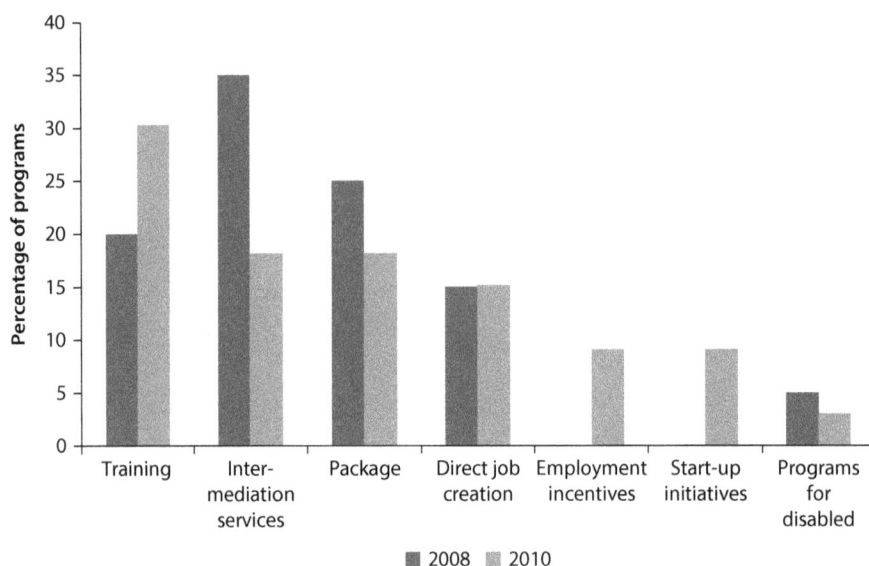

Source: Angel-Urdinola, Kuddo, and Semlali 2013.
Note: Countries included are Egypt, Jordan, Lebanon, Morocco, Syria, Tunisia, and the Republic of Yemen.

by social funds (Egypt and the Republic of Yemen), microcredit institutions (Tunisia), or donors (Egypt, Lebanon) (Angel-Urdinola, Semlali, and Brodmann 2010). Indeed, data indicate that in 2008 none of the national PEAs offered start-up assistance, although the PEA in Tunisia did offer to link promising entrepreneurs to microfinance institutions. By 2010, start-up assistance programs were offered by the national PEAs in Egypt, Lebanon, Morocco, and Syria. These programs typically provide financial and advisory assistance to microcredit institutions; some also include mentoring and training in entrepreneurial skills.

Wage subsidies are also taking a prominent role in countries where unemployment disproportionally affects first-time job seekers (as in Jordan, Morocco, and Tunisia). Wage subsidies aim to facilitate recruitment or ensure continued employment for targeted segments of the population. Jordan, for example, subsidizes 100 percent of the employee's contribution and 50 percent of the employer's contribution to social security for a two-year period. In Tunisia, subsidized paid internships for a maximum of one year, also covering social security contributions, are offered to a significant number of first-time job seekers.

Almost half of the programs delivered by PEAs in MENA (47 percent) target highly educated individuals and 53 percent target young adults or youth. The tendency to target programs at educated young people reflects the fact that in some countries, especially in North Africa, high-skilled youth face higher than average, and increasing, rates of unemployment. Recent regional data indicate that high-skilled individuals (proxied by those who attained a tertiary education

Figure 1.2 Targeting of Publicly Provided ALMPs, Selected MENA Countries, 2010

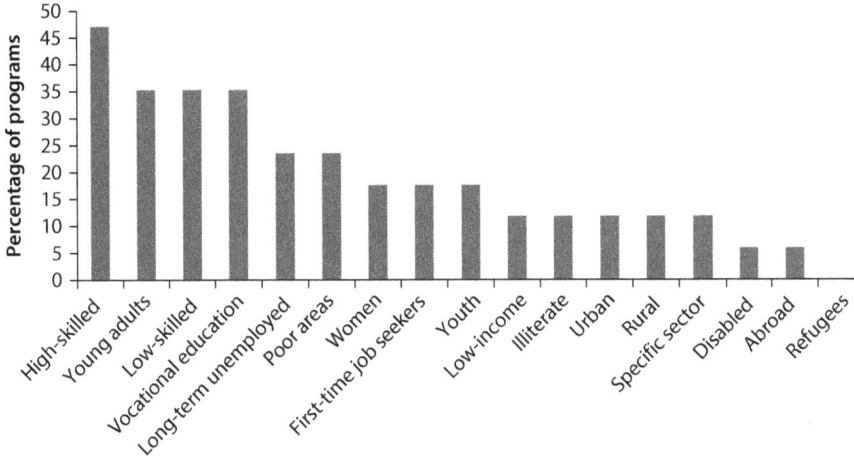

Source: Angel-Urdinola, Kuddo, and Semlali 2013.
Note: Data from Egypt, Jordan, Lebanon, Morocco, Syria, Tunisia, and the Republic of Yemen. Youth are ages 15–24;
young adults are ages 25–34.

degree) account for 20–30 percent of the stock of unemployed (World Bank 2013). Indeed, many programs in MENA are designed to help individuals find formal employment, something for which low-skilled individuals are unlikely to qualify (Gatti et al. 2012). Nevertheless, some ALMPs do target low-skilled individuals, rural areas, and minority groups who are likely to belong to vulnerable segments of the population (figure 1.2).

Women in MENA have much higher rates of unemployment than men. According to ILO data from 2008, the average unemployment rate among women in MENA was 17 versus 8 percent among men (World Bank 2013). Nonetheless, only 18 percent of the ALMPs in the region specifically target women. Many ALMPs, notably training, are conducted during working hours and/or require full-time participation, making it difficult for women with young children to participate. Cultural and social constraints may also affect the participation of women in ALMPs.[2]

Training Programs

Most training programs reviewed in the inventory are conducted in class only, with a minority providing on-the-job training. Practical experience is crucial in order to create well-trained and qualified workers. International evidence indicates that the most efficient way to acquire knowledge and skills for employment is to apply the material learned in class in a real-world workplace setting through on-the-job training and internships. Unfortunately, only a fraction of the training programs analyzed offer on-the-job training in addition to classroom sessions. As shown in figure 1.3, 62 percent of the training programs are conducted in class only, while 15 percent are conducted on the job only. Thus the majority of programs use very classical ways of transmitting knowledge and skills. Indeed,

Figure 1.3 Training Provided by ALMPs by Type of Training, Selected MENA Countries, 2009
percent

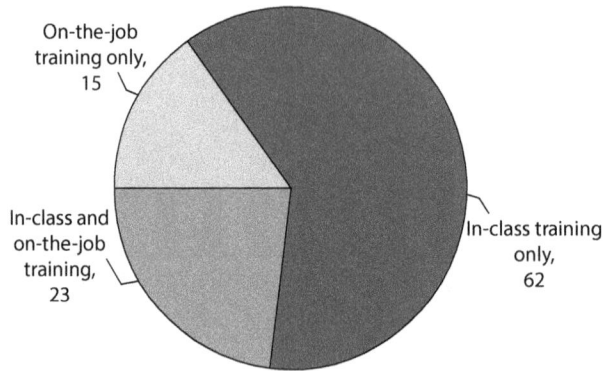

On-the-job training only, 15

In-class and on-the-job training, 23

In-class training only, 62

Source: Angel-Urdinola, Kuddo, and Semlali 2012.
Note: Countries included are Egypt, Jordan, Lebanon, Morocco, Syria, Tunisia, and the Republic of Yemen.

some PEA staff seem to lack understanding of the benefits of combining in-class and on-the-job training. One interviewee commented, "Why should we insist that program beneficiaries work also during their training? They will eventually spend their lives working, but training is training and that should be in class, no?"

Among training programs in the inventory, the large majority focus solely on the provision of hard skills—that is, the specific technical, mechanical, or other skills needed to do a particular job. Only a few of the programs focus on the provision of soft skills. Soft skills are the cluster of personality traits and interpersonal skills that help a person function effectively in the workplace, including social graces, language and communication abilities, amenability to training, ability to get along with other people, and ability to think creatively and independently. The acquisition of both hard and soft skills is crucial in order to create well-rounded and qualified workers. Moreover, employers in the MENA region often express their dissatisfaction about deficiencies in the skill sets of job seekers. This is an obstacle to hiring, especially of young workers.

Most of the nontraining programs reviewed do not focus on skills development of any kind. In Tunisia, internship programs, most of which are accompanied by wage subsidies, are required by law to provide some training to beneficiaries. In practice, this rarely happens, and skills enhancement is largely absent from all programs provided by the national PEA.

A further weakness of training programs is the systematic prevalence of inconsistent certification practices. In the MENA region, as in most regions of the world, a diploma has a "credentialing" value: it signals that its bearer has achieved a particular level of knowledge and competence. This allows access to higher levels of instruction and/or signals readiness for the workplace. Given the restrictions on hiring and firing in the MENA region (see World Bank 2013), employers give considerable weight to diplomas, degrees, test scores, and the like as predictors of productivity and competence, thereby reinforcing the importance of these credentials.

Only half of all training programs delivered by PEAs in MENA provide some type of certification, and certification practices vary from country to country. For example, Syria and the Republic of Yemen largely lack standard certification and accreditation systems and national qualifications networks, while Jordan and Lebanon have accreditation systems that are better developed. In order to signal the value added of training programs, it is important that both skills and service providers be accredited so that the certification has a signaling value in the labor market. This becomes quite relevant in countries like Lebanon, where training programs offered by the PEA are actually implemented by private training providers.

Although its performance is far from ideal, the public sector is doing better than the private sector when it comes to certification. A review of privately provided ALMPs revealed that only 10 percent of all private training programs included in the inventory provided beneficiaries with some type of recognized credential upon program completion (Angel-Urdinola, Semlali, and Brodmann 2010).

Intermediation Services

All countries in the region provide some type of intermediation services. All of the reviewed countries have walk-in employment centers, most of which allow job seekers to post a curriculum vitae (CV) and search the database for job offers. Egypt, Jordan, Morocco, and Tunisia also provide online services, including electronic matching platforms. The list of intermediation services provided by the PEAs to job seekers and employers in the reviewed countries is presented in tables 1.4–1.6.

For example, in Jordan, the MoL's Department of Employment and Training offers labor intermediation through its electronic labor exchange (ELE) platform. Unemployed job seekers who want to register can access the platform online or visit a regional office to receive assistance. In addition to posting a CV, job seekers can access career and job search advice on the website. Employers can register and view job seeker profiles only if they have a job vacancy to post. Employers outside Jordan also have access to the platform and can post vacancies. In 2009, 27,961 job seekers posted their CVs on the ELE, and 8,775 of them (31 percent) were successfully placed in firms.

Certain intermediation services are available to employers in most of the reviewed countries, such as posting of vacancies, database search for job profiles, prescreening of job applicants, and matchmaking. In order to participate in labor intermediation programs, employers usually have to register at the PEA; for example, in connection with vacancies they have to report to the PEA. The PEAs in all of the reviewed countries except Jordan also conduct interviews with firms to assess the needs of the labor market.

Most countries in the region partner with the private sector for the provision of intermediation services. Traditionally, national PEAs in the region had

Table 1.4 Public Intermediation Services for Registered Job Seekers, Selected MENA Countries, 2010

Country	Walk-in centers	Database search for job offers	Posting of job profiles	Posting of CVs	Alerts for matching
Egypt, Arab Rep.	Yes	Yes	No	Yes	No
Jordan	Yes	Yes	Yes	Yes	Yes
Lebanon	Yes	No	No	No	No
Morocco	Yes	Yes	No	Yes	No
Syrian Arab Republic	Yes	Yes	Yes	Yes	Yes
Tunisia	Yes	Yes	Yes	Yes	No

Source: Angel-Urdinola, Kuddo, and Semlali 2013.

Table 1.5 Public Intermediation Services for Registered Job Seekers and Employers, Selected MENA Countries, 2010

Country	Firm interviews to assess needs of labor market	Electronic matching platform	Provide services on internet
Egypt, Arab Rep.	Yes	Yes	Yes
Jordan	No	Yes	Yes
Lebanon	Yes	No	No
Morocco	Yes	Yes	Yes
Syrian Arab Republic	Yes	No	No
Tunisia	Yes	Yes	Yes

Source: Angel-Urdinola, Kuddo, and Semlali 2013.

Table 1.6 Public Intermediation Services for Employers, Selected MENA Countries, 2010

Country	Posting of job vacancies	Database search for job profiles	Matching	Alert function for matching	Automated collection of applications	Prescreening
Egypt, Arab Rep.	Yes	Yes	Yes	Yes	No	Yes
Jordan	Yes	Yes	Yes	Yes	Yes	No
Lebanon	Yes	Yes	Yes	No	No	No
Morocco	Yes	Yes	No	No	No	Yes
Syrian Arab Republic	No	No	No	No	No	Yes
Tunisia	Yes	Yes	Yes	No	Yes	Yes

Source: Angel-Urdinola, Kuddo, and Semlali 2013.

a monopoly status for the provision of intermediation services. However, in recent years there has been a shift toward more cooperation between the PEA and other institutions, such as private employment agencies, training and education institutions, local authorities, employers' organizations, NGOs, and universities. The PEA needs to assume the role of manager of relations with various relevant institutions and external service providers (European Commission 2009). This trend was recognized and boosted by the Private Employment Agencies Convention adopted by the ILO in 1997 (Convention 181 supported by Recommendation 188). This convention encourages "cooperation between the public employment service and private employment agencies in relation to the implementation of a national policy on organizing the labor market."

In Jordan, the MoL licenses private employment agencies, which are then granted access to the ministry's ELE platform to post vacancies and share information about job seekers. According to the data collected in the inventory, there are 45 licensed private employment agencies in Jordan and 54 private agencies in Egypt. Up until 2010, private employment agencies were illegal in Syria, with the exception of those recruiting foreign workers. The 2010 Labor Law reform legalized private employment agencies in Syria, allowing them to act as an intermediary between job seekers and private businesses, and mandated MoSAL to license them and regulate their activities.

Nevertheless, in some countries in the region, provision of employment services continues to be a monopoly of the state. For instance, the Tunisian labor code (Articles 280–285) gives ANETI a monopoly in the provision of placement and intermediation services. Private providers of placement services, whether free or fee-based, are forbidden by law. However, ANETI by itself does not have the capacity to provide services to all registered job seekers. In 2011 each ANETI counselor served on average 267 job seekers, a figure that is significantly above international standards for upper-middle-income or high-income countries (for example, the ratios of counselors to job seekers are 1:88 in the Czech Republic, 1:97 in Slovenia, and 1:133 in Bulgaria) (Kuddo 2012). The Jasmine Revolution exacerbated the problem, as hordes of unemployed youth registered with ANETI in order to receive unemployment assistance through the Active Employment Search Program for Higher Education Graduates (AMAL) program.[3] This placed an unexpected additional burden on ANETI's counselors, most of whom became involved in the registration and payment of AMAL beneficiaries, hindering their capacity to provide employment services to the registered job seekers.

Despite their availability, intermediation services provided by the PEAs in the region are not widely used by either employers or job seekers. This is partly explained by the fact that most firms in MENA do not believe that public employment agencies have the capacity to do effective matching. This is true to a large extent, as PEAs generally do not have a systematic way (or staff dedicated) to match registered unemployed to available vacancies. While the PEAs typically offer platforms for posting CVs and vacancies, more effective types of intermediation, such as counseling, job search training, and job clubs and fairs, hardly exist. Indeed, the PEAs in many countries play only a limited role in labor intermediation. Also, PEA staff have generally little incentives to engage in effective intermediation, since there are no extra incentives provided for better performance and/or for attaining effective matching. In Lebanon, Syria, and the Republic of Yemen, fewer than 4 percent of all workers report having found a job through labor offices. In Egypt, however, almost 50 percent of all workers report to have found a job through intermediation services in year 2010. These findings are largely misleading and do not necessarily reflect success in the provision of intermediation services, but rather the fact that Egypt's employment agency still plays an important role in public sector recruiting. (figure 1.4).

Lack of proper job-matching platforms and procedures undermines the role of intermediation services in many MENA countries.

The NEO in Lebanon receives announcements of job vacancies from firms and CVs from job seekers via fax, phone, e-mail, and personal visits to its walk-in center. Staff enter the requests into an electronic platform, but this is not available online, so neither firms nor job seekers have access to it. This leaves NEO solely responsible for matching vacancies with job seekers by selecting candidates and forwarding their CVs to the firms. The lack of automated and systematized processes results in unsystematic follow-up on the recruitment of job seekers by prospective employers and the use of an unreliable paper record system for program monitoring. Moreover, the databases of the offices in Saida and Tripoli are not linked to the central office in Beirut. Lebanon (Beirut only) is rather active in registering job vacancies, although the ratio of registered job seekers per vacancy is quite modest by international standards (table 1.7).

In Tunisia, the national PEA, known as ANETI, has a special unit in charge of reaching out to potential employers (Unité d'Information et d'Orientation Professionnelle). In 2011, personnel from this unit were able to collect approximately 100,000 job offers for internships and permanent positions. However,

Figure 1.4 How Workers Find Jobs, Selected MENA Countries, Various Years

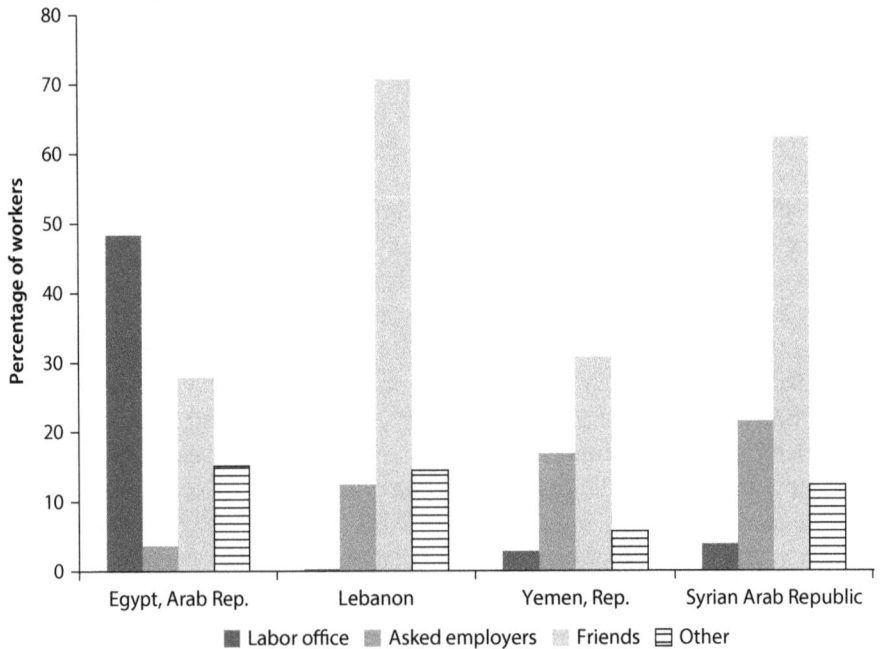

Source: Data from Gatti et al. 2012.
Note: Available years are Egypt 2006, Lebanon 2004, Syria 2010, and the Republic of Yemen 2005–06. Syria data are only for formal workers.

Table 1.7 Job-Seekers-to-Vacancy Ratio and Number of Job Placements per 1,000 Registered Job Seekers, Selected MENA Countries, 2010

Country	Number of registered job seekers (thousands)	Number of registered job vacancies (thousands)	Number of job seekers per one registered vacancy	Average placements per year (thousands)	Job placements per 1,000 job seekers per month
Egypt, Arab Rep.	895.1	222.9	4.0	40.1	45
Jordan	28.0	2.6	10.8	0.7	25
Lebanon[a]	12.2	3.6	3.4	—	—
Morocco	517.0	27.7	18.7	4.4	9
Tunisia	281	100.4	2.8	45.6	4.7

Source: Angel-Urdinola, Kuddo, and Semlali 2013.
Note: — = not available. Data for Tunisia are for the year 2011.
a. Beirut only.

46 percent of these vacancies were filled. Vacancies are entered in a database open to job seekers, but there is no systematic way to match the registered job seekers with available vacancies.

In Egypt, the PEA is quite active in registering job vacancies, having registered about 222,888 vacancies in the private sector in 2010. Employers in Egypt are required by law to send a detailed statement to the MoMM reporting the qualifications, age, nationality, gender, and salary of each new employee within 30 days of hiring. The companies have to meet certain criteria regarding work sites, salaries, and type of work in order to receive a license. Despite these efforts, less than 5 percent of all registered job seekers in Egypt are hired every month.

In Jordan and Morocco, the job-seekers-to-vacancy ratio is relatively high, and job placement rates are not high enough to absorb the growing number of unemployed individuals.

Monitoring and Evaluation of ALMPs

It is important to carefully monitor and evaluate employment programs as this makes it possible to introduce and scale up interventions on the basis of what has been shown to work. Rigorous, independent impact evaluations are critical to achieving real progress in addressing the major employment challenges. They provide evidence of best practices and promote wider use of these practices. Impact evaluations can be seen as a public good; they are often financed by the public sector or large donors, given high costs and positive externalities on the design of future programs. Absence of rigorous evaluations almost certainly leads to an overestimation of program effectiveness by policy makers.

Process evaluations are also useful in identifying bottlenecks and implementation problems. Typically, a process evaluation consists of interviews with beneficiaries and providers in order to assess whether a program is being implemented according to plan and whether it is achieving its objectives. Process evaluations, which are faster and less expensive than impact evaluations, can be carried out on a yearly basis and used to make midcourse adjustments to implementation.

Most programs included in the inventory lacked impact or process evaluations. However, most of them have output-based monitoring systems, typically providing data on the number of beneficiaries served. Indeed, data on program outcomes, such as job placement rates and wages after program completion, were not available for most programs included in the study (box 1.1). The majority of programs (93 percent) did not have a procedure for assessing program cost-effectiveness, and only a minority (15 percent) had conducted a program evaluation (figure 1.5). Moreover, most of the evaluations conducted lacked scientific rigor, rarely using control groups to allow for an estimation of the programs' net impact. Some programs did, however, provide some information on placement rates after program completion, at least for the first year. Only three programs provided information on earnings after program completion. Morocco conducted qualitative evaluations, in three of its four programs. In this case, the program administrators hired an external evaluator. In Tunisia there have been some attempts to use impact evaluations to assess programs delivered by ANETI, but results are outdated, sporadic, donor-driven, and lacking in scientific credibility (Belghazi 2012).

Box 1.1 Monitoring and Evaluation Processes

Monitoring entails the periodic collection of data to assess program performance. It can serve as a learning tool for organizations implementing and funding ALMPs to help them understand whether program objectives are being met and whether resources are being used to achieve those objectives. Monitoring indicators should generate relevant information for quantifying program performance.

Impact evaluation is the process of assessing the impact of a particular ALMP on program participants. The main difference between monitoring and evaluation is that evaluation aims to attribute causality, that is, the actual effects of ALMPs on employment outcomes in the short or long term. Evaluations are highly desirable because they provide evidence that could lead to more efficient allocation of public resources and to improved targeting of existing or new programs at the appropriate clients. Evaluations are intended to show what would have happened in the absence of the program, something that cannot be observed directly. Thus, evaluators have to find a way to estimate what participants' outcomes would have been in the absence of the program (the counterfactual). This is usually done by measuring the outcomes of a control group whose members resemble the beneficiaries in key characteristics.

Finally, process evaluations are systemic assessments to determine whether programs are operating as described in the operations manual. While they cannot attribute causality, they provide useful information about bottlenecks in service delivery, beneficiaries' satisfaction, quality of services provided, and the functioning of service delivery systems.

Source: Betcherman et al. 2010.

Figure 1.5 Percentage of Publicly Provided ALMPs that Have Conducted an Impact Evaluation or Cost-Benefit Comparison, Selected MENA Countries, 2009
percent

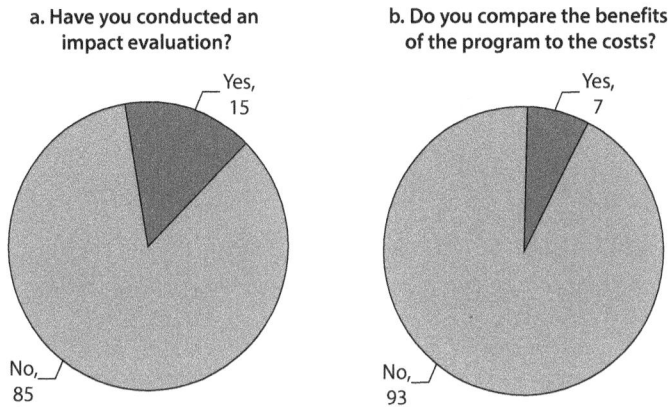

a. Have you conducted an impact evaluation?

Yes, 15

No, 85

b. Do you compare the benefits of the program to the costs?

Yes, 7

No, 93

Source: Angel-Urdinola, Kuddo, and Semlali 2013.
Note: Countries included are Egypt, Jordan, Lebanon, Morocco, Syria, Tunisia, and the Republic of Yemen.

Nevertheless, most programs did conduct some form of internal evaluation, though less than half attempted to quantify the benefits of the program (figure 1.6). Many of the programs gathered qualitative information through informal interviews with staff and beneficiaries, questionnaire surveys, and focus group discussions. Some programs administered skills tests before, during, and after project completion in order to assess progress, but they did so without including control groups. The quality and relevance of these various evaluations remain largely unassessed (box 1.2). In short, because of the lack of knowledge regarding the effectiveness of these evaluation instruments and the lack of substantial program information, it is difficult to say whether any given program works well or not.

Conclusions and Policy Recommendations

The MENA region is facing serious challenges affecting its labor markets. These include sluggish labor demand, high rates of joblessness among youth and women, prevalence of skills mismatches, stagnant labor mobility, high rates of informal employment, and lack of formal employment networks.

Given these challenges, ALMPs could play an important role in addressing market failures related to labor demand, labor supply, and information asymmetries, thus increasing the employability and employment chances of program beneficiaries. ALMPs have been widely used in the MENA region. However, the efficiency and effectiveness of these programs depend largely on their design, as well as on the country's institutional capacity to implement them.

In several countries in the region, the number of caseworkers and counselors is inadequate for delivering ALMPs through effective and personalized

Figure 1.6 Monitoring and Evaluation Practices in Publicly Provided ALMPs, Selected MENA Countries, 2009

percent

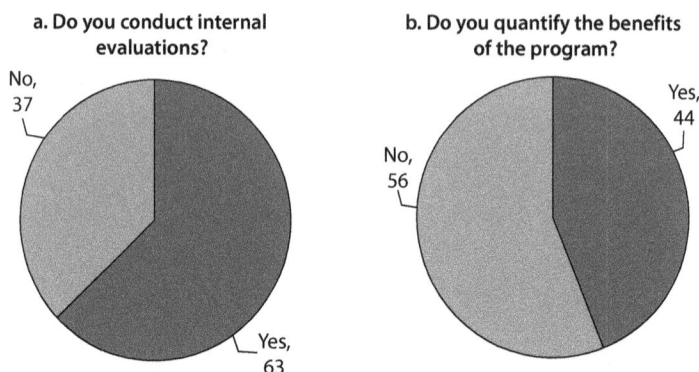

a. Do you conduct internal evaluations?

No, 37

Yes, 63

b. Do you quantify the benefits of the program?

Yes, 44

No, 56

Source: Angel-Urdinola, Kuddo, and Semlali 2013.
Note: Countries included are Egypt, Jordan, Lebanon, Morocco, Syria, Tunisia, and the Republic of Yemen.

Box 1.2 Basic Results-Based Indicators for Employment Programs

The following basic indicators are used widely by national employment agencies to measure fundamental outcomes:

• *Job placement rate.* The number of registered job seekers in quarter t who are employed in quarter $t+1$.
• *Job retention rate.* The number of registered job seekers in quarter t who are employed in both quarters $t+2$ and $t+3$.
• *Average earnings.* Average earnings in quarters $t+2$ and $t+3$ for those registered job seekers in quarter t who retained employment in these quarters.
• *Filled vacancy rate.* The number of registered job vacancies in quarter t that are filled by registered job seekers in quarter $t+1$.

While these are proposed as core performance indicators, three additional indicators could be considered at a later stage: average length of time required per job placement, average length of time per filled vacancy, and annual cost per program participant. At a minimum, this set of indicators should be calculated annually, but it is preferable if they are calculated quarterly or semiannually.

Source: Betcherman et al. 2010.

---

mediation services. While there might be limitations on hiring new staff, the efficiency and quality of services could be improved by moving more staff to the front line to deal with clients, periodically updating the roster of registered job seekers to exclude individuals who are no longer looking for jobs, and building effective, results-based partnerships with the private sector for service delivery. Indeed, given the needs of the labor market and the important capacity constraints faced by PEAs in the region, there is a strong rationale for increasing reliance on private delivery of services in the areas of training, employment services, and public works. Contracting out is a means to ensure more effective and efficient partnerships with private providers. Service contracts with private providers should be based on results to encourage providers to improve job placement.

There is ample space to reform the provision of vocational training programs. Vocational training continues to be the main type of program provided by PEAs in MENA, targeting mainly high-skilled unemployed youth. But international experience shows that training programs have limitations. First, they are relatively costly, which means that participation is necessarily limited. Second, their impact will be limited when job opportunities for trained workers are scarce. Finally, training programs are also associated with deadweight losses (that is, some workers would have found jobs without the training). It is important to enhance coordination with the private sector to ensure that training programs are demand-driven and relevant.

The content and structure of training programs also needs improvement. Most training programs reviewed in the inventory are conducted in class only, with only a minority providing on-the-job training. Recent evidence indicates that programs that combine' different training approaches are more likely to yield positive impacts on employment and/or earnings outcomes of trainees. In particular, the combination of in-class and workplace training increases the likelihood of positive labor market impacts by 30 percentage points compared to in-class training alone. When such combined training is bundled with other services, the probability of a positive impact increases by 53 percentage points.[4] Employers in the region often express their dissatisfaction with deficiencies in the skills of job seekers, not only technical/occupational skills but also the more generic soft skills. However, very few training programs focus on provision of soft skills. Only 10 percent of all training programs reviewed give beneficiaries some type of recognized credential after program completion that could make trainees more attractive to potential employers. Finally, most programs are conducted during the day, often full-time, making it difficult for women who care for children to attend. In sum, training programs could be reformed by (a) complementing in-class, hard-skills training with on-the-job training and provision of soft skills; (b) improving certification practices so that participation in training programs provides a positive signal to employers; and (c) making programs flexible (especially in terms of schedules) to facilitate the participation of women.

While most countries in the region offer intermediation services, there is scope for improving their effectiveness. All of the reviewed countries have walk-in employment centers, and most of them allow job seekers to post their CVs and search the database for job offers. Despite their availability, intermediation services are not widely used by either employers or employees. This is partly because most firms in MENA do not believe that public employment agencies have the capacity to do effective matching. Beyond providing platforms for posting CVs, intermediation services could be improved by offering more group-based activities for job seekers. These might include collective sessions in which the unemployed learn about the local and regional labor market situation, including jobs offered and the qualifications needed to apply for them; receive job counseling about the skills and qualifications they need to improve in order to increase their employability; obtain information about education, training, and alternative job opportunities; and receive training in job search skills, such as filling out job applications and attending job interviews.

PEAs in MENA should sustain their efforts to support entrepreneurship promotion. Data collected for this study indicate a positive tendency in this regard: while none of the national PEAs offered start-up assistance in 2008, by 2010 such programs were offered by the PEAs in Egypt, Lebanon, Morocco, and Syria. Most MENA countries have developed entrepreneurship programs, and these have had, for the most part, a positive impact on youth employment. However, these efforts are limited in scale and scope and target primarily the low-skilled, whose businesses tend to remain small and thus have a limited impact on job creation. Several studies show that providing education to the owners of micro and small informal enterprises is an important determinant of innovation, rate of return on capital, and employment growth (World Bank 2012). Evidence from a World Bank entrepreneurship program in Tunisia, which allows university students to develop a business plan rather than a traditional thesis to meet graduation requirements, shows that the provision of entrepreneurship training and personalized coaching is effective in increasing the rate of self-employment among university graduates. Of course, these types of initiatives need to be complemented with information, coaching, access to credit, and other instruments such as incubators and guarantee funds. Moreover, there is a need to develop mechanisms for effective job matching through, for example, electronic platforms, mobile technology, and/or providing financial incentives to councilors who succeed at effective employment matching. Partnership with private providers of intermediation services will also be pivotal as these providers generally know the needs of the labor market better than public agencies, and have a profit-driven incentive to deliver successful services.

Finally, there is an urgent need to improve governance and accountability of program delivery by establishing results-based monitoring and evaluation frameworks. Most programs included in the inventory have output-based monitoring systems but lack results-based systems and/or rigorous program evaluations. The majority of all programs (93 percent) did not have any type of method or procedure for assessing program cost-effectiveness, and only a minority (15 percent) had conducted an impact evaluation. MENA countries need to establish a clear governance structure, quality assurance mechanisms, and an M&E strategy based on results, not merely outputs, to increase program efficiency and effectiveness and improve the use of public resources. Rigorous, independent impact evaluations are needed to demonstrate what works, encourage sharing of best practices, enhance capacity in the region, and improve overall policy making.

Notes

1. This EU average figure hides considerable variation: for example, Germany has a ratio of about 1:200 and the Netherlands 1:60.

2. To improve female take-up, training programs may have a female teacher and/or offer classes for women only. However, because labor demand is constrained in the region, there is a belief that encouraging women to increase their labor force participation will lead to higher unemployment for men, who are considered to be the main breadwinners.

3. After the Jasmine Revolution, Tunisia's interim government launched the AMAL ("hope" in Arabic) program in February 2011. AMAL is a comprehensive youth employment program that seeks to provide unemployed university graduates with employment services for a maximum of 12 months.

4. The evidence is based on recent meta-analysis of 345 studies of training programs from 90 countries around the world (Fares and Puerto 2009). In Argentina, Chile, Peru, and Uruguay, the Joven training programs have been widely recognized as successful in reaching disadvantaged youth. Critical to their success is the nature of the training—which includes both technical and life skills, lectures and internships—and the support services and course certifications that foster continuing participation.

References

Angel-Urdinola, D., and A. Kuddo. 2010. "Key Characteristics of Employment Regulation in the Middle East and North Africa." Social Protection Discussion Paper 55674, World Bank, Washington, DC.

Angel-Urdinola, D., A. Kuddo, and A. Semlali. 2013. *Public Employment Agencies in the Middle East and North Africa*. Washington, DC: World Bank.

Angel-Urdinola, D., A. Semlali, and S. Brodmann. 2010. "Non-Public Provision of Active Labor Market Programs in Arab-Mediterranean Countries: An Inventory of Youth Programs." Social Protection Discussion Paper 1005, World Bank, Washington, DC.

Belghazi, S. 2012. "Evaluation Stratégique du Fonds National pour l'Emploi de la Tunisie." Tunis.

Betcherman, G., R. Gussing, P. Jones, R. Can, and J. Benus. 2010. "Policy Note on Turkey's Active Labor Market Programs." World Bank, Washington, DC.

Card, D., J. Kluve, and A. Weber. 2010. "Active Labor Market Policy Evaluations: A Meta-Analysis." NBER Working Paper 16173, National Bureau of Economic Research, Cambridge, MA.

European Commission. 2009. *The Role of the Public Employment Services Related to 'Flexicurity' in the European Labour Markets*. VC/2007/0927, European Community, Brussels.

Fares, J., and O. S. Puerto. 2009. "Towards Comprehensive Training." Social Protection Discussion Paper 0924, World Bank, Washington, DC.

Gatti, R., D. F. Angel-Urdinola, J. Silva, and A. Bodor. 2012. *Striving for Better Jobs: The Challenge of Informality in the Middle East and North Africa*. Washington, DC: World Bank.

Kuddo, A. 2009. "Employment Services and Active Labor Market Programs in Eastern European and Central Asian Countries." Social Protection Discussion Paper 0918, World Bank, Washington, DC.

————. 2012. "Public Employment Services, and Activation Policies." Social Protection Discussion Paper 1215, World Bank, Washington, DC.

Lippoldt, D., and M. Brodsky. 2004. "Public Provision of Employment Services in Selected OECD Countries: The Job Brokerage Function." In *Labor Exchange Policy in the United States*, edited by D. E. Balducchi, R. W. Eberts, and C. J. O'Leary, 211–48. Kalamazoo, MI: W. E. Upjohn Institute.

Martín, I. 2010. "Labour Markets Performance and Migration Flows in Arab Mediterranean Countries. A Regional Perspective." In *Labour Markets Performance and Migration Flows in Arab Mediterranean Countries: Determinants and Effects*. European Economy, Occasional Paper 60. Brussels: European Commission. doi:10.2765/26101.

World Bank. 2012. *World Development Report 2013: Jobs*. Washington, DC: World Bank.

————. 2013. *Jobs for Shared Prosperity: Time for Action in the Middle East and North Africa*. Washington, DC: World Bank.

CHAPTER 2

Public Employment Programs in Egypt

Amina Semlali and Diego F. Angel-Urdinola

Introduction

The Arab Republic of Egypt has the fourth-largest economy in the Middle East and North Africa (MENA). Egypt has implemented economic reforms since 2004 that have led to economic growth, notably a fast-growing technology sector. The country has been recognized as one of the top offshoring destinations in the region for international companies.

However, Egypt's economic development has been undermined by a number of factors. In particular, the country has been struggling with structural unemployment, especially among women and youth. The rates of long-term unemployment (12+ months) are high among women and high-skilled youth, as they generally queue for public sector jobs (figure 2.1). Furthermore, the quality of employment has deteriorated. There is stagnation in the creation of formal private sector jobs, and public sector employment is not growing fast enough to absorb the estimated 600,000 new entrants to the labor market annually.[1]

Paradoxically, employers experience difficulty in recruiting personnel for the few positions available, as they feel that young workers often lack the skills and experience needed to fill vacancies. Results from enterprise surveys in Egypt indicate that 50 percent of all firms interviewed identify worker skills mismatches among their top five constraints to business development (Angel-Urdinola and Semlali 2010). The education and training systems are often unrelated to the demands of the job market, resulting in inadequate curricula that are not aligned with the competencies required by employers. Neither higher education nor technical and vocational education and training (TVET) have offered a critical level of skills enhancement that qualifies young people to successfully find jobs in the formal economy. To cope with the situation, young workers, both educated and uneducated, are opting to work in the informal sector in low-quality, low-paying jobs, while those who can afford to do so may withdraw from the labor force (Angel-Urdinola and Semlali 2010).

Labor offices in Egypt are one of the main mechanisms that job seekers use to find formal jobs, notably in the public sector (figure 2.2). Close to 50 percent of all workers in Egypt report having obtained employment through some labor

Figure 2.1 Percentage of Labor Force Experiencing Long-Term Unemployment in Egypt, by Category of Worker, 2006

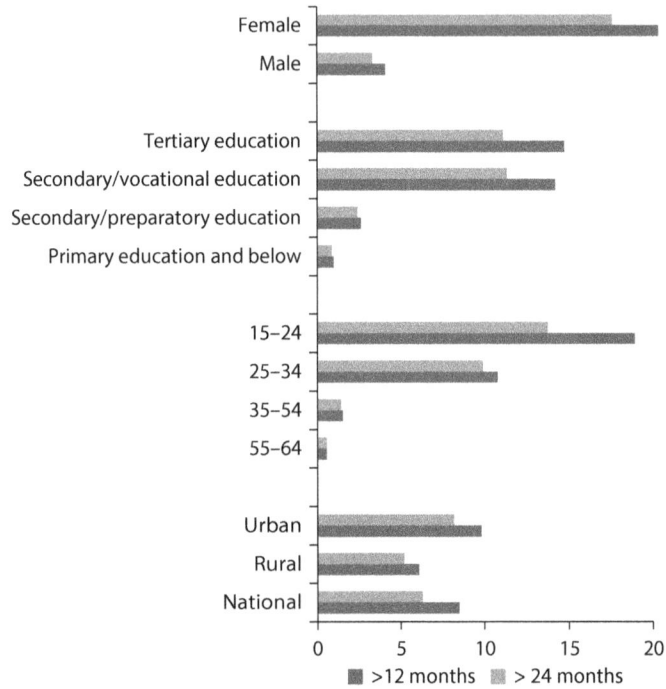

Source: Based on data from the Egypt Labor Market Panel Survey 2006.

Figure 2.2 How Workers Find Jobs in Egypt, by Employment Sector, 2006

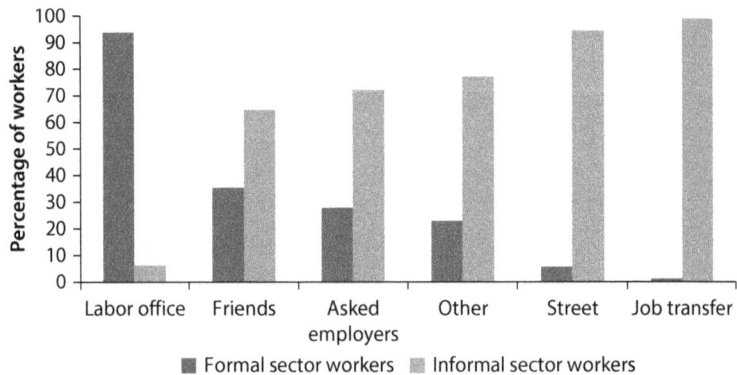

Source: Based on data from the Egypt Labor Market Panel Survey 2006, multiple-choice question.

intermediation mechanism, either through public labor offices run by the Ministry of Manpower and Migration (MoMM) or through private providers (see chapter 1, figure 1.4). Indeed, Egypt is one of the countries where public labor intermediation, despite capacity constraints, seems to be a widely used instrument that allows unemployed individuals to find jobs. The broad utilization of labor offices by the unemployed is largely a legacy of the past when the government guaranteed public employment to university graduates.

Beyond intermediation, Egypt has a complex system of active labor market programs (ALMPs) in the areas of vocational training, entrepreneurship, and public works. These aim to enhance employability, provide a safety net, and encourage employment creation among the unemployed. In particular, Egypt has implemented large public works and microcredit programs that have benefited a significant share of the population. However, the technical and vocational education system is fragmented and suffers from a lack of coordination. Services are often supply-driven and of low quality, and most interventions remain largely unassessed.

Institutional Framework for Employment Programs in Egypt

Ministry of Manpower and Migration

The MoMM is Egypt's primary public employment services agency. It is responsible for labor policy, managing labor supply, increasing the employability of the labor force, and monitoring and managing labor market demand (box 2.1). Established in 1961, the ministry has seen its role change dramatically over the past 10 years as the national employment strategy has shifted from public sector employment guarantees to job creation in the private sector. Approximately

---

Box 2.1 Legal Framework for Public Employment Programs in Egypt

Unified Labor Law 12/2003 and its executive decisions and regulations control employment rules in the Arab Republic of Egypt.

Article 11. This article establishes a higher committee for regulating public employment services for workers inside and outside the country. The committee is headed by the competent minister and includes representatives from related ministries, the Egyptian Trade Union Federation, and business owners' organizations. The committee is responsible for conceptualizing policies, systems, rules, and procedures for labor intermediation, domestically and internationally.

Articles 12–15. Everyone able and willing to work must submit an application to register with the administrative labor office nearest his or her place of residence, indicating name, age, profession, qualifications, and experience. The labor office shall register these applications in serial numbers and give the applicant a certificate of registration; no fee is charged. For workers in certain professions, specified by ministerial decision, the applicant should attach a certificate to the registration indicating skill level and grade. Employers are obliged to submit a detailed statement of their workforce, specifying the number of workers employed according to their qualifications, careers, experience, nationalities, gender, and salaries. Employers are also obliged to register vacancies in the labor offices, and the labor offices are responsible for identifying suitable candidates for open positions. These articles shall be applied without prejudice to provisions of Law 39/1975 and its amendments in Law 49/1982.

1,600 staff are employed at the MoMM, and the ministry claims that the majority of them are in contact with job seekers. One of the main responsibilities of the MoMM is to match job seekers and job vacancies through a network of 307 employment offices throughout Egypt. In 2010 there were 895,078 registered unemployed, while the number of vacancies registered with the MoMM was 222,888. The average number of job placements per month in that year was 40,101. The MoMM's main functions in relation to labor intermediation include the following:

- Registration of job seekers (mandatory by law). Job seekers need to present certification indicating their skills and educational level.
- Registration of vacancies. Employers are required by law to send detailed statements to the MoMM of the employees they hire within 30 days of hiring (qualifications, age, nationality, gender, and salary). A company has to meet certain criteria regarding work sites, salaries, types of work, and so on, in order to receive a license, which enables the company to be matched to employees.
- Helping job seekers find suitable jobs according to their skills and the requirements of the labor market.
- Helping job seekers pursue professional training in order to become more employable.
- Making job seekers aware of how to better present their abilities to employers through preparation of interviews and curricula vitae (CVs).
- Making employers aware of laws and regulations concerning employment provision.

Beyond labor intermediation, the MoMM collaborates with employers and workers through the Supreme Council for Human Resources Development (SCHRD). The SCHRD is responsible for coordinating the training policies of all ministries. Its role is to "set up a national policy related to planning and developing manpower and training and set up comprehensive and global national program for the development and optimum use thereof" (ETES 2000). The MoMM is also in charge of the coordination and implementation of the "national plan for employing youth," with the participation of partners such as the Higher Council for Youth and Sport, civic organizations, the International Labour Organization, and donors. The main objectives of the national plan include increasing youth employability, developing training centers, and encouraging small projects, all with the intention of maximizing economic growth. The MoMM leads the establishment of a National Framework of Qualifications and is responsible for the implementation of a skills and occupational standards system in the tourism, hotel, construction, agriculture, and industrial sectors.

The MoMM also performs labor mediation as an alternative to litigation. Mediation plays an important role, given the high numbers of time-consuming labor lawsuits and disputes between employees and employers before the courts. Finally, the MoMM supports Egyptian workers who wish to emigrate, as well as workers who have already emigrated, through information on laws, contacts, and

Table 2.1 Summary of Public Employment Programs in Egypt Provided by the MoMM, 2010

Program	Description	Targeting/characteristics of beneficiaries	Number of beneficiaries (annual)
Most-needed jobs for the job market (quarterly program)	Announces the most-required jobs within the internal and external job markets, using data from sources such as newspapers, the national employment bulletin, foreigner labor permits, public labor offices, and compliance programs.	Most job seekers: high- and low-skilled, women and men, younger and older, urban and rural areas, with the exception of refugees seeking employment.	—
National employment bulletin	Reviews needs of businesses and their job vacancies and offers them to employment seekers, acting as a link between them.	Most job seekers: high- and low-skilled, women and men, younger and older, urban and rural areas, with the exception of individuals seeking employment overseas and refugees seeking employment.	281,274
Services to disabled	Provides people with disabilities with employment services to foster labor market and societal integration.	Job seekers with disabilities.	3,529
Local recruitment agencies (licensing)	Provides job opportunities within Egypt through licensing of recruitment agencies.	Most job seekers: high- and low-skilled, women and men, younger and older, urban and rural areas, with the exception of individuals seeking employment overseas and refugees seeking employment.	29 agencies
Irregular employment program	Provides social security and health care for informal sector employees, such as farmers, part-time workers, construction employees, mine and quarry workers, and fishermen.	Low-skilled males.	2,560,963
Regularizing employees within the informal sector	Works to regularize employees within the informal sector and incorporate them into the formal sector by providing social security and health care.	Semi-skilled and high-skilled workers in the informal sector.	290

Source: Based on administrative data collected through World Bank interviews with Egyptian government officials from the Ministry of Manpower and Migration in 2010.
Note: — = not available.

so forth. As of 2009, the MoMM had a number of ALMPs under way. Brief descriptions of the programs with their objectives, targeting, and numbers of beneficiaries are summarized in table 2.1.

Social Fund for Development

The Social Fund for Development (SFD) is a semi-autonomous government agency under the direct supervision of the prime minister. It was created in 1991 as a joint initiative between the Egyptian government, the World Bank, and the United Nations Development Programme. It promotes economic development and improved employment services, with a special focus on mitigating the negative effects of economic reform on the most vulnerable groups of people.

Labor Intermediation and Direct Job Creation

One of the main responsibilities of MoMM is employment matching through a network of 307 employment offices throughout Egypt. As mentioned previously, Egypt has been quite active at matching employees to employment opportunities, notably in the public sector, with about 50 percent of job seekers reporting that they found employment through labor intermediation. In other MENA countries labor intermediation is less developed and serves a smaller share of job seekers. For instance, in Lebanon only 0.3 percent of all job seekers report finding employment through an employment service; comparable figures are 2.8 percent in the Republic of Yemen and 3.8 percent in Syria. Even in Egypt, however, job seekers with higher education use formal means of finding employment—such as registering with public or private employment offices—to a much larger extent than do less-educated individuals. The latter mainly rely on their networks of family and friends, who are often lacking in influence.[2]

Although Egyptian employment offices have been doing comparatively well in the MENA context, there is much room for improvement. Offices need to become more relevant and more able to efficiently assist both job seekers and employers in the private sector. According to interviews with MoMM staff, of the 307 offices, 127 need substantial investments in facilities and equipment. Moreover, the employment offices operate with very limited funding, as the Ministry of Finance has prioritized other sectors. This has made it difficult to train staff and upgrade office equipment. The offices operate at low capacity because of understaffing. Staff focus mainly on intermediation and spend little time interacting with job seekers; employment services such as counseling and life skills training are rarely provided. Furthermore, there is not much interaction and information exchange between the various offices across regions/governorates; rather, each employment office in each governorate works individually, seldom communicating with other offices. This suggests that job seekers are not referred to potentially suitable jobs in other regions and governorates—a large gap in the Egyptian employment matching apparatus.

The MoMM has developed a comprehensive database that maps vacancies, indicating the vacancy's profile, key function areas, and skills/competences needed. The dataset also contains a comprehensive list of job seekers and their competences and registers information on how many of them are hired. However, the database has been underused, and the MoMM lacks the capacity to analyze the data and produce monitoring reports. This dataset could potentially be very useful within the Egyptian labor market context, making job matching more efficient and providing a better picture of labor demand in Egypt. Box 2.2 shows the main challenges facing employment offices in Egypt, based on information collected by a visiting World Bank team and provided by other international donors.

Egyptian Labor Market Service Reform Project

Efforts have been made to upgrade and modernize public employment services through the Egyptian Labor Market Service Reform Project (ELMSR). Initiated in 2001, the ELMSR was implemented by the SFD in partnership with

Box 2.2 Main Challenges Facing Labor Offices in Egypt

Office infrastructure

- Some of the offices lack Internet connection, telephone/fax lines, computers, and even basic furniture such as desks.

Staff allocation and competencies

- Offices are understaffed and staff members do not have time to input data in computer systems, when appropriate equipment exists, or provide counseling services. Division of functions is not clearly defined, resulting in duplicate work.
- Most staff have not received training on how to perform employment counseling.
- There is no partnership between the various offices. Employment offices in each governorate operate without communicating or sharing data with other offices.
- Many staff lack sufficient computer skills. This affects productivity, since they cannot communicate with employers through e-mail or fax in a prompt manner.
- Staff lack strong understanding of the needs of the Egyptian labor market, including local labor market needs.
- Monitoring of office/staff performance seems nonexistent.

Provision of services

- Staff do not always register walk-in clients in the main database, nor do they share information on all available opportunities, since they themselves are not aware of all the options. Instead, job matching is done manually, based on connections the office managers might have with employers in their local district.
- Job seekers cannot go online to upload their CVs or search for jobs registered with the employment offices.
- There is a significant time lag in announcing vacancies, typically one to two months from the time that the employment office receives the employer's request for hiring.
- No written materials such as booklets or brochures are provided in the offices for job seekers to take home and use as reference.
- Employment counseling is very rarely carried out.

Job seekers/employers

- There is a mismatch between the jobs available and the qualifications of job seekers. Many of the job seekers who approach employment offices have higher levels of education, a bachelor's degree or more, although this varies according to location. Thus they may be overqualified for the jobs available on the market.
- At the same time, the positions that employers often need to fill—such as cashiers, waiters, cleaners, nurses, sales clerks, and drivers—often are not registered with the employment offices.
- The lack of cooperation between the private sector and employment offices leads to further discrepancies in job-matching efforts.

Source: World Bank field visits to employment offices and conversations with MoMM staff at local and central levels, as well as information collected by other international donors.

the MoMM. It was funded by the Canadian International Development Agency (CIDA) at $4.98 million and the Egyptian government at $4.64 million. The project's objective was to be achieved by (a) establishing a comprehensive system for delivering programs and services in a network of offices throughout Egypt; (b) training professional staff to operate an employment service, and training of trainers; and (c) expanding the usage and relevance of the Egyptian National Occupational Classification System. The initial plan was to establish 60 additional employment offices in the country by 2006 and an additional 15 by 2007; however, only 37 offices were actually established. The implementation strategy also called for training office staff in various skills, including employment counseling and case management, in workshops organized by CIDA.

Upon the project's completion, an independent team from CIDA conducted an evaluation of its impact using a strengths, weaknesses, opportunities, and threats (SWOT) analysis. Overall, the evaluation found that even though the project's area of intervention was very relevant to national and local priorities, its impact was limited. The main achievement was a clear improvement in office facilities and equipment, but this had only minor impacts on the quality and efficiency of service delivery. The challenges encountered were mainly related to bureaucratic inefficiencies within the MoMM itself (box 2.3).

Box 2.3 Main Challenges Facing the Egyptian Labor Market Service Reform Project

- Fully automated and accessible electronic labor exchange system to facilitate rapid job matching was not achieved, even though Internet connection has been installed in the offices that lacked it. Office staff continue to perform job matching manually, as before. No explanations were given as to why this facilitating service was not utilized.
- Employment counseling services were mostly not provided to job seekers, despite extensive training of staff. Staff mentioned lack of personnel and time as the reasons they are not able to provide counseling.
- Staff were trained as trainers. However, continued training of other staff did not take place, partly because personnel were regularly relocated or rotated to other posts, thus hindering their ability to train others.
- Staff members selected for training by the MoMM were mostly close to retirement age (assignment to newly established offices was treated as a reward). This led to an extra cost to the project for training additional employees when those already trained retired.
- The MoMM did not monitor employment offices or maintain new equipment.
- A network designed to facilitate information sharing between the various employment offices and the MoMM was not implemented by the ministry.
- Employment-related information was not consistently provided to clients. For example, a career handbook was produced to assist job seekers in making informed career choices; however, the evaluation team noticed that the handbook was only available in a few offices.

box continues next page

Box 2.3 Main Challenges Facing the Egyptian Labor Market Service Reform Project *(continued)*

- After completion of the project, the team observed large variations between offices in terms of their use of technology and office upkeep and cleanliness. This reflected the uneven willingness of employment office staff to sustain and implement project activities and keep the premises in a presentable condition.
- The evaluation team assumed that it would find beneficiaries such as job seekers, employers, and trained employees to interview. This was not the case, as the offices were often empty and office staff did not often share job seekers' contact information.
- The evaluation team found it difficult to obtain data from employment offices after project completion, as staff kept this information private.

Source: Internal CIDA documents.

Technical and Vocational Education and Training

TVET can, ideally, help young entrants enhance their skills and make them more employable. TVET has been at the core of employment policy in Egypt, yet the system largely fails to achieve its objective. Labor market outcomes, especially employment outcomes of TVET beneficiaries are inadequate. Even though the weaknesses of the system are well documented and there is wide agreement on needed reforms, there is little momentum to implement these reforms as yet.

Various initiatives have been launched to improve the Egyptian TVET system (Amer 2007). In 2002 the government decided that the SCHRD would be responsible for implementation of the TVET reform. Following this, a number of programs were developed, including the National Skills Standards and Certification Project, the National Training Fund, the World Bank Higher Education Enhancement project, the Mubarak Kohl Initiative, the Skill Development Program of the World Bank, and the TVET project supported by the European Commission.

Challenges to the TVET System in Egypt

Egypt's vocational training system faces numerous challenges (for more information see ILO 2007). A key problem is the institutional framework. Training is provided by both public and private providers but unfortunately little is known about training provided by the private sector. Public provision of TVET in Egypt is very fragmented, as a myriad of ministries oversee TVET programs and facilities (figure 2.3). The large number of agencies involved in regulating and providing programs leads to a troublesome lack of coordination.

A major player in the TVET system is the Ministry of Education, which administers around 1,600 technical and vocational schools at the secondary level. The Ministry of Higher Education manages 47 middle technical institutes, which provide two-year postsecondary courses. Numerous specializations are provided, particularly within the industrial institutes, including, for example, electrical installation, printing, and sheet metal work. However, much of this specialized technical training is geared to producing skilled workers rather than technicians.

Figure 2.3 Structure of the Technical and Vocational Education and Training System in Egypt

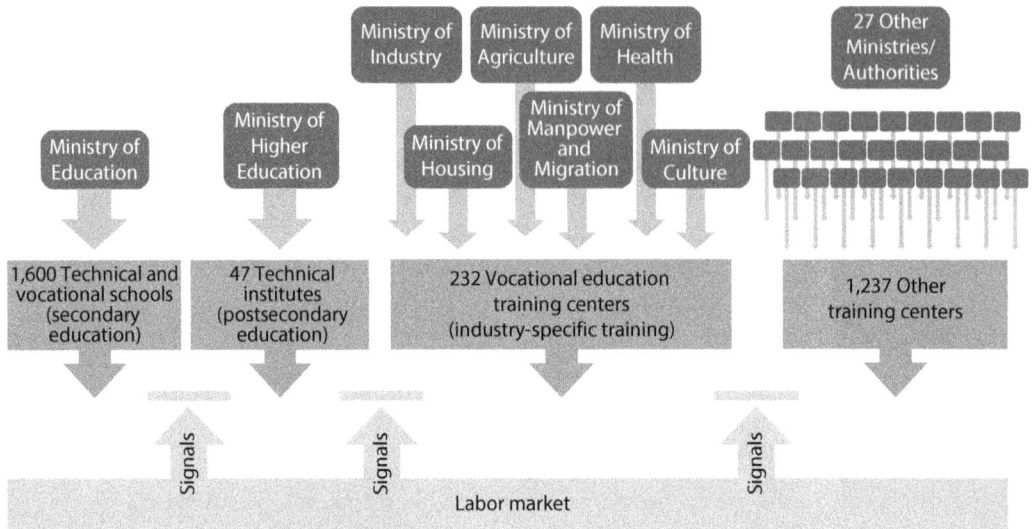

Source: Kamel 2006.

Six other ministries run a total of 232 vocational training centers (VTCs) providing industry-specific training. In addition, there are 1,237 other training centers affiliated to 27 ministries or authorities, which operate somewhat independently in 19 governorates. Although all the training centers might be broadly classified as VTCs, this classification is somewhat misleading, as courses can last anywhere from a few weeks to four years. However, in all cases the training is essentially vocational; it focuses more on practice than does the technical education provided by the Ministry of Education, where at least 30 percent of time is spent on general subjects. Each center decides its own program content, conditions, curriculum, and examination standards. Most of them provide only in-house certificates (in effect, certificates of attendance). However, five agencies provide diplomas endorsed by the ministry.

Beyond system fragmentation, a second problem with the TVET system is that services are often supply-driven, and there is little coordination with the needs of the labor market. Ministries in Egypt allocate their vocational training budgets to their providers on an ad hoc basis, not necessarily based on performance (ILO 2007). Training programs fail to adjust to the type and quality of skills that employers need. The World Bank, in a survey of 211 Egyptian employers, found that employers consider the training provided by the VTCs to be deficient in quality and market relevance (Angel-Urdinola and Semlali 2010). Employer federations representing small and medium enterprises have reported that the demand for semiskilled workers and trained technicians is increasing rapidly, but that such personnel are in short supply.

The efficiency and quality of training are low. This reflects the insufficient budget allocation, the separation of theory from practice, and the low qualifications of trainers. According to a survey by Egypt's central statistical agency, only

35 percent of instructors had any pedagogical training, and only 50 percent had attended any advanced practical training (ILO 2007). The VTCs suffer from a lack of knowledge about curriculum development methodologies and an inability to monitor, evaluate, and modify curricula. In some cases, trainers are left to prepare their own notes based on personal experience and knowledge, since authorities have not distributed the printed training materials that exist. In addition, the vast majority of equipment in training centers is poorly maintained, dilapidated, depleted, and/or underutilized.

Finally, monitoring and evaluation of the training programs' impacts on labor market outcomes is deficient. Documentation regarding program outcomes, such as placement rates and wages after program completion, was not available for most programs, and interventions do not assess program cost-effectiveness. Few rigorous program evaluations have been done.

Human Resource Development Program

The Human Resource Development Program (HRDP) was set up to target unemployed youth, providing them with the skills needed to obtain jobs. It also helps public and private enterprise employees stay in their jobs or redeploy to other jobs. The services are geared to literate people with basic education. The program is jointly funded by the Egyptian government and international partners through the SFD with a budget of approximately 30 million Egyptian pounds (LE) ($5 million) a year. The HRDP has two main components (table 2.2):

- *Provision of contracted training to unemployed youth.* The training is tailored to the needs of enterprises that are looking for specific skill sets and that intend eventually to hire the trainees. The training is jointly financed by the enterprises and HRDP. It also includes improving the capacity of the training system to respond to rapid developments in the labor market by providing relevant skills. This has involved reequipping some training centers, redesigning curricula, and training instructors.
- *Egyptian Labor Adjustment Services (ELAS)*, operated as part of the HRDP. ELAS works with public or private enterprise employees to enable them to either stay in their current position or acquire new employment elsewhere. ELAS provides financial incentives to businesses, organizations, communities, and sector groups to help employers and workers meet the challenges of adjusting to industrial change. Within enterprises that have to reduce

Table 2.2 Projects and Beneficiaries of the Human Resource Development Program, Egypt, 2010

Type of project	Number of projects	Contracted amount (Egyptian pounds, millions)	Planned number of beneficiaries
Training for unemployed youth	23	45.9	16,371
Assistance for public enterprise workers	9	185.3	31,142

their workforce, ELAS will set up adjustment committees comprising equal numbers of employee and management representatives to assess the situation and recommend appropriate solutions for retraining or redeployment of staff.

The main challenges facing the HRDP concern the following issues:

- *Type of training.* Both hard and soft skills, as well as practical, on-the-job experience, are crucial in order to create well-rounded and qualified workers. However, few training programs under HRDP provide soft skills or on-the-job training.
- *Targeting.* Beneficiaries of youth unemployment programs are mainly educated males, often university graduates from middle- or high-income groups. There are several reasons why low-income people and women do not benefit as much from these programs. One is the lack of flexible scheduling that would allow beneficiaries to combine program attendance with work and family responsibilities. Many women and rural people, moreover, do not meet the basic education requirements for participation in the programs. Additional factors are the urban focus of the programs and the failure to disseminate information about training options to target groups.
- *Stakeholder coordination.* Most youth unemployment programs are characterized by a weak coordination among relevant stakeholders. Training providers face great difficulties coordinating with the private sector to identify programs that employers deem relevant.
- *Monitoring and evaluation (M&E).* Most programs lack rigorous M&E, and as a result, the benefits of interventions remain largely unknown.

Public Works and Regional Development Programs

The government's principal public works and regional development programs are administered by the Ministry of Local Development through its Shoroukh program and by the SFD.

Shoroukh Program

The National Program for Integrated Rural Development, known as Shoroukh, was launched in 1994 by the Organization for Reconstruction and Development of the Egyptian Village (ORDEV). Program implementation relies mainly on the coordination between various partners in the rural development process, including local community representatives, government administrators, and nongovernmental organizations (NGOs). The program's executive arms are the rural development committees at various administrative levels.

The objective of the program is to combat unemployment by creating income-generating opportunities in rural areas. This is expected to lead in turn to a reduction in migration, increased productivity, and a greater role for local communities in the development process. The program aims to expand the enterprise base and increase the economic capacity of enterprises. NGOs play a crucial role, especially by increasing community awareness of the benefits of participating in the development process. Capacity building of NGOs constitutes a main component of the program.

The government agencies' interventions include both financial and technical assistance. Initially, projects were fully funded by the government, but gradually community funding has taken on a more prominent role. A funding mechanism affiliated with ORDEV facilitates the establishment of small enterprises. Credit is only given to enterprise activities that are in line with the program development plan, mainly environmental and basic infrastructure projects. Within a four-year period the program established 9,188 economic projects that led to 25,628 job opportunities within the enterprises, most of them permanent jobs. Moreover, the program created an additional 55,225 job opportunities, around half of which were temporary jobs, at a cost per job ranging between LE 4,087 and LE 9,760 (approximately $675 and $1,614).

Public Works Program

The primary aim of the Public Works Program (PWP) is to supply basic infrastructure and services to impoverished rural communities and urban poverty pockets in order to generate employment and improve poor people's access to basic infrastructure and municipal services. This is done through investments in roads, water systems, sewerage, buildings, and environmental projects. The PWP's operational guidelines call for the employment of large numbers of workers on its labor-based projects and require contractors to hire individuals from areas adjacent to their project sites. At least 25 percent of a project's value should go to the labor component, and 50 percent of workers should be recruited locally. The PWP discourages the use of machinery and construction equipment unless needed to attain specified quality levels.

It appears that the number of permanent jobs created by PWP programs is small, mainly due to the temporary nature of public works activities. Wages received for these mostly temporary jobs directly benefit laborers and inject money into the local economy, but the income is not enough to reduce poverty sustainably. However, important infrastructure and services have been provided or improved through this PWP. A number of the PWP implemented have addressed poor people's lack of access to basic services by providing potable water, sanitation, and health care, and lessen their exclusion from economic life by improving road access to remote rural areas.

Entrepreneurship Programs

Community Development Program

The Community Development Program (CDP) is financed by the SFD. It has a number of subprograms, including education and microcredit activities. While these programs place less emphasis on job creation than other programs, considerable efforts have been made in practice to provide earning opportunities and increase the incomes of poor families. The CDP provides small microcredit loans of up to LE 5,000 (approximately $1,827), mainly to very poor families. A significant number of beneficiaries are reached: approximately 15,000 beneficiaries had access to microcredit in 1999, of which 40 percent were women. The loans enable women with family responsibilities to engage in home-based activities that contribute substantially to household incomes. In some cases the financed activity provides only part-time employment; in other cases, several family members become involved in the project on a full-time basis. Overall, the CDP provides the equivalent of one "permanent" job to each beneficiary family.

Loans are provided at 7 percent interest to NGOs; these then lend to individuals, usually charging borrowers 8 percent and retaining a 1 percent margin to manage risks. The margin has to be returned to the SFD if there is no default on the loan. The interest rate is considerably lower than the market interest rate. Repayments to the SFD take place in tranches. Individuals who have already benefited from a loan are either ineligible for a second loan or must wait until first-time applicants are served. Operating costs are covered by a grant, using public and international funding. Additional funds can also be provided for training NGOs in credit management and borrowers in developing their activities. Overall repayment rates are very high. However, there are some difficulties in calculating the on-time repayment rates, as loans are rescheduled readily when borrowers encounter problems. In a well-run microcredit program operating in one municipality, one loan officer could be expected to serve between 150 and 400 loans per year, depending on the type of loans involved. Programs that use interest rates high enough to cover operating expenses as well as the cost of capital are quickly able to leverage grant and concessional loans with resources from the private sector.

Small Enterprise Development Organization

The main objectives of the Small Enterprise Development Organization (SEDO), also under the SFD, are to create new small enterprises and help existing ones grow. Program beneficiaries range widely from unemployed youth to medium-sized enterprises. Although the program does not directly target poor people, they benefit through the jobs that are created by small enterprises. A wide range of loan types and sizes are provided to all nonagricultural sectors of the economy through a large network of banks in all regions. Three types of services are provided:

- The Financial Services Department deals with contracting, disbursements, negotiations with new partners, portfolio control, database development, and direct lending through banks.
- The Business Services Department provides a wide range of direct services to potential clients through a network of field officers.

- The Institutional Business Services Department provides replicable standard loan packages and local area development projects that are implemented through tripartite agreements between SEDO as the financier, a bank as the sponsor and credit manager, and an NGO as the executing agent.

The SFD has adopted a comprehensive policy that emphasizes women's role in the small enterprise sector. It prioritizes the development of women's skills and capabilities to enable them to establish and expand small enterprises. It also seeks to feminize the culture of entrepreneurship through a media campaign and establish a businesswomen's network. Women account for 27 percent of entrepreneurs who benefit from SEDO loans. Affirmative action is not used, and female and male clients are treated equally.

Conclusions and Policy Recommendations

Egypt has a complex system of labor intermediation and ALMPs in the areas of vocational training, entrepreneurship, and temporary employment schemes through public works. These programs seek to respond to the needs of the unemployed, enhance employability of the workforce, provide safety nets, and encourage employment creation. The performance of the various programs in meeting these objectives, however, is mixed.

Although there is ample room for improvement, public labor intermediation in Egypt is already an important mechanism by which unemployed individuals obtain formal employment, especially in the public sector. Investments in capacity building and modernization of the public labor offices have great potential to further improve labor market intermediation and reduce frictional unemployment. In particular, labor offices could expand their scope to include job search assistance, counseling, and referral of job seekers to ALMPs, but this would require investments in training labor office staff. Labor offices in Egypt could also benefit from improving their labor market information systems and from more collaboration with private employment agencies. Although the MoMM has developed a comprehensive database that maps information on registered unemployed and vacancies, the data are underutilized. The database, if better used, could be a useful instrument to assess labor demand within the Egyptian labor market.

The technical and vocational training system in Egypt, although widely used, faces important challenges. As described above, the TVET system is highly fragmented and loosely coordinated, with thousands of training centers and institutes operating under several dozen ministries or other authorities. Services are often supply-driven and of low quality. At the same time, Egypt has implemented large public works and microcredit programs that have benefited a significant share of the population. Despite significant investments in these programs, most interventions remain largely unassessed.

Given the size of investments and the urgent need to improve labor market outcomes among new entrants, the system of public employment programs in

Egypt could make significant improvements in service delivery by focusing on 5 priority areas, as outlined below.

Stakeholder Coordination

Public-private partnerships should be increased. This could be achieved by (a) establishing a coordinating body to facilitate interaction and knowledge exchange between training providers and the private sector; (b) designing provider contracts based on performance and intermediation, with pay bonuses to performers achieving higher placement rates; and (c) expanding programs that offer apprenticeships and on-the-job training. Partnerships between the private sector and universities are highly encouraged. Universities could modify their curricula so that practical experience is credited toward students' graduation.

Quality Assurance Mechanisms and Signaling

There is a need to establish mechanisms for quality assurance of ALMP providers and increase the signaling effect of ALMPs. This could be achieved by (a) introducing systems to accredit training providers while ensuring that the skills taught are in demand and also accredited, (b) disseminating information about providers' performance and quality, and (c) establishing a National Qualifications Authority to define occupational norms and relevant skills training in consultation with the private sector.

Program Design

The emphasis should be on a mutual obligations approach through activation policies. Activation policies encourage job seekers to become more active in improving their employability and searching for work. In return for a range of employment services, individuals must comply with a set of eligibility requirements. They might be required to participate in training or other employment programs, attend interviews with employment counselors, or independently search and apply for job vacancies. The main target groups for activation programs are recipients of income-replacement benefits, a very small population, which are conditional on availability for work. Moreover, a general increase in the number of programs focused on job search assistance is desirable; such programs include job fairs, job clubs, CV/interview training, and matching services. These programs are generally found to have a positive impact in the short run and to be cost-effective (Kuddo 2009).

Content of Training Programs

Training has traditionally been delivered in-class and has focused on occupation-specific hard skills. There needs to be a shift to comprehensive training packages that also provide practical, on-the-job experience—such as through internships with private employers—and develop a mix of hard and soft skills. Employment services should be provided as part of the training to address information asymmetries. Future skills needs and regional and global integration should be considered when designing new programs in order to increase portability of the skills acquired. This might involve expanding training in the areas of computers, other information technologies, and languages.

Monitoring and Evaluation

Well-functioning M&E systems require information systems, data availability, data collection, selection of meaningful indicators, and periodic reporting. There is a need to develop a culture that favors data collection and provision of monitoring reports. For large programs, impact evaluation should be integrated in the program design and interventions in order to provide real-time feedback and facilitate midcourse corrections, as well as to evaluate the efficiency and effectiveness of expenditures. Evaluations should ideally be conducted on pilot interventions before these are scaled up. For smaller programs, involvement of the public sector in financing or subsidizing evaluations is important. Developing comprehensive datasets, identifying and tracing beneficiaries over time, and linking programs across different institutions are steps toward greater integration and harmonization of social protection and labor policies.

Notes

1. Based on data from the Egypt Labor Market Panel Survey of 2006.
2. Ibid.

References

Amer, M. 2007. "Transition from Education to Work: Egypt Country Report." Working Paper, European Training Foundation, Turin, Italy.

Angel-Urdinola, D., and A. Semlali. 2010. "Labor Markets and School-to-Work Transition in Egypt: Diagnostics, Constraints, and Policy Framework." MPRA Paper 27674, Munich Personal RePEc Archive. http://mpra.ub.uni-muenchen.de/27674.

Angel-Urdinola, D., A. Semlali, and S. Brodmann. 2010. "Non-Public Provision of Active Labor Market Programs in Arab-Mediterranean Countries: An Inventory of Youth Programs." Social Protection Discussion Paper 1005, World Bank, Washington, DC.

ETES (Education, Training, and Employment Sub-committee). 2000. *Report by the Education, Training and Employment Sub-committee, 3 August 2000.* Government of Egypt, Cairo.

ILO (International Labour Organization). 2007. "School-to-Work Transition: Evidence from Egypt." Employment Policy Paper 2007/2, ILO, Geneva, Switzerland.

Kamel, M. 2006. *Situation Analysis of Youth Employment in Egypt.* Centre for Project Evaluation and Macroeconomic Analysis, Ministry of International Cooperation, Cairo.

Kuddo, A. 2009. "Employment Services and Active Labor Market Programs in Eastern European and Central Asian Countries." Social Protection Discussion Paper 0918, World Bank, Washington, DC.

CHAPTER 3

Public Employment Programs in Jordan

May Wazzan and Diane Zovighian

Introduction

In Jordan, positive economic growth and good overall levels of job creation coexist with high rates of unemployment of the labor force. Between 2000 and 2008, the Jordanian economy grew at an average annual rate of 6.2 percent and created up to 70,000 jobs per year. The economy was negatively affected by the global financial and economic crisis, resulting in a sharp drop in the growth rate to 2.3 percent in 2009. Yet signs of recovery were noticeable early in 2010, a year when the economy grew at an average rate of 3.1 percent. Though Jordan has performed relatively well in terms of economic growth and job creation in the last decade, labor force participation rates remain low (40 percent in 2009) and unemployment rates among nationals have remained high, especially among youth (table 3.1).

Jordanian women, youth, and university graduates have particularly constrained access to full and productive employment (table 3.1). Women and youth have considerably lower labor force participation rates and higher unemployment rates than the national average. Only 14.9 percent of women participate in the labor force, and the unemployment rate among economically active women is as high as 24 percent, compared to 10 percent for men. Similarly, only 28 percent of youth participate in the labor force, and active youth constitute half of the unemployed, with an unemployment rate of 27 percent. University graduates constitute one-third of the unemployed, with an unemployment rate of 16 percent (figure 3.1). Women and youth with no previous work experience are more vulnerable than other groups to long-term unemployment (Alhawarin and Kreishan 2010).

Labor market outcomes in Jordan are negatively affected by geographic mismatches, skills mismatches, and expectations mismatches between labor demand and supply (World Bank 2008):

- *Geographic mismatch.* Jobs are mostly created in the capital and the main cities, while the majority of the unemployed are located outside of these areas.

Table 3.1 Jordan Labor Market Indicators, 2000 and 2009
percent

Indicator	2000	2009
Labor force participation rate (age 15+)		
Male	66.0	64.8
Female	12.3	14.9
Youth (ages 15–24)	27.8	28.0
Total	39.4	40.1
Unemployment rate		
Male	12.3	10.3
Female	21.0	24.1
Youth (ages 15–24)	26.7	27.0
Total	13.7	12.9

Source: Based on data from Jordan Department of Statistics, Employment and Unemployment Survey, 2000 and 2009.

Figure 3.1 Unemployment Rates by Age Group and Educational Attainment in Jordan, 2009

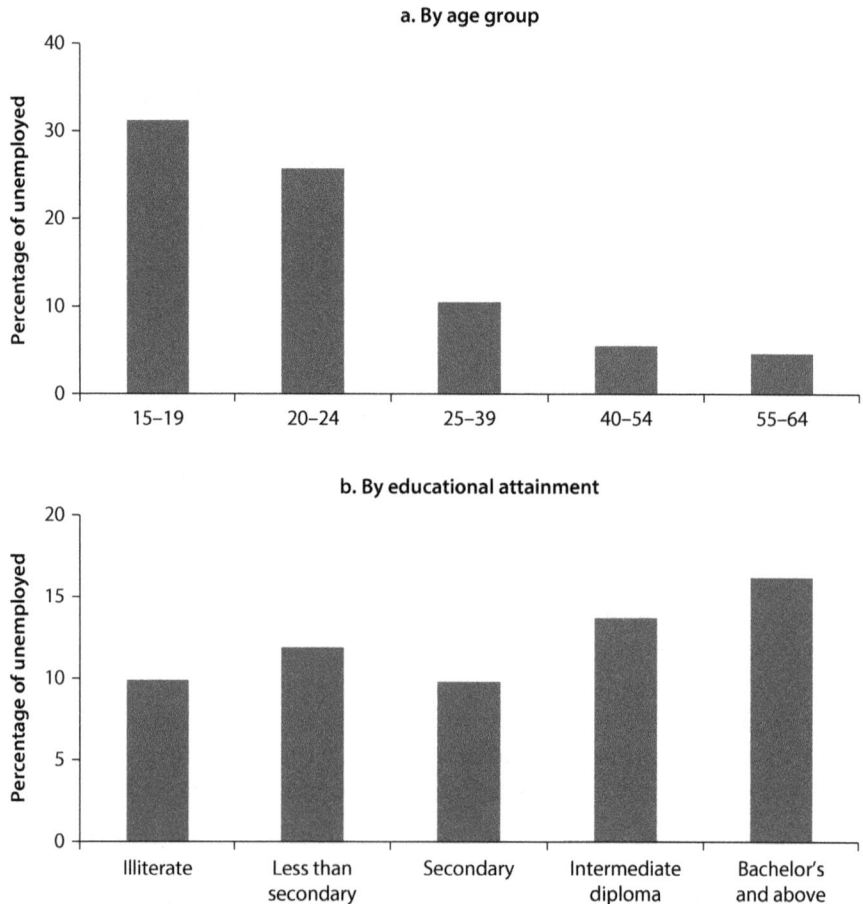

a. By age group

b. By educational attainment

Source: Based on data from Jordan Department of Statistics, Employment and Unemployment Survey, 2009.

- *Skills mismatch.* The skills provided by the educational and training systems tend not to be in line with the needs of the labor market. One of the consequences is the difficult school-to-work transition of Jordanian youth, which underlies their high level of unemployment and tendency toward long-term joblessness.
- *Expectations mismatch.* Job seekers and employers have divergent expectations with regard to working conditions and wages. Some segments of the Jordanian labor force are unwilling to take existing jobs because they do not match their expectations. Evidence indicates that only 54 percent of the unemployed are unwilling to take available jobs at prevailing wages (Razzaz and Iqbal 2008). Partly as a result, employers tend to be biased toward hiring foreign workers, who often have lower wage expectations than Jordanians. The expectations mismatch between employers and job seekers is particularly marked for low-skilled, low-paying jobs, which account for the bulk of job creation. Women are also significantly affected: Jordanian female workers are often discouraged to take up jobs with poor working conditions, and many have a strong preference for public sector jobs.

One challenge faced by the Jordanian government is gradually replacing foreign labor with Jordanian labor, especially in jobs that provide wages and working conditions compatible with the expectations of the national labor force. The labor market receives a high influx of foreign workers: there were approximately 298,241 foreign workers in Jordan in 2010, making up approximately 20 percent of the labor force (NCHRD 2010). Job creation surveys by the Department of Statistics indicate that 30 percent of the net jobs created in 2008 and 2009 went to foreign workers. Foreign workers tend to have low educational attainment (91 percent have not completed secondary school) and are concentrated in agriculture, construction, and services.

Measures to overcome barriers to employment are at the core of Jordan's policy agenda. Employment support and vocational training are key priorities of the government's National Agenda for 2011–13. This area was allocated a total budget of 151 million Jordanian dinars (JD) ($212 million) for the three years, accounting for about 2.4 percent of total spending foreseen under this development plan (MoPIC 2011). The objective of this component of the National Agenda is to improve the employability and participation rates of the workforce. Jordan puts a strong focus on institutions and governance with a view to reforming the structures in charge of policy making and service delivery in the field of human resource development. A series of measures and policies have been developed within the framework set by the National Agenda, including (a) enactment of a law supporting the establishment of an Employment—Technical and Vocational Education and Training (E-TVET) Council in charge of policy coordination and funding of human resource development programs, and (b) preparation of a National Employment Strategy that opens space for investments in active labor market programs (ALMPs) to support skills upgrading and facilitate job matching.

The various mismatches and barriers to employment identified above call for sustained public intervention in Jordan to expand and strengthen employment programs. These programs can facilitate intermediation between prospective employers and job seekers to bridge information gaps, which are often at the source of inefficient job matching and expectation gaps. They can help bridge the skills mismatch by bringing unemployed workers' skills into closer alignment with the needs of private businesses. At the same time, ALMPs can help bridge the gap in wage expectations between the national workforce and private businesses through temporary wage subsidies.

The main categories of ALMPs implemented in Jordan, and examined in this chapter, include:

- Public employment services
- Training programs, particularly for the unemployed
- Employment subsidies, including those linked with training programs
- Programs supporting micro, small, and medium enterprise (MSME) development

The chapter first outlines the institutional framework governing the public delivery of ALMPs in Jordan and the main stakeholders. It then reviews ALMPs provided by the Jordanian government, discusses some design and relevance issues, and offers recommendations to strengthen these programs and improve their effectiveness.

Institutional Framework for Employment Programs in Jordan

An array of ministries and agencies in Jordan are involved in policy making and service provision related to ALMPs and to human resource development more generally (figure 3.2). With regard to ALMPs, most of the responsibilities lie with the Ministry of Labor (MoL) and its related agencies, including the Vocational Training Center (VTC) and the Department of Employment and Training (DET), with the latter in charge of delivering employment services. Several other public ministries and agencies also have stand-alone ALMPs. For example, the Jordanian Armed Forces provide training programs; the National Center for Human Resources Development (NCHRD) provides selected employment services; and the Development and Employment Fund provides support to MSME development projects. Traditionally, institutional coordination between the different public agencies and ministries engaged in ALMP provision has been weak to nonexistent.

Jordan has embarked on a series of governance reforms to address the fragmentation of policy making and service provision in the area of human resource development. In particular, the reform of E-TVET governance systems is a major component of Jordan's National Agenda. This reform effort is geared toward strengthening policy and institutional coordination among the various agencies involved in human resource development, enhancing the efficiency of their

Figure 3.2 Institutional Framework for the Public Provision of ALMPs in Jordan

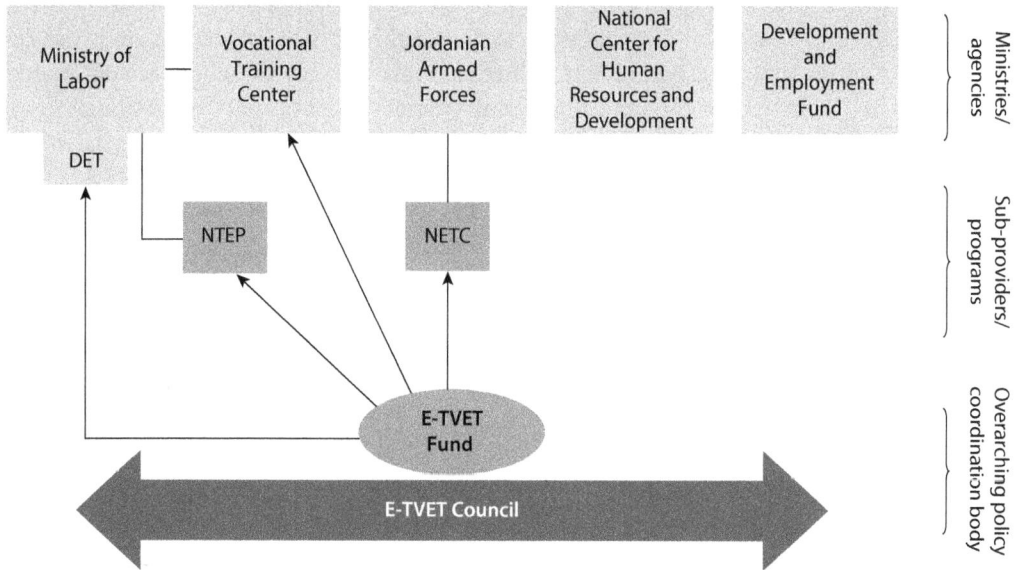

Note: DET = Department of Employment and Training; NETC = National Employment and Training Company; NTEP = National Training and Employment Project; E-TVET = Employment—Technical and Vocational Education and Training.

financial and management systems, regulating their functions, and providing increased resources to the E-TVET system. One of the main results of such reforms is the establishment of a multi-stakeholder body, the E-TVET Council, in charge of policy making and coordination in the field of human resource development. Jordan has received considerable support from foreign donors for the implementation of these reforms, including the World Bank, the Canadian International Development Agency (CIDA), and the European Commission.[1] Yet it is still too early to assess the overall impact of efforts to reform the E-TVET governance systems.

Ministry of Labor

The MoL is the core provider of public employment services through the DET. The ministry also supports the provision of training programs through its VTC and through affiliated agencies.

The DET has 14 regional branches, covering all of Jordan's governorates, but its human and financial resources remain constrained. It has 133 staff, only 63 of whom are in direct contact with job seekers and employers; they include registration officers, caseworkers, counselors, and marketing officers. In addition to the direct provision of public employment services, DET also licenses and regulates private employment agencies (which numbered 45 as of December 2009).

The VTC, established in 1976, is the main agency directly providing short-term vocational training programs and accrediting training providers in Jordan.

It is a semi-autonomous agency governed by a board of directors that is chaired by the minister of labor and includes, among others, representatives of the private sector. The VTC oversees 46 centers, employs 1,400 permanent staff, and runs on an annual budget of $14 million, allocated mainly from government budget.

The National Training and Employment Project (NTEP) is a training agency established in 2001, affiliated with but independent from the MoL. It has 40 staff and a budget that ranged from JD 3.5 million to JD 5.7 million ($5–8 million) per year in 2007–10. Though it is affiliated with the MoL, the extent to which it coordinates with and reports to the ministry remains unclear.

In addition to the direct provision of ALMPs, the MoL is a key player in the implementation of governance reforms for the human resource development sector. It plays a central role in policy coordination, notably as the chair of the newly established E-TVET Council.

E-TVET Council and Fund

The E-TVET Council is one of the main instruments of Jordan's governance reforms in the human resource development sector. A multi-stakeholder umbrella body, it develops overarching policies and standards in the area of employment and technical/vocational education and training, with a specific focus on the training sector. Its establishment under Law 46 of 2008 followed recommendations of the National Agenda, which acknowledged the multiplicity of providers and lack of coordination in the human resource development sector. The E-TVET Council replaced an older TVET Council established in 2001, which had a similar mandate but lacked the required institutional infrastructure and capacities and was largely ineffective.

The E-TVET Council aims at "improving the standard of technical and vocational education and training and providing employment opportunities that develop human resources to meet the requirements of comprehensive development in the Kingdom."[2] Its responsibilities encompass policy guidance, regulation, quality assurance, assessment of providers, and harmonization of programs. It includes, among others, representatives of the MoL (the Minister chairs the council), Ministry of Education, Ministry of Social Development, Ministry of Higher Education and Scientific Research, NCHRD, and VTC, as well as representatives from trade unions, the private sector, and the Chamber of Commerce.

The E-TVET Fund is the funding arm of the council, but its resources have been repeatedly cut down, and the fund faces difficulties in fulfilling its original mandate. Established under the E-TVET Council Law of 2008 and chaired by the MoL, the E-TVET Fund is mandated to finance employment and technical/vocational education and training programs that are in line with the council's policy priorities. It is therefore one of the main sources of financing for ALMPs, which tend to be funded either by their respective implementing agency or by the E-TVET Fund. The fund is expected to provide financial support to selected employers/sectors and training providers after assessing whether proposed programs fit the overall objectives, criteria, and skill requirements of the sector. In 2009, approximately JD 29 million ($41 million) was disbursed by the fund;

80 percent of this amount was allocated to the National Employment and Training Company (NETC), run by the Jordanian Armed Forces. Funding was also allocated to the VTC and to the MoL's NTEP.

Though the E-TVET Fund is mandated to provide funding to market-driven programs, in practice it has been rather reactive and supply-driven in allocating funding. In addition, its revenue schemes face a number of limitations that relate to cash flow risks and have resulted in decreasing resources. Indeed, according to its original bylaws, the fund's revenues should derive mainly from a 1 percent tax on net profits of companies in the form of a "training levy." However, the tax on profits was annulled in 2009. Currently, the E-TVET Fund is financed through revenues raised from the issuance of work permits to foreign workers. The fund has faced a serious cash flow crisis as a result of that change in funding schemes, shrinking by 38 percent between 2008 and 2009 and by a further 50 percent in 2010.

Other Public Agencies Engaged in the Delivery of ALMPs

In addition to the MoL and its related agencies and the E-TVET Council and Fund, several other agencies are involved in the provision of ALMPs in Jordan. However, there is little or no coordination between these other agencies and the MoL or the E-TVET system.

The NCHRD was established in 1990 to generate knowledge on human resource development and to provide policy guidance and support to the government. The NCHRD has been providing selected employment services, including through the establishment of a publicly accessible labor market information system, an online labor exchange platform, and a system of career guidance services. Despite obvious complementarities with the DET, institutional coordination between the NCHRD and the MoL remains limited.

The Jordanian Armed Forces manage an independent entity, the NETC, which runs a specialized training program for the construction sector. The construction sector was chosen as a target for this program because it is dominated by foreign workers who the government believes could be replaced by Jordanians. Established in 2007, the NETC is a legally autonomous entity governed by a board of directors that is chaired by the prime minister and accountable to a higher steering committee in which the private sector is well represented. The NETC has 595 staff, all of whom are armed forces personnel seconded to the project.

The Development and Employment Fund is a major provider of MSME development programs. Established in 1989, the fund has 12 branches across the country and provides lending and training services to microenterprises.

Public Employment Services and Other Publicly Provided ALMPs

Employment Services

The employment services offered by the DET focus mainly on labor intermediation services and a yearly job fair; they do not include personalized career guidance or counseling. DET operates and maintains an electronic labor exchange (ELE) platform and matches job seekers and employers; it does not perform any screening of job applications or engage in any step of the selection process. The ELE can be accessed by registered job seekers and employers, whether based in Jordan or abroad, as well as by municipalities and selected nongovernmental organizations. Registered, unemployed job seekers can access the platform online or visit the regional offices to get assistance. Besides the opportunity to post curricula vitae (CVs), the website offers career and job search advice. Employers can register and view job seeker profiles only if they have a job opportunity to post.

There is obvious demand for employment services. According to the MoL, 27,961 job seekers posted their CVs on the ELE in 2009; of these, 8,775 (31 percent) were successfully placed in firms. A study conducted in 2008 shows that roughly 80 percent of registered unemployed are below the age of 40, 70 percent are male, and 60 percent have not gone beyond secondary school.[3]

Recognizing the need to enhance the quality and impact of its public employment services, the government of Jordan has undertaken reform projects focused on strengthening databases and diversifying service provision. These include the Al Manar project, supported by CIDA, and the National Employment Center (NEC) project, supported by the United States Agency for International Development (USAID).

Al Manar was launched in 2004 under the NCHRD. It aimed to establish a publicly accessible labor market information system, an ELE platform for employers and job seekers (launched in 2006), and a system of career guidance services. Job seekers would have the opportunity to create online profiles and search job vacancies posted by employers, free of charge. However, the platform does not perform any intermediation or matching role. A total of 91,000 job seeker profiles were registered by the end of 2009, with an average of 17,000 new registrations per year. Two-thirds of registrants were males, and almost half held a bachelor's degree. In 2009 over 101,000 new job vacancies were advertised by both local and overseas employers. The project also entailed the training of career counselors in various institutions in Jordan, as well as the direct provision of career services through online tools such as manuals, scales, and tests.

The NEC, which started in 2004 under the MoL, is another initiative geared toward the provision of high-quality employment services. It aims to provide comprehensive labor intermediation services, including a platform linking job seekers and available jobs, matching services, and screening services in which staff interview applicants and select qualified ones. The NEC also offers specialized career consultations and short courses dealing with work skills, work environment, and work ethics. The project's total budget allocation for 2009–12 was about JD 1.5 million ($2.2 million). Between 2004 and 2010, 64,118 job seekers registered at the NEC, while 466 companies are registered in their database. Yet the project's placement rate is quite low. In the same period, only 1,739 candidates were employed.

Thus far, these parallel labor intermediation systems have not been stream-lined. DET, NEC, and Al Manar operate comparable online tools, offer similar types of services, and, in the case of DET and NEC, are affiliated with the same ministry. Yet the consolidation of their databases and information remains a challenge, partly because of gaps in institutional coordination between the different agencies.

Training Programs

The VTC is mandated to prepare the technical workforce and upgrade its efficiency in various nonacademic vocational training levels and specializations. It provides diverse vocational training through apprenticeships, training of institutions' employees in specialized training centers and at work sites, extensive and speedy training for various professions, and training in occupational safety and health. It also provides support for the establishment and development of small and medium enterprises.[4]

For a nominal fee of JD 15–30 ($21–42), the VTC offers vocational training courses at three levels and in over 200 specializations, ranging from 700 to 1,800 hours each. In most cases, in-class training is combined with supervised practical experience. VTC training programs cater mainly to low-skilled workers. The majority of students entering the program are dropouts who have not gone beyond the tenth grade.

The VTC is facing challenges in fulfilling its mandate. Enrollment rates are decreasing, resulting in, among other things, an increase in unit costs. The VTC reports that the per-student cost for training before 2008 ranged from JD 700 to 900 ($987–1,269). In 2008, with decreasing enrollment rates (5,867 students enrolled), per-student costs rose to JD 1,300 ($1,832). Unit costs and internal efficiencies vary, however, between different VTC institutes.

In general, the curricula of the training courses provided by the VTC are outdated and not in line with the needs of the labor market. In addition, Jordan lacks a vocational qualification framework that would set common criteria for training content and certification and provide prospective employers with clear signals about the skill level and aptitudes of vocational training graduates. The low quality and market relevance of some training programs partly explains the pattern of graduates' job placements. Based on available data, the VTC reports a 75 percent employment rate of its graduates; of those who found employment, 47 percent were employed within their specializations. The low quality of some of the training programs exacerbates the stigma that has traditionally been attached to vocational education and training in Jordan and provides a partial explanation of the difficulties experienced by the VTC in sustaining enrollment. Monitoring and evaluation systems are in place but remain weak. The VTC implements tracer studies of graduates and collects feedback from employers, but data collection is rudimentary and irregular.

The government has acknowledged the need for wide-ranging reforms of the vocational training system, including in the areas of data collection and quality regulation. At the policy level, the E-TVET reform plan emphasizes the need to enhance the quality of training provision by building efficient information systems to support evidence-based policy making, developing regulatory frameworks, and providing training that is relevant to the needs of the labor market. In addition, at the programmatic level, the VTC has taken some practical steps to enhance the quality of its programs and move toward a demand-driven business model. The USAID-supported Siyaha project, which targets training programs in the hotel and tourism industry, is an example of such effort (box 3.1). The VTC is developing similar training plans for other economic sectors.

Box 3.1 The Siyaha Project in Jordan

The Jordan Tourism Development Project, known as Siyaha, is viewed as an example of best practice in the design of demand-driven training programs in Jordan. For this program, USAID partnered with the VTC, the MoL, and the Ministry of Tourism to develop and implement a strategic plan for the hotel and tourism unit of the VTC. The main objective is to enhance the quality of training offered within the unit's 11 vocational centers around the country, with centers of excellence established in Madaba and Aqaba. The project offers internationally accredited certification.

Besides the physical upgrading of the centers, the project includes the revision and modernization of curriculum, with the production of new textbooks in cooperation with industry specialists, the use of lecturer exchange programs, and the introduction of soft-skills modules. Most importantly, the program is supplemented by a mandatory practical experience component: trainees are required to complete 24 weeks in the training center and 24 weeks on-site in the industry. The project has established close relationships with the private sector. The VTC signs contracts with accredited hotels and restaurants to provide practical on-the-job training, and it monitors the trainees placed in work sites. Establishments are encouraged to visit the training center to interview and select students. Low-income youth are the main target group of the project, which also seeks to reach out to women and encourage their employment in the hotel industry.

The Siyaha project monitors its performance on a monthly basis. It also collects feedback and information from participating industries and program graduates. From the launch of the program in October 2006 through 2010, a total of 3,000 students enrolled, and 1,100 graduated. Demand for enrollment increased in 2010, when students were waitlisted or given priority based on existing skill levels. Student information from 2008 to 2009 shows that the dropout rates are at 13 percent during theoretical training and 17 percent during practical training. Family responsibilities are cited as the main reason for dropping out. Of those who graduated, 57 percent were accepted in jobs.

Source: Interview with USAID Siyaha team, September 2010.

Employment Subsidies

A large number of employment subsidy programs, many of them linked to training programs, have been implemented in Jordan. The MoL is a core provider of such programs, both directly and through its affiliate, the NTEP. The Jordanian Armed Forces also operate a large program combining training and subsidized employment through the NETC.

Employment subsidy programs tend to be geared toward vulnerable segments of the labor force, in particular women, youth, and low-skilled workers. The programs subsidize the costs associated with the employment of target groups in order to bridge the wage expectation gap between employers and job seekers. Some programs also upgrade the skills of workers to address the mismatch between the skills offered by job seekers and those needed by private business. Table 3.2 provides an overview of the employment subsidy programs provided by the MoL, NTEP, and the Armed Forces' NETC in 2009.

It is difficult to assess the impact of employment subsidies, whether stand-alone or combined with training programs, in Jordan. The absence or weakness of monitoring and evaluation (M&E) systems across all such programs in Jordan translates into a limited availability of data on the labor market outcomes, including earnings, of program beneficiaries. In addition, international research is hardly conclusive as to the potential of employment subsidy programs and calls for caution in their use. Most evidence on the impact of subsidies on employment and earnings is based on the experience of developed countries, where their deadweight losses and substitution effects have been found to be important and their cost-effectiveness is regularly questioned.

Available data for existing employment subsidy programs (including those combined with training) in Jordan seem to indicate internal inefficiencies. Programs tend to have low take-up rates, high dropout rates, and low placement rates (see performance indicators in table 3.2). Arguably, low take-up rates and high dropout rates are an indication that programs do not provide adequate incentives to beneficiaries to participate in these programs as currently designed, given wages and work conditions. Still, low placement rates could be an indication of employers' abusing the system in order to get access to subsidized labor and/or their dissatisfaction with beneficiaries' skills sets.

These performance indicators point to the challenge of designing employment subsidy programs that address the expectations and skills mismatches in an efficient manner. Meeting this challenge requires more regular and comprehensive data collection to inform policy makers' understanding of workers' and firms' expectations and needs. Strengthened M&E systems would facilitate the tracking of beneficiaries and build a body of knowledge on the use of employment subsidies in Jordan. Some examples of best practices could serve as a starting point when considering alternatives to the current system, which is predominantly based on informal tracking (box 3.2).

Table 3.2 Summary of Public Employment Subsidy Programs in Jordan, 2008–09

Program	Description	Targeting/characteristics of beneficiaries	Number of beneficiaries (2009)	Budget/cost	Performance indicators
Ministry of Labor					
Employing Women in Villages (2008)	*Objective:* Support the employment of women in industrial zones. *Type of program:* Employment subsidy. *Design:* Contracts with firms in industrial zones (garment sector) to employ groups of women and fully subsidizes accommodation, transportation, meals, and social security contributions for the first six months.	Women	143	Budgeted at 146,000 Jordanian dinars (JD); cost per beneficiary is JD 1,110 ($1,565).	Half of participants drop out before completing six months.
Employment Support for Unemployed with Low Educational Attainment (2009)	*Objective:* Support the employment of low-skilled unemployed. *Type of program:* Employment subsidy. *Design:* Fully subsidizes employees' contributions and half of employers' contributions to social security for a two-year period.	Unemployed > four months, with education below secondary diploma.	4,306, of whom 64% are men	—	No exact figures, but dropout rates are estimated to be high.
Employment Support for Agricultural Workers (2009)	*Objective:* Support the employment of agricultural workers. *Type of program:* Employment subsidy. *Design:* Fully subsidizes social security contributions for two years and subsidizes 50% of contributions in the third year.	Employed agricultural workers.	243, of whom 65% are women	—	Take-up rates are considered low and dropout rates high.
National Training and Employment Program					
Waged Employment Program (2009)	*Objective:* Support the employment of unemployed youth in specific industries including textiles, assembly, sales, hospitality, and jewelry production. *Type of program:* Employment subsidy and training. *Design:* Contracts with firms in certain industries to take on workers for a three- to six-month training period during which 50% of wages, all off-the-job training costs, 50% of on-the-job training costs, and 50% of employees' social security contributions are subsidized. The industries must agree to offer beneficiaries a fixed one-year employment contract after the training period.	Young unemployed job seekers.	—	—	Dropout rates are reported to be quite high, mostly as a result of employees being dissatisfied with working conditions.

table continues next page

Table 3.2 Summary of Public Employment Subsidy Programs in Jordan, 2008–09 *(continued)*

Program	Description	Targeting/characteristics of beneficiaries	Number of beneficiaries (2009)	Budget/cost	Performance indicators
Satellite Units (2008)	*Objective:* Support the employment of unemployed youth, especially young women, in poor areas. *Type of program:* Employment subsidy and training. *Design:* Offers incentives for businesses to open in remote areas, including free sites from which to operate for five years; financing of 30% of wages, transportation, meals, and employees' social security contribution costs for 18 months; and any costs associated with pre-employment training specific to their needs.	Unemployed youth, with a focus on women. Program areas should have high poverty, unemployment, and population density, with an absence of companies that can provide employment for young job seekers.	1,137, of whom 90% are women	—	Dropout rates are high (around 40%) due to dissatisfaction of women with their working conditions.
Employment Support for ICT Graduates (2008)	*Objective:* Support the employment of first-time job seekers who are graduates in information and communication technologies (ICT). *Type of program:* Employment subsidy and training. *Design:* Supports the employment of new graduates in ICT by subsidizing 50% of wages for the first year and 25% for the next six months. Also finances two-week sessions of soft-skills training and professional training by Microsoft (sponsored by USAID). The ceiling on the subsidy is JD 300/month.	Holders of bachelor's degree or diploma in ICT who graduated less than two years ago and are first-time job seekers.	600 in 2008–09	—	—
Employment Support for Male Nursing Graduates (2009)	*Objective:* Support the employment of male nursing graduates. *Type of program:* Employment subsidy. *Design:* Places male nursing graduates and subsidizes 50% of their wages for two years. The ceiling on the subsidy is JD 135/month for BA holders and JD 90/month for tertiary education graduates.	Male holders of bachelor's degree or diploma in nursing.	450	—	—

table continues next page

Table 3.2 Summary of Public Employment Subsidy Programs in Jordan, 2008–09 *(continued)*

Program	Description	Targeting/characteristics of beneficiaries	Number of beneficiaries (2009)	Budget/cost	Performance indicators
Jordanian Armed Forces					
National Employment and Training Company	*Objective:* Train and place 30,000 young male nationals in the construction sector over a period of six years (2007–13). *Type of program:* Employment subsidy and training. *Design:* Has three phases: (a) Two months of military training; (b) Four months of vocational training; and (c) Six months of on-the-job training in construction companies, during which allowance, accommodation, transportation, meals, social security, and health insurance costs are financed up to JD 191 ($269).	Lower-income young males and school dropouts. 80% of beneficiaries are 18–21 years of age and have not completed secondary school.	2007–09: 12,600 completed military and vocational training; 3,200 placed in on-the-job training	NETC estimates annual cost per beneficiary at JD 365 ($514), but the actual cost could be higher.	Dropout rate is around 13%.

Source: Based on administrative data collected through World Bank interviews with Jordanian government officials.

Note: — = not available.

Box 3.2 The NOW Project: Employment for Young Female Graduates in Jordan

Jordan New Work Opportunities for Women (NOW) is a pilot project that aims to increase female labor force participation by providing young female community college graduates with employment support. This may take the form of (a) job vouchers that serve as a short-term (six-month) subsidy to firms that employ the beneficiaries; (b) employability training, focusing on soft skills; or (c) a combination of both. A total of 900 female graduates have been randomly selected to receive one or the other of these forms of support. The project is supported by the World Bank and is implemented in partnership with the Ministry of Planning and International Cooperation.

In addition, the project seeks to produce hard evidence on the effectiveness of such active labor market interventions. The pilot will be rigorously evaluated by tracing the labor market outcomes of participants and of a randomly selected control group. The evaluation is designed to allow assessment of the impacts of the two different interventions (subsidy versus training) and of a combination of both. Such a rigorous impact evaluation methodology of an active labor market program is unprecedented in Jordan.

Source: World Bank 2011.

MSME Development Programs

The Development and Employment Fund supports the development of micro-enterprises, with a strong focus on poverty reduction. Its lending and training services, which target poor and unemployed Jordanians, include the provision of loans directly and indirectly (through microfinance institutions) and the provision of business training. In 2009, 5,590 loans were provided for a total amount of nearly JD 13.5 million ($19 million). The majority of these loans (4,713) financed new projects, each project creating an average of 1.3 jobs. Arguably, widening the fund's focus to support small and medium enterprises as well as microenterprises would increase its impact on unemployment in Jordan.

Lessons Learned and Policy Recommendations

Under its ambitious reform agenda, including through the establishment of the E-TVET Council and Fund, Jordan has taken bold steps to strengthen coordination among the public agencies involved in the provision of ALMPs and to rationalize the funding of these programs. Yet a number of areas still need to be addressed.

First of all, innovative and sustainable financing schemes for ALMPs can be explored to leverage funding for the programs. The funding challenges faced by the E-TVET Fund illustrate the need to diversify the sources of funding for ALMPs, including, for example, by levying fees on private businesses.

Further streamlining of reform efforts is needed to ensure that policies and programs are not duplicated. For example, in the area of employment services,

Building Effective Employment Programs for Unemployed Youth in the Middle East and North Africa •
http://dx.doi.org/10.1596/978-0-8213-9904-0

the concurrent efforts of the DET, NEC, and NCHRD to provide labor market information and intermediation would benefit from being consolidated. Further integration of ALMP provision would present opportunities to better respond to job seekers' needs. International experience has demonstrated that ALMPs have a stronger impact when services are offered to job seekers in an integrated manner—for example, when employment services are linked to training programs. But ALMP provision in Jordan remains, to a large extent, fragmented.

Regulatory frameworks for the provision of ALMPs, whether by public or private providers, would positively affect the quality of services. In particular, training provision in Jordan would benefit from coherent nationwide regulation, including the establishment of a vocational qualification framework, setting standards for the delivery of training programs with regard to curricula, skills acquisition, and certification. Strengthened regulation would also ensure better quality standards for the services provided to job seekers and provide clearer signals to employers on the skills and capacities of job seekers.

Diversifying services offered by public agencies can leverage their impact. In particular, there is considerable space to diversify the set of employment services offered. The current focus on labor intermediation (in particular, job posting and matching) should be enlarged to encompass career guidance and counseling, among other services.

Across all programs, a stronger focus on young graduates could help address the high level of unemployment among educated youth. While data indicate that this group is the most vulnerable to unemployment, programs seem to cater predominantly to low-skilled workers.

Enhanced partnerships with private businesses would help ensure that programs respond to the needs and demands of the private sector and allow public agencies to tap the expertise that the private sector can provide. For example, systematically involving private businesses in the design of training curricula would ensure that skills provided by training programs correspond to the actual needs of the labor market. In addition, partnerships with private businesses would create opportunities to leverage their financial resources, including in the framework of on-the-job training programs.

Finally, strengthened M&E systems could allow public agencies to better track the outcomes and impact of publicly provided ALMPs. While data are available on the number of program beneficiaries, there does not appear to be any systematic evaluation of the programs' short- or long-term impacts on beneficiaries' employment and wage outcomes. Systematic program monitoring and rigorous impact evaluations would provide an opportunity to better design and target publicly provided ALMPs, ensuring better returns on public investment. This is particularly true for employment subsidy programs, which should be subject to close examination. Available data reveal high dropout rates and low placement rates, indicating that both beneficiaries and employers are prone to dissatisfaction with the programs. Data on the short-term, medium-term, and long-term outcomes of employment subsidies are needed to better understand their actual impact and inform the design and targeting of future programs.

Notes

1. Assistance from these donors includes the Employer Driven Skills Development Project funded by the World Bank, which aims to realign policy formulation with Employment—Technical and Vocational Education and Training (E-TVET) operational mechanisms through the development of employers' participation in sector policy formulation, institutional development of training providers, and skills development program design; the Building and Extending Skills Training Systems (BEST) project funded by CIDA; and budget support from the European Commission.

2. "About the Council," on the Jordan Ministry of Labor website, http://www.mol .gov.jo/tabid/273/default.aspx.

3. Figures from personal conversations with MoL staff.

4. "About the Jordan VTC," on the New VTC website, http://www.thenewvtc.com/ about-the-jordan-vtc/.

References

Alhawarin, I., and F. Kreishan. 2010. "An Analysis of Long-Term Unemployment (LTU) in Jordan's Labor Market." *European Journal of Social Sciences* 15 (1): 56–66.

MoPIC (Ministry of Planning and International Cooperation). 2011. *Overview: Jordan's Executive Development Program (2011–2013)*. MoPIC, Amman.

NCHRD (National Center for Human Resources Development). 2010. *Human Resources Indicators in Jordan for the Year 2010*. Al Manar project, Amman.

Razzaz, S., and F. Iqbal. 2008. *Job Growth without Unemployment Reduction: The Experience of Jordan*. World Bank, Washington, DC. http://www.iza.org/conference_files/ worldb2008/razzaz_s4349.pdf.

World Bank. 2008. *Resolving Jordan's Labour Market Paradox of Concurrent Economic Growth and High Unemployment*. Report No. 39201-JO, World Bank, Washington, DC.

———. 2011. *Concept Note for 'Jordan New Work Opportunities.'* World Bank, Washington, DC.

CHAPTER 4

Public Employment Programs in Lebanon

May Wazzan and Diane Zovighian

Introduction

Despite positive economic growth, unemployment in Lebanon has been increasing, with higher rates among women, youth, and educated workers. According to the Employer-Employee Survey conducted by the World Bank in 2010, the unemployment rate reached 11 percent that year. Joblessness is concentrated among youth, with unemployment rates reaching 34 percent among those between 15 and 24 years old. The unemployment rate decreases with age: 11 and 6 percent of people aged 25–34 and 35–44, respectively, are unemployed. Skilled individuals, with secondary or tertiary education, have the highest unemployment rate, at 12 percent, compared to 9 percent for people with no formal education and 10 percent for people with primary education (World Bank 2010). Despite the high number of educated workers leaving the country to seek work abroad, unemployment among university degree holders has increased rapidly in recent years, most likely reflecting higher reservation wages and lack of acceptable jobs. The rate of unemployment among women, at 18 percent, is twice as large as that of men, at 8 percent.

A significant share of employed workers are either underemployed or working in fields unrelated to their educational backgrounds. This is particularly true for young and skilled workers. A recent survey of young workers shows that 16 percent are either overqualified for the job they hold or work in a field unrelated to their specialty (Kasparian 2009). Among graduates with higher education and with technical and vocational education, the share of young workers working in an unrelated field rises to 21 and 23 percent, respectively. This reality generates low expectations in terms of jobs, job quality, and earning prospects among university and vocational education graduates.

Low levels of job creation and significant skills mismatches provide a partial explanation for this suboptimal utilization of human resources in Lebanon.

Moreover, the jobs available tend not to correspond to the skills sets available in the workforce. For instance, 55 percent of firms consider that the "skills and education of available workers" are a serious constraint to their business. In particular, employers identify the lack of soft skills, including leadership, communication, and writing skills, as a major gap in the preparation of graduate recruits (World Bank 2009).

Formal labor market intermediation mechanisms, whether public or private, do not play a significant role in matching employers and job seekers. Public institutions play a residual role in facilitating information exchange between employers and job seekers: only 5 percent of young job seekers were employed through the help of their education institutions, and 1 percent through the National Employment Office (NEO). Similarly, only 1 percent were employed through a private employment office. At the same time, 55 percent of young job seekers resort to personal or family connections to find their first job, while another 3 percent are employed in their family business (Kasparian 2009).

Capital constraints seem to be an important source of barriers to employment in Lebanon. The self-employed make up as much as 36 percent of the labor force in Lebanon, while employers (those who report hiring workers) account for 5 percent of the labor force. Self-employment appears to be a preferred employment status of the labor force in Lebanon: 88 percent of the self-employed prefer to stay self-employed, and 66 percent of employees wish they were self-employed (World Bank 2010). Despite the prevalence of and preference for self-employment, access to credit for the self-employed and for micro and small enterprises through the formal banking system in Lebanon is very limited.

Stronger public intervention in the area of active labor market programs (ALMPs) in Lebanon could help alleviate some of these barriers in the short term. The rationale for intervention lies in the potential of ALMPs to (a) strengthen labor intermediation and matching mechanisms to bridge the information and communication gap between employers and workers; (b) overcome, in the short term, the mismatch between the skills of the available workforce and the needs of the labor market; and (c) facilitate self-employment opportunities.

This chapter examines the public provision of ALMPs in Lebanon. The main types of publicly provided ALMPs in Lebanon include:

- Public employment services, especially services facilitating labor market intermediation
- Training programs, particularly for the unemployed
- Programs supporting small and medium enterprise (SME) development

The chapter first reviews the institutional setup for service delivery, followed by a discussion of the design and relevance of the programs provided. Ways to leverage the relevance, effectiveness, and impact of these programs are then proposed.

Institutional Framework for Employment Programs in Lebanon

A number of public agencies are engaged in the delivery of ALMPs in Lebanon, yet there is no overarching policy framework, and institutional coordination remains limited. The NEO is the only public agency providing employment services. It is, however, one of many public agencies providing training programs. In addition to NEO, other ministerial agencies are also involved in the provision of ALMPs. In particular, agencies in three different ministries (Ministry of Labor [MoL], Ministry of Social Affairs [MoSA], and Ministry of Education and Higher Education [MEHE]) directly provide vocational training programs, in parallel and with virtually no coordination with NEO. The Ministry of Economy and Trade (MoET) is also involved in the provision of ALMPs through the delivery of an SME development program.

National Employment Office

Established in 1977, the NEO is a financially and administratively independent agency under the authority of the minister of labor, who chairs its board of directors. The board includes both employer and worker representatives, as well as representatives from the education sector and academia. In theory, NEO's mandate goes beyond the provision of employment services and other ALMPs: it was initially mandated to design and implement a comprehensive national employment strategy for Lebanon. Its responsibilities therefore include conducting research on labor trends and issues, providing employment services through its employment offices in Beirut and other Lebanese regions, and improving the organization of the labor market and the quality of the labor force.

Despite this ambitious mandate, NEO's role remains quite constrained, partly as a result of its limited financial and institutional capacity. NEO has a stagnant annual budget of 2 billion Lebanese pounds (LL) ($1.3 million) and only three offices (in Beirut, Tripoli, and Sidon). These are seriously understaffed, with only 32 staff in 2009. Given its restricted institutional capacity, NEO's mandate is largely unattainable. In practice, its role is limited to (a) running an electronic labor intermediation platform; (b) conducting occasional studies and labor market needs assessments, for which a small budget is reserved (around $33,000); and (c) subsidizing some vocational training programs implemented by nongovernmental organizations (NGOs).

In 2011 NEO's budget was doubled, with the increase intended mainly to finance the establishment of two new regional offices and the recruitment of 41 additional staff. NEO is also working on strengthening its capacity to provide job counseling and career guidance services.

Other Agencies Engaged in ALMP Provision

In addition to NEO, at least three government agencies are directly providing short-term vocational training courses (figure 4.1). These agencies include:

- *The Vocational Training Center (VTC)*. An independent agency, the VTC is financed by the MoL at an annual budget of $2 million and is institutionally

Building Effective Employment Programs for Unemployed Youth in the Middle East and North Africa • http://dx.doi.org/10.1596/978-0-8213-9904-0

Figure 4.1 Institutions and Providers of Training Programs in Lebanon

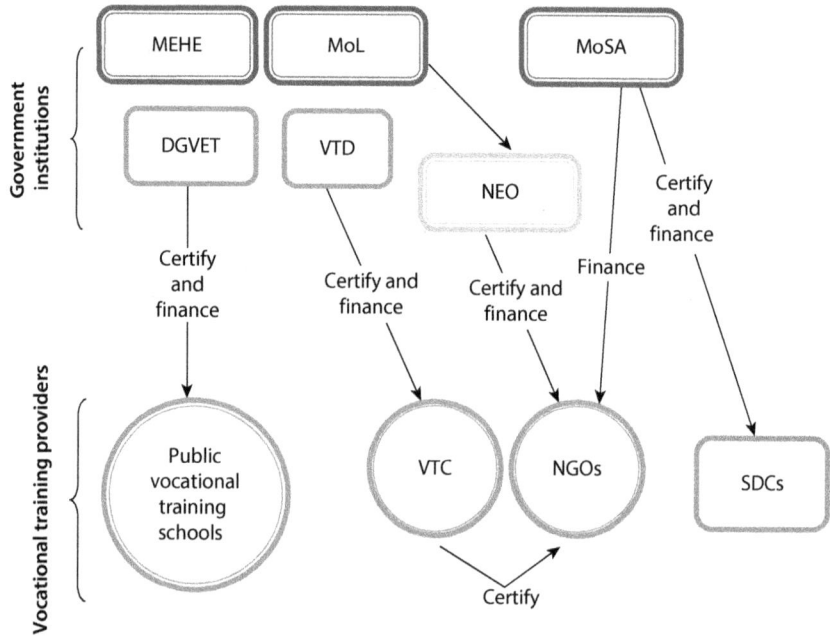

Note: MEHE = Ministry of Education and Higher Education; DGVET = Directorate General of Vocational Education and Training; VTD = Vocational Training Department; MoL = Ministry of Labor; NEO = National Employment Office; NGOs = nongovernmental organizations; VTC = Vocational Training Center; MoSA = Ministry of Social Affairs; SDCs = Social Development Centers.

affiliated with the ministry's Vocational Training Department (VTD). Established in 1998 in response to demands of the industrial sector, the VTC is governed by a board of directors chaired by the minister of labor and managed by a director general.

- *The Directorate General of Vocational Education and Training (DGVET)*. Under the MEHE, DGVET provides vocational training programs through public vocational training schools. It also licenses private vocational training providers and certifies their courses.
- *MoSA*. MoSA provides short vocational training programs in at least 58 of its Social Development Centers (SDCs) located nationwide. It also finances NGOs that provide these services.

Overall, the provision of training programs suffers from the absence of institutional coordination and a weak regulatory framework. First, the limited public resources invested in training programs are allocated in a very fragmented manner. There is virtually no institutional mechanism organizing or encouraging any coordination between the different providers, whether to identify training needs within the workforce, develop a training and skills development strategy, design curricula, or provide training courses. Second, the role of NGOs in the provision of publicly financed programs is not regulated. Public resources are channeled through NEO and MoSA to NGOs that provide training with limited accountability and follow-up. Third, training lacks a unified system of institutional accreditation and program certification. MoSA, NEO, the VTD, and the DGVET all play a role in certifying some of the courses offered by NGOs and private training institutions (figure 4.1). Yet this certification is based on each NGO and private institution following its own curriculum, rather than a curriculum common to all public training providers.

With regard to SME development programs, the MoET is the main public agency engaging in providing loan guarantees and business support to small entrepreneurs. Under the ministry's Integrated SME Support Program (ISSP), with assistance from the European Union, three business centers were created in three different regions to provide business support services to nascent businesses and serve as business incubators. Loan guarantees are provided through a public financial company, Kafalat.

Public Employment Services and Other Publicly Provided ALMPs

ALMP provision in Lebanon is limited in scope. Public intervention has been geared mainly to the financing and implementation of public employment services, training programs, and SME development programs. Overall, programs tend to have insufficient budget; their coverage is limited; and their quality and impact are questionable. Some program reforms and budget increases are under way, but there is still considerable scope for increased and better-targeted investments in ALMPs.

Employment Services

NEO urgently needs to strengthen its weak labor intermediation function and provide a more diversified set of employment services. Employment services currently provided are mainly limited to registering job seekers and available vacancies. Other services usually performed by public employment offices, such as career guidance and counseling, labor market studies, or the organization of job fairs, are not offered by NEO. There has been an impetus in recent years to reform public employment services, including moving toward more diversified services, but such reforms are still in their early stages (box 4.1).

The coverage of employment services is limited and is concentrated on young, male university graduates in Beirut. In 2010 NEO forwarded the curricula vitae (CVs) of 398 job seekers to employers. A total of 98 successful placements were registered (though the number of actual placements could be higher since placements are not necessarily reported). A snapshot of the database with all entries since 2007 shows that three-quarters of registered job seekers at NEO are young adults between the ages of 20 and 35, 56 percent are male, and 80 percent hold an undergraduate university degree or higher. Only 15 percent of applications are registered in the regional offices (Tripoli and Saida).

There is considerable space to enhance the delivery of employment services in Lebanon, starting with some critical system modernization. NEO lacks systematized and fully automated processes to fulfill its job-matching role efficiently.

Box 4.1 Donor-Supported NEO Reform in Lebanon

Under a project funded by the Canadian International Development Agency (CIDA), the International Labour Organization (ILO) provided support to strengthen the delivery of public employment services in Lebanon. Launched in 2008, the four-year project focused on building the capacity of NEO to deliver services to the unemployed, as well as enhancing the labor market information system (LMIS), developing an occupational information system, and increasing opportunities for self-employment. A number of deviations from the original plan took place due to unforeseen challenges related to the institutional environment surrounding NEO and its capacity. The project funded a needs assessment study for the hospitality sector, produced an action plan for the development of an LMIS, upgraded NEO's electronic labor exchange platform (with plans to place it online), and provided training to NEO's employment officers, among other activities. The ILO is also working with NEO to develop plans for career counseling services and a self-employment training program.

A major constraint lies in NEO's dysfunctional electronic labor exchange platform and its reliance on the limited human resources of the office to perform job matching between employers and job seekers. NEO receives announcements of job vacancies from firms and CVs from job seekers by fax, phone, e-mail, and personal visits to its walk-in center. Staff enter the requests into an electronic platform that is not available online; thus neither firms nor job seekers have access to the database. This means that NEO is solely responsible for matching vacancies to job seekers and forwarding the CVs of selected candidates to the firms. The lack of automated and systematized processes also results in unsystematic follow-up on the recruitment of job seekers by prospective employers and the use of an unreliable paper system for program monitoring. In addition, the database contains errors, and data entry is often interrupted by technical difficulties. It is also not fully consolidated, in that the databases of the offices in Saida and Tripoli are not linked to the one at the central office in Beirut.

Data collection is a critical challenge for the delivery of relevant employment services. Though one of NEO's functions is to conduct labor market needs assessment that can inform the design of employment services and facilitate job matching and career guidance, the office does not collect data on labor market trends or conduct regular studies and needs assessments. An action plan for the development of a labor market information system (LMIS) has been developed, but translating this action plan into practice will require sustained financial and technical support.

Partnerships with the private sector remain underdeveloped. Outreach to business is weak, and the modalities of private sector engagement with NEO are mainly ad hoc and informal. NEO has not managed to position itself strategically vis-à-vis private businesses: it has yet to demonstrate its added value, whether through the provision of readily available information to private businesses on job seekers or through the organization of job fairs, which could provide businesses with visibility and facilitate their access to job seekers.

Training Programs

Training is, to a large extent, the most prominent type of publicly provided ALMP in Lebanon. Still, public provision is fragmented and poorly regulated: delivery schemes, training curricula, and certification are not harmonized across the agencies providing training programs. With regard to service delivery schemes, while some agencies act as direct service providers, others subcontract NGOs for service provision. There are no common guidelines or approaches to the regulation of training provision by NGOs. Lebanon also lacks a nationwide vocational qualification framework that would set common criteria for training content and certification, thus providing employers with clear signals about the skill level and aptitudes of vocational training graduates.

The main training programs in Lebanon are summarized in table 4.1.

Training programs provided by NEO:

- *Accelerated vocational training programs* (indirect provision). Since 1981, NEO has subsidized, supervised, and certified accelerated vocational training programs provided by contracted NGOs (31 in 2009). In 2009, NEO contributed a fixed amount of $400 for each of the 833 beneficiaries who received a six-month training. In addition to financing, NEO's role includes selecting and contracting NGOs from the pool of applicants on a yearly basis; identifying the number of trainees to be financed per NGO; deciding upon training specializations (38 in 2009); and supervising and certifying training.

- *Training program for people with disabilities* (indirect provision). NEO subsidizes three to six months of vocational training for persons with disabilities, at a rate of $533 per trainee. It also contributes to equipping specialized sheltered workshops, run by NGOs, where registered disabled workers are employed for a wage. In 2009, NEO financed the training of 125 persons with disabilities, 61 percent of whom were between the ages of 15 and 24, in 11 different NGOs. The implementation mechanisms are similar to those of accelerated vocational training programs. Certification is only offered to trainees with physical disabilities; trainees with other types of disabilities, including mental, receive training but no certification.

Training programs provided by the VTC:

- *Vocational training courses* (direct provision). The VTC runs a total of 12 vocational training courses, but because of budget constraints, only four are currently operational. The courses provided concentrate on electrical and mechanic vocations as well as basic computer courses. All programs run for six months, except for computer-related courses, which run for three

Table 4.1 Summary of Public Employment Training Programs in Lebanon, 2009

Agency	Program	Delivery scheme	Description	Targeting	Number of beneficiaries (2009)	Average cost or budget (2009)
National Employment Office (NEO), Ministry of Labor (MoL)	Accelerated vocational training programs	Indirect provision through nongovernmental organizations (NGOs)	NEO subsidizes, supervises, and certifies accelerated vocational training programs (six months) provided by 31 contracted NGOs in 38 specializations.	Unemployed	833	$400 per trainee
NEO, MoL	Training program for persons with disabilities	Indirect provision through NGOs	NEO subsidizes 3–6 months of vocational training programs for persons with disabilities offered by 11 specialized NGOs.	Persons with disabilities.	125	$533 per trainee
Vocational Training Center (VTC), MoL	Vocational training courses	Direct provision	VTC provides four courses that concentrate on electrical and mechanic vocations (six months) and basic computer courses (three months).	Programs supposed to target unemployed, but in practice, no selection criteria.	150	—
Directorate General of Vocational Education and Training (DGVET), Ministry of Education and Higher Education (MEHE)	Vocational training courses	Direct provision	DGVET provides training courses in 23 different subjects for three months (120 hours), six months (240 hours), or nine months (450 hours), taught at public vocational schools.	Primarily targets school dropouts.	—	$366 per trainee for 100 hours

table continues next page

Table 4.1 Summary of Public Employment Training Programs in Lebanon, 2009 *(continued)*

Agency	Program	Delivery scheme	Description	Targeting	Number of beneficiaries (2009)	Average cost or budget (2009)
DGVET, MEHE	International Labour Organization (ILO)-supported vocational training in construction sector	Direct provision	DGVET provides training courses in 10 schools in southern Lebanon with a focus on vocations relevant to the construction sector.	Primarily targets school dropouts.	338 (2010)	—
Ministry of Social Affairs (MoSA)	Vocational training courses	Direct provision	MoSA provides, through its Social Development Centers (SDCs), vocational training courses with varying durations (30 hours to 9 months). Specializations focus mainly on language and computer skills as well as crafts and beautician skills.	No specific targeting or eligibility criteria, though over 85% of trainees are women.	1,179	Total budget estimated at $46,000 (average unit costs applied to SDCs with missing budget data)
MoSA	Vocational training courses	Indirect provision through NGOs	MoSA finances 30 NGOs providing training programs.	—	677	—

Source: Based on administrative data collected through World Bank interviews with Lebanese government officials.
Note: — = not available.

months. In general, 80 percent of the course time is spent on applied skills and 20 percent on theoretical subjects. The center currently services around 150 trainees annually, though the demand for training is higher and there is a waiting list. Successful graduates receive a certificate from the MoL. The VTC evaluates courses based on questionnaires distributed to students for feedback on course content and administration.

Training programs provided by the DGVET:

- *Vocational training courses* (direct provision). The work plan of the DGVET at the MEHE includes the provision of vocational training courses in 23 different subjects, taught at public vocational schools. Duration of the courses is three months (120 hours), six months (240 hours), or nine months (450 hours), depending on the subject. The average cost is estimated at around $366 per trainee per 100 training hours, and graduates receive a certificate from the MEHE upon completion. In recent years, however, the DGVET has focused on vocational education—within the formal education track—and has been unable to provide the vocational training courses because of budget constraints.
- *ILO-supported vocational training in the construction sector* (direct provision). In 2010, the ILO provided financing for the provision of training courses in 10 schools in southern Lebanon with a focus on vocations relevant to the construction sector. A total of 338 trainees were served by this program.

Training programs provided by MoSA:

- *Vocational training courses* (direct provision). MoSA is involved in the direct provision of training programs through its SDCs. There are 88 SDCs distributed nationwide, at least 58 of which provide vocational training on their premises. The training focuses mostly on subjects that do not require large investments in materials, including languages, computer skills, beautician skills, and crafts. Beneficiaries are predominantly women, though there are no specific targeting or eligibility criteria.
- *Vocational training courses* (indirect provision). MoSA also finances approximately 30 NGOs that provide training programs. The contracts between MoSA and these NGOs are not exclusive to training provision. The NGOs report annually on the number of trainees subsidized through their contracts with MoSA (677 beneficiaries in 2009).

Public providers of training programs tend to face severe budget constraints. Limited resources have led to the suspension of training programs in selected agencies and to very low enrollment in others. DGVET, for example, has not been able to provide vocational training in recent years, as its limited budget ($2 million) has been entirely allocated to vocational education. Similarly, budget constraints have resulted in the VTC providing only four of 12 courses, with a waiting list for students demanding to enroll.

The quality and content of publicly provided training programs pose a concern in terms of their potential impact on the labor outcomes of participants. Most of these programs are supply-driven, and the choice of specializations provided is seldom coordinated with private businesses. As a result, curricula are generally considered to be outdated, raising concerns about the relevance of the skills provided through training. In addition, courses consist mainly of in-class training and are rarely linked to on-the-job training or internships.

Targeting of training programs is either nonexistent or weak. Some agencies do not target at all: for example, MoSA does not impose any selection criteria. Most agencies do identify a target group and set eligibility criteria, but the choice of target group tends not to be evidence-based, partly because of a lack of data availability. Moreover, targeting mechanisms are generally weak and do not systematically result in proper identification and selection. For example, the mission of the VTC is to train unemployed school dropouts. In effect, however, its program enrolls students registered in the vocational education systems, employed workers who want to upgrade their skills, and even persons who are neither employed nor seeking employment (especially in computer courses). In cases where training programs are provided by NGOs, the enforcement of selection criteria is challenging. NEO, which outsources training delivery to NGOs, has no direct control over the selection of training beneficiaries. They are often existing beneficiaries of the contracted NGOs and, to a lesser extent, job seekers whom NEO has referred to the NGOs.

Monitoring of programs is basic and unsystematic, and program impact evaluations are virtually nonexistent. Data, whether on training output (e.g., number of trainees) or outcomes (e.g., job placements of training graduates), are not systematically collected by training providers. When program outputs are monitored, monitoring typically is almost entirely based on a paper system.

Private training institutes and NGOs (in addition to those contracted by NEO and MoSA) are actively engaged in providing vocational training in Lebanon. Their courses are considered more advanced and of better quality than the publicly provided ones, which are to some extent stigmatized. While private training providers are abundant, the government has limited knowledge about their services and rarely explores private-public partnerships or coordination in the area of training. Regulation is limited to licensing at the time of establishment and certification of curricula.

SME Development Programs

The ISSP, implemented by the MoET with support from the European Union, combines service provision and a policy component to promote the development of SMEs in Lebanon. Efforts to reform the legal and regulatory business environment complement the delivery of financial and business services to SMEs. Two basic types of services are provided:

- *Loan guarantees*. These totaled $85 million in 2009. ISSP supports access to finance through Kafalat, a Lebanese financial company, which provides loan guarantees to SMEs upon approval of a business plan or feasibility study. Kafalat offers three loan guarantee schemes: Basic, guaranteeing loans of up to $200,000 at 75 percent of the value of the loan; Plus, up to $400,000 at 85 percent; and Innovative, up to $200,000 at 90 percent for very innovative projects. Guaranteed loans are provided by Lebanese banks and benefit from interest rate subsidies financed by the Lebanese treasury. As of April 2010, 474 projects had been guaranteed under the Kafalat Plus scheme; the total loan amount was approximately $143 million, and the average loan amount was approximately $300,000.[1]

- *Business support services*. ISSP supports access to nonfinancial services through three Business Development Centers (Berytech, BIAT, and SouthBIC) established across Lebanon. The centers provide a range of services to start-ups, existing SMEs, and entrepreneurs, including business skills training, technical advice, and assistance on finance, accounting, marketing, sales, exporting, mentoring and networking opportunities, incubation opportunities, and company hosting.

The majority of businesses supported through ISSP focus on industrial development: 61.5 percent of Kafalat-supported loans have been provided to SMEs in the industrial sector, followed by 23.4 percent in the tourism sector and only 5.9 percent in the new technologies sector. Loans are also concentrated geographically, with 66 percent of loans issued to beneficiaries in the Mount Lebanon region, followed by 13.1 percent in Beirut. Only 6.1 percent of loans are issued in the Bekaa region, 4.5 percent in the South, and 1 percent in Nabatieh.

The extent and quality of the monitoring and evaluation of SME development programs is unclear. Though some data on program outputs, such as numbers of loans, are readily available, other important information is largely absent (such as the number of beneficiaries of the Business Development Centers). Data on the quality of services, including loan repayment rates, also seem to be lacking. As for program impact, Kafalat staff estimated in interviews that as of August 2008, 19,887 jobs had been created under the Kafalat Plus and Kafalat Innovative schemes, based on the number of employees working at the newly created companies. Yet such figures are scarce and the methodology for data collection is unclear.

Lessons Learned and Policy Recommendations

In sum, ALMP provision in Lebanon is severely fragmented and poorly regulated. Stronger institutional, policy, and regulatory frameworks for ALMPs would allow the provision of more, higher-quality, and better-integrated services. Lebanon could consider defining mechanisms for institutional coordination across all public agencies engaged in ALMP development and provision to ensure more integrated provision of services and help avoid duplication. Designing a comprehensive vision for the provision of ALMPs in Lebanon would make it possible to define

Building Effective Employment Programs for Unemployed Youth in the Middle East and North Africa •
http://dx.doi.org/10.1596/978-0-8213-9904-0

clear objectives, resources, roles, and responsibilities at the national level for both management and provision within the ALMP sector. Ideally, such a policy framework would be set within a broader labor market strategy.

Developing regulatory frameworks and setting rules and standards for the provision of ALMPs, whether by public or private providers, would improve the quality of these programs. ALMP provision in Lebanon lacks coherent nationwide regulations. For example, at the national level there is no vocational qualification framework to set standards for the delivery of training programs with regard to curricula, skills acquisition, and certification. Stronger regulation would ensure better quality standards for the services provided to job seekers. In the case of training programs, it would also provide clearer signals to employers about the skills and capacities of job seekers.

Increased public investment in strengthening the institutional capacity of public providers, especially NEO, would help leverage their efforts to provide services to the unemployed and to regulate the provision of services by private actors. Most public providers of ALMPs, in particular NEO, suffer from inadequate financing and insufficient staffing. The result has been an incapacity to fulfill their mandate (whether as providers or regulators of employment services and other ALMPs), the suspension of some programs, and limitations on the coverage and number of beneficiaries of programs still operating.

Scaled up and diversified service provision would allow public and private agencies to cater to more job seekers and to better respond to their needs. Given institutional capacity and financial constraints, most public agencies provide a limited number of services to a limited number of beneficiaries. NEO, in particular, serves an extremely low share of the unemployed, and its employment services focus exclusively on job matching, with no resources directed toward, for example, career guidance or counseling. In parallel, the lack of regulatory frameworks for the provision of employment services and other ALMPs by private agencies results in suboptimal levels and quality of service provision. If service provision is financed, managed, and implemented by the private sector, the key role of public agencies would be to ensure proper regulation and policy coordination between public and private providers.

Strengthened labor data and information systems would facilitate the design of evidence-based ALMPs. Labor data and information in Lebanon are scarce, and the use of existing data by policy makers is low. The role and resources of NEO could be leveraged to enable the agency to fulfill its role as a provider (and user) of labor market data and studies.

Strengthened monitoring and evaluation systems would allow policy makers to better track the outcomes and impact of publicly provided ALMPs. Most of the programs are neither regularly monitored nor properly evaluated: little or no data are available to track implementation, and the short-, medium-, and long-term impacts of the programs do not appear to be evaluated. Systematic program monitoring and rigorous impact evaluations would provide an opportunity to better design and target publicly provided ALMPs and ensure better returns on public investment.

Innovative targeting mechanisms could be explored to ensure better coverage of vulnerable groups. Most ALMPs have no defined target group or do not cater to their target group, possibly as a result of weak administrative or selection processes. The national poverty targeting program in Lebanon offers an opportunity to target ALMPs to those individuals most in need of government support.

Partnerships with private businesses could help leverage resources and expertise to enhance the quality and impact of ALMPs. Most agencies tend to develop their programs in isolation from, rather than in response to, the needs of the private sector, disregarding the potential resources and expertise that private businesses can provide. For example, the possibility of levying fees on private businesses to finance training programs is not explored, and businesses are not systematically involved in the design of training curricula. In this context, building partnerships with the private sector would create opportunities to leverage their financial resources and technical expertise to enhance the quantity and quality of publicly provided ALMPs. Equally important, it would ensure that ALMPs are demand-driven and respond to the actual needs of the labor market.

Note

1. Information from the Kafalat website, http://www.kafalat.com.lb/. Also see website of the Investment Development Authority of Lebanon, http://www.idal.com.lb /WhyLebanon.aspx?ID=68.

References

Kasparian, C. 2009. *L'Emigration des jeunes Libanais et leurs projets d'avenir*. Beirut: Presses de l'Université Saint-Joseph.

World Bank. 2009. "Lebanon: A Survey-Based Investment Climate Update." World Bank, Washington, DC.

———. 2010. "Employer-Employee Survey (EES)". World Bank, Washington, DC.

CHAPTER 5

Public Employment Programs in Morocco

Saad Belghazi

Rationale for Public Employment Services and Active Labor Market Programs in Morocco

Unemployment rates in Morocco are high for youth, women, and university graduates. In urban settings, the general rate of unemployment reached almost 14 percent in 2010 (figure 5.1, panel a). That year, unemployment was about 20 percent for urban women and around 18 percent for youth aged 15–24 (figure 5.1, panels b and c). High unemployment rates among university graduates emerged as the country's main employment problem in 2000, with nearly 39 percent of degree holders unemployed. Since then, the Moroccan government has increased its efforts to tackle this problem with some success as unemployment rates have decreased rapidly among high school and university graduates in recent years (figure 5.1, panel d).

While trends in economic growth have contributed to the decrease in unemployment among university graduates, joblessness among educated youth remains high, which has led to some social unrest. Furthermore, a large share of the economy is informal, and labor market segmentation is persistent. During the past decade, Moroccan labor market dynamics have been driven mainly by demand-side growth as the Moroccan economy has opened its markets. Productivity grew significantly in the main sectors of employment, contributing to hiring of university graduates in the growing manufacturing, transport, telecommunications, services, and agricultural export sectors. Nevertheless, the public sector, which currently employs less than 10 percent of the active population, remains as the preferred employer for university graduates. This contributes to queuing for public sector employment and thus to high levels of unemployment.

Institutional Framework for Employment Programs in Morocco

Employment policy in Morocco is developed through periodic consultations involving many actors, including the national and provincial levels of government as well as social partners. The two main national agencies involved are the Ministry of Employment and Professional Training and the Ministry of Social Development, Solidarity, and the Family. However, other institutions participate in the consultation process, including the Department of Home Affairs and the Ministries of Commerce and Industry, Education, Health, Agriculture, Energy, Tourism, and Youth and Sports.

The Moroccan parliament discusses and votes on texts of state law and the budget together with various consultative bodies, including the Economic and

Figure 5.1 Unemployment by Area, Gender, Age, and Education in Morocco, 1999–2010

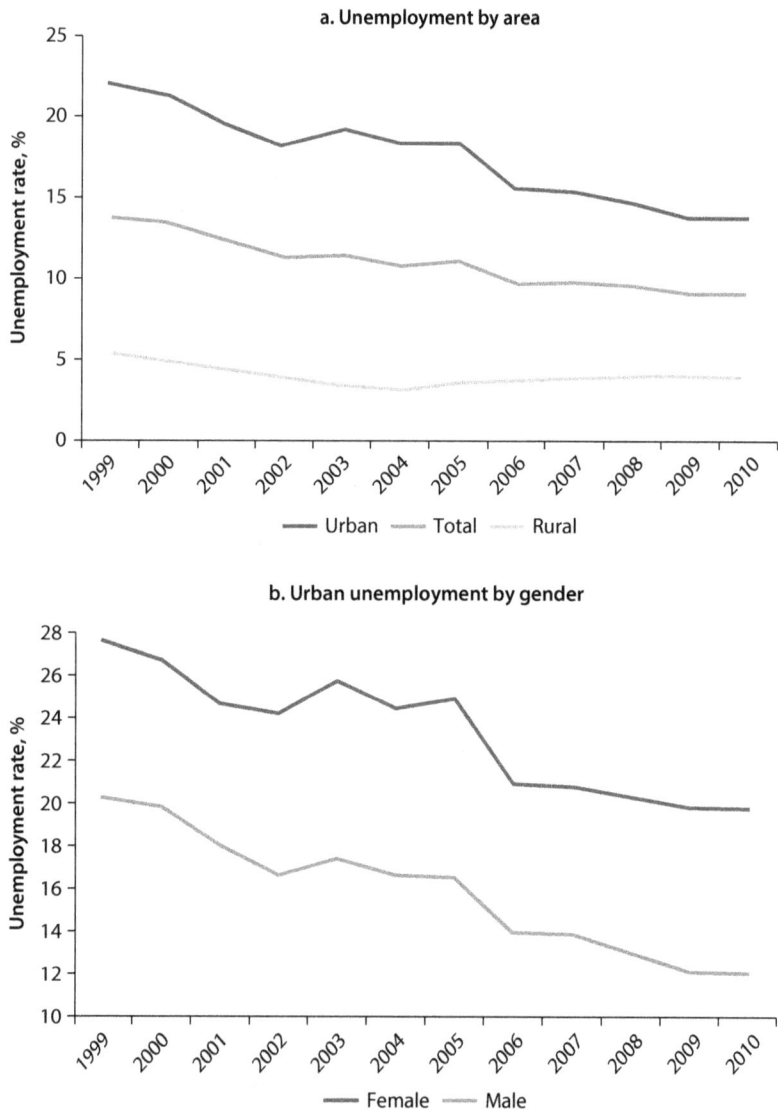

a. Unemployment by area

b. Urban unemployment by gender

figure continues next page

Figure 5.1 Unemployment by Area, Gender, Age, and Education in Morocco, 1999–2010 *(continued)*

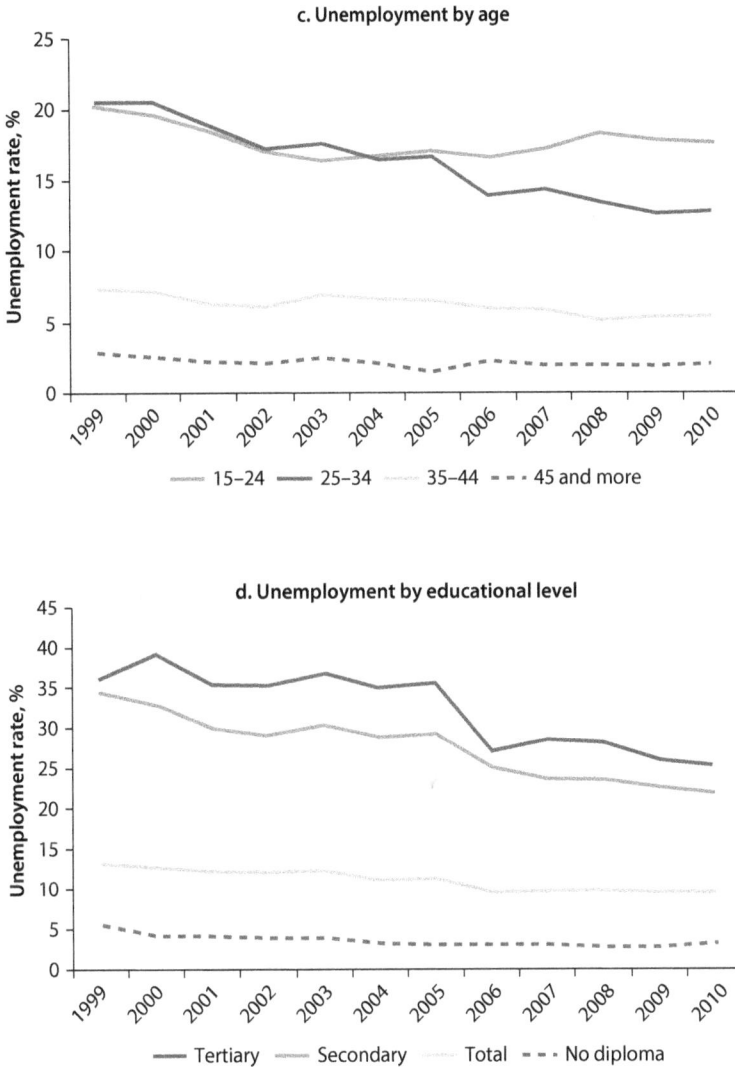

c. Unemployment by age

Legend: 15–24 25–34 35–44 - - - 45 and more

d. Unemployment by educational level

Legend: Tertiary Secondary Total - - - No diploma

Source: Haut Commissariat au Plan 2011.

Social Council, the Higher Council for Employment Promotion, and the Regional and Provincial Councils for Employment Promotion.[1] These are tripartite bodies, representing administration, employers, and employees. The degree of involvement in the implementation and financing of active labor market programs (ALMPs) varies by department and agency: some programs are carried out directly by a department, others are run by local authorities, and still others are managed by nonprofit organizations. The main departments and agencies responsible for the development and public provision of ALMPs are described below.

National Agency for Employment and Skills Promotion (ANAPEC)

Created in 2001, the National Agency for Employment and Skills Promotion (Agence Nationale de Promotion de l'Emploi et des Compétences, ANAPEC) is the principal agency responsible for organizing and implementing ALMPs in Morocco. It is a public agency that acts as a labor market intermediary, providing information to job seekers and employers. The agency collects information on vacancies and potential candidates and assists in matching the two. In 2009, ANAPEC collected information about 27,678 vacancies and helped about 4,355 job seekers find employment. At the end of 2009, ANAPEC had registered nearly 517,000 job seekers—41 percent of them women, 18 percent below 24 years of age, 33 percent university graduates, 33 percent professional training graduates, and 30 percent with a secondary diploma. Only 3 percent of all unemployed registered with the agency had lower than secondary-level schooling.

In 2009, ANAPEC had a budget of 808 million Moroccan dirhams (DH) ($100 million) and 547 staff, of whom 343 were in direct contact with job seekers. The agency has a network of 74 branches across the country. In remote areas where local branches are hard to access, local professional associations and nongovernmental organizations (NGOs) partner with ANAPEC to provide services through self-service job terminals. The aforementioned figures indicate that less than 1 percent of all registered job-seekers in Morocco found a job through ANAPEC and that the average number of job placements achieved by their staff is about 10 per year. These figures suggest very low levels of performance and effectiveness of the agency in their job-matching efforts.

Economic and Social Council

The Economic and Social Council is a constitutional body established in 2011. It works to find solutions to issues brought up by the government, the parliament, or the head of state concerning economic and social policies, including those related to employment. It includes a panel of experts appointed by civil society.

Higher Council for Employment Promotion

The Higher Council for Employment Promotion was established in 2004 and is supported by regional and provincial councils. It provides guidance to the government on employment-promoting policy measures, such as the integration of youth in the labor market and labor market management. The council is also responsible for monitoring and evaluating employment promotion measures supported by the government and for developing regional employment programs and plans.

Strategic Committee

Introduced in 2009, the Strategic Committee is under the chairmanship of the minister of economy and finance. It is responsible for monitoring the effects of the global and financial crisis, introducing measures related to employment in certain export sectors to improve their competitiveness, and undertaking emergency measures. Unlike the other committees, it operates on a very ad hoc basis.

Building Effective Employment Programs for Unemployed Youth in the Middle East and North Africa •
http://dx.doi.org/10.1596/978-0-8213-9904-0

Department of Employment

The Department of Employment is part of the Ministry of Employment and Professional Training. It comprises four directorates—Employment, Labor, Social Protection, and Human Resources, Budget and General Affairs—along with the National Institute of Labor and Social Protection. The mission of the Directorate of Employment is to develop, monitor, and evaluate ALMPs in Morocco. It conducts studies and presents projections on the factors determining employment and unemployment both nationally and globally. It works in coordination with the Higher Council for Employment Promotion. The program is implemented by ANAPEC.

Entraide Nationale

Entraide Nationale is a public enterprise that has been granted legal and financial autonomy. Its mission is to ensure the economic inclusion of vulnerable segments of society. It is responsible for a vast network of social protection establishments such as orphanages and boarding schools, and it also provides training services to make this subpopulation more employable. It also helps carry out initiatives of the Ministry of Social Development and the Ministry of Family and Solidarity.

Promotion Nationale

Promotion Nationale was established in 1961 as an autonomous agency in charge of the implementation of public works in rural areas. Since 1983, it has been attached to the Department of Interior. Its main mission is to promote direct job creation in labor-intensive activities. Toward this end, it carries out works in both rural and urban areas, as well as special programs focused on southern Morocco.

Vocational Training Institutions

Vocational training institutions that oversee apprenticeships may also be considered contributors to ALMPs in Morocco. Apprenticeships are a tool developed to facilitate school-to-job transition for young workers with low and intermediate education. Apprenticeships are provided by the Office of Vocational Training and Labor Promotion (Office de la Formation Professionnelle et de la Promotion du Travail, OFPPT), diverse vocational training public institutions, public departments, and private schools.

Financing

The Ministry of Economy and Finance supports various employment interventions and public ALMPs through special treasury accounts. These accounts are managed by the relevant public departments, depending on their sector prerogatives. For each program, there is a budget line managed directly by the associated public department, although the ministry carefully monitors all public expenses. Two funds are worthy of special note:

Building Effective Employment Programs for Unemployed Youth in the Middle East and North Africa •
http://dx.doi.org/10.1596/978-0-8213-9904-0

- *The Fund for the Promotion of Youth Employment*, created in 1994, is managed by the Ministry of Employment and Professional Training and the Ministry of Industry, Trade, and New Technologies. Its original aim was to develop conditions and a structure around granting loans to young entrepreneurs and financing activities to promote the integration of young people into the labor market. The fund was modified in 2009 to contribute to the financing of the Self-Employment Support Fund, managed by the Central Guarantee Fund (Caisse Centrale de Garantie), which provides loan advances without interest to young people with business projects, both graduates and nongraduates.
- *Financing for Installation Expenses and to Combat Unemployment* is a special account intended to finance public works programs.

Public Employment Services and Other Publicly Provided ALMPs

Morocco's ALMPs carry out five basic functions: intermediation, employment training, direct job creation, business start-up support, and provision of employment incentives.

Employment offices played an important role in labor market intermediation during colonial times, but their role and outreach has decreased since then, although the offices still play an important role in finding employment for Moroccans abroad. Since the 1960s, job seekers have relied less on public employment offices as a means to find existing job opportunities. Also, employers make less use of employment offices to report vacancies or hiring of recruits. In recognition of this, the Employment Department launched a pilot program between 1995 and 2001 to reinvigorate the labor market intermediation system by developing Centers of Information and Orientation for Employment. These centers matched graduate job seekers with appropriate job openings.

Employment training programs in Morocco target two main categories of beneficiaries: those with higher education and those who drop out of school or have lower education. The highly educated are reached mainly through programs implemented by ANAPEC (such as the Taehil program, described below), as well as by universities and executive training establishments. Those with less education receive training mainly through apprenticeship programs run by the Department of Professional Training of the Ministry of Employment and Professional Training (in collaboration with a number of public operators) and through specific programs implemented by Entraide Nationale. Although training programs in Morocco have notable achievements, they still face important challenges: responding to the needs of all job seekers, adapting training to meet the needs of the Moroccan labor market, acquiring sufficient financing for training, and effectively coordinating activities of the government, training providers, trainees, and the private sector.

Since the end of the 1990s, the number of micro and small enterprises has increased in Morocco as a result of the new financing policies and ALMPs supporting entrepreneurship. At the end of the 1980s, in accordance with Morocco's structural adjustment program, new employment policies were adopted, mainly aimed at promoting employment of youth with higher education. With support from the World Bank and the United States Agency for International Development (USAID), the Moroccan authorities developed an institutional framework for the development of microcredit provision. Initially this model seemed to be successful; however, the rate of outstanding unpaid debts has been growing in recent years.

Public ALMPs Provided by ANAPEC

ANAPEC delivers four main programs: Idmaj, Infitah, Taehil, and Moukawalati. Table 5.1 summarizes the characteristics of these programs.

The Idmaj program is responsible for labor market integration of the unemployed through provision of short- and medium-term employment contracts with a private firm for up to 24 months. Its target population consists of higher education graduates who have been registered with ANAPEC for more than six months. The trainee receives a minimum monthly tax-free salary of $198 and maximum of $743, paid by the enterprise. If the trainee is hired, this income tax break is extended for another year. This arrangement allows the graduate to acquire professional experience and skills while also contributing to the firm. Normally, an employer is required to give a notice period before terminating an employee. However, this program provides an exception so that employers can terminate an employee at any time, making employers more willing to recruit young graduates. ANAPEC has not estimated the unit cost per successful placement.

An independent evaluation showed that almost two-thirds (65 percent) of Idmaj beneficiaries reported that they had finished their training/job contract.[2] However, according to employers, just over half (52 percent) of the contracts were terminated before the full contract period had elapsed. Employers initiated the termination in 79 percent of the cases; most of the remaining candidates (83 percent) were offered a permanent position upon training completion. Only 10 percent of employers interviewed hired all their trainees. Half of employers said they wished candidates possessed more relevant skills and qualifications (Directorate of Employment 2011).

Infitah was launched in 2008 with a focus on international intermediation, seasonal labor provision, and circular migration. Program financing was $4.3 million from January 2008 to February 2010. The majority of beneficiaries were female workers who performed farm labor (such as strawberry picking) in Spain and France. Workers had to be between 18 and 40 years of age and in very good physical condition. They had to be from rural areas and have young children (up to 14 years old) whom they had to leave at home as a guarantee that they would return to Morocco after the employment period was over. Almost all (95 percent) of the women who participated in the program finished their contracts and returned.

The program was successful in achieving its goal of providing seasonal employment and income support to rural women. In 2009, 85 percent of female beneficiaries felt more self-assured after participating in the program, and nearly

Table 5.1 Summary of Public Employment Programs Provided by ANAPEC in Morocco

Program	Description	Targeting/characteristics of beneficiaries	Company obligation	Number of beneficiaries (annual)	Performance indicators/budget
Idmaj	Intermediation; first job contract (6–24 months) with private sector enterprise.	Higher education graduates, registered with ANAPEC for more than six months.	Maximum salary around DH 6,000 ($743), tax free. If the trainee is hired, this is extended for another year.	2009: 52,257 44% women 28% 15–24 years of age 41% higher education graduates	Out of all job seekers who signed an integration contract, 80% were integrated into an enterprise; 64% completed their training course within the enterprise; 83% of those who completed were offered a permanent job by the enterprise.
Infitah	Intermediation on the international market. Seasonal labor/circular migration.	Persons 18–40 years old. Must originate from rural areas. Must have young children (up to 14 years old) whom they leave at home as a guarantee that they will return to Morocco.	None.	2009: 10,853 2010: 6,222 Job placements mainly in Spain and France Mainly farm workers Mainly women	95% of the women selected finish their contract and return to their home country. Program evaluation shows that some beneficiaries can live all year on the savings from their earnings. Nearly 70% of women polled identified positive economic and financial change. Challenges: the workers are uneducated and socially vulnerable in host countries.
Taehil	Training for the labor market and labor market integration. Short- to medium-term training, with work contracts of six months to three years.	Persons with a high school diploma, registered with ANAPEC.	Company commits to hire the beneficiaries who are being trained within the field of company.	2009: 14,033 48% women 87% with a professional training or higher 23% less than 24 years old	Cost: DH 10,000 per beneficiary ($1,238). Budget: $24.75 million. 72% of beneficiaries finish the program. 58% of employers surveyed hired more than 50% of training candidates, 37% hired 100%, and 17% hired none.
Moukawalati	Self-employment support. Grant amount of DH 25,000 ($3,094) in the form of a loan, if the project is eligible for financing. Loan divided into two parts: (a) for support services in the form of business training; (b) financing project/product start-up expenses.	Graduates below 45 years of age, registered with ANAPEC, with an innovative business idea.	Part of the support must be granted in the form of an advance without interest to be reimbursed within six years.	2009: 10,786	8,634 jobs generated (3.38 jobs per business created): 34% in industry, 21% in services, 14% in crafts, 12% in information and communication, 11% in tourism, 8% in agriculture.

Source: Based on administrative data collected through World Bank interviews with Moroccan government officials from ANAPEC, the Ministry of Finance, and the Treasury.

70 percent reported that their income improved as a consequence of the program. Several beneficiary families were even able to live on their savings for the remainder of the year. However, the women found the enforced separation from their children for long periods of time to be inhumane and cruel, and they often felt exposed and vulnerable in the host country, given cultural and linguistic barriers. Moreover, working conditions were often harsh, with long hours spent doing heavy labor in the hot sun. Several proposals have been made to improve the program, such as lifting the strict family separation requirement, improving the work conditions, and letting men participate in the program to an increasing extent.

Taehil was launched in May 2006 as a national program to improve the employability of job seekers while contributing to labor market integration. The program sponsors contractual employment training for young graduates to provide them with specific skills requested by firms, which commit to hiring trainees for a short- or medium-term contract of six months to three years. Regional studies are first undertaken to identify the various regions' employment needs by sector of activity, by firm, and by profession. Afterward, the specific needs of individual firms are identified. The actual training is carried out by both public and private training providers, with customized matching in which program counselors match each trainee or job seeker with an appropriate training and firm. The demand for training is greater than current program capacity. Before selection, participants are interviewed to determine their qualifications and where they might be a good fit. Monthly salaries range from DH 2,000 to 4,500 (approximately $248–558).

Of those who received customized training, 70 percent were integrated into firms with short- or medium-term contracts. Of the surveyed firms, 37 percent hired all trainees upon completion of contract, 58 percent hired half, and 17 percent hired none. Employers' stated reasons for not hiring included candidates' inadequate training (35 percent) and lack of competence and experience (23 percent); in addition, some candidates declined to remain with the firm (19 percent). Most beneficiaries (83 percent) were satisfied with the training and felt that it facilitated labor market integration. Among employers, 59 percent felt that the program was partially effective at developing the trainees' skills according to the needs of the enterprise, while 39 percent felt it was effective. Both beneficiaries and employers called for the training period to be extended and to include more practical training.

In collaboration with 70 associations and firms, Moukawalati provides self-employment support to young people who want to start their own business. Support is provided both through business training and through the financing of project start-up/product expenses. Young entrepreneurs registered with ANAPEC can apply for a loan. The program first evaluates the sustainability of their project. If eligible, the entrepreneur receives DH 25,000 ($3,094) in the form of a loan divided into two parts: one for training and the other for product purchases/start-up costs. The loan is given without interest and must be reimbursed within six years. The program monitors and follows the start-ups for two years.

Building Effective Employment Programs for Unemployed Youth in the Middle East and North Africa • http://dx.doi.org/10.1596/978-0-8213-9904-0

Public ALMPs Provided by Institutions Other than ANAPEC
Offshoring Training Program[3]

There is an estimated need for 81,000 employees within the offshore telecom-munications services and aerospace sectors between the years 2008 and 2015. These offshore firms are looking for recruits with improved skills and qualifica-tions. To meet this need, the Fund for the Promotion of Youth Employment financed a training program provided by universities and OFPPT during 2007–09. The universities trained 4,700 youth at a cost of DH 81 million ($10 million). The OFPPT trained 6,900 candidates, at a cost of DH 151 million ($18.5 million), of whom 5,393 completed the training successfully. The average training cost was DH 50,000 ($6,188) per beneficiary.

Competence Development/Anti-Crisis Measures Training[4]

This training is part of a larger program that focuses on skills development within the textile, leather goods, and automobile equipment sectors. Participants acquire skills to produce better products, which in turn improves their employability and productivity. For the automobile sector, the goal is mainly to strengthen indus-trial and project management skills. Eligible firms are those that made at least 20 percent of their turnover in exports in 2008 and that have maintained a steady level of salaried staff. The firms are reimbursed for a large part of the staff training costs. In the first year, 2008, reimbursements amounted to DH 75 million ($9.28 million), benefiting 144 enterprises and 9,500 individuals. The program has not yet been evaluated.

Apprenticeship Training

This program is run by the Department of Professional Training in coopera-tion with the technical departments in charge of diverse economic sectors (crafts, tourism, agriculture, fishing, industry) and with Entraide Nationale, which runs the apprenticeship training centers. Participants receive practical training in a firm for 80 percent of the training time, while the remaining 20 percent is spent on general and technical classroom training in the training centers. The main objective of the program is to help young people acquire practical know-how on the job, which will make them more employable. The program also provides small enterprises with qualified staff and helps certain craft industries remain viable in the face of increasing automation. The state provides participating firms within the craft industries (only) with DH 250 ($31) per month per apprentice (Ministry of Economy and Finance 2009, 56–58).

In 2008–09, there were 96,982 beneficiaries, 17,711 of whom were women; in 2009–10, there were 31,948, including 11,072 women. More than 13,900 enterprises contributed to training apprentices during 2009. Twenty-nine percent of the training courses were provided within the agricultural sector, 20 percent in artisanal production, 15 percent in services and education, 12 percent in the hotel trade, 7 percent in the maritime fishing industry, 6 percent in artisanal services, and 6 percent in construction.

Entraide Nationale's Centers of Education and Training[5]

Entraide Nationale's 1,040 training centers are open to all, with no condition set for admission. They offer training in subjects ranging from basic literacy to the acquisition of specific skills. Apprenticeships constitute the core of the program, and certificates are issued at the end of the training. There is a plan to include provision of life skills as part of the training. As of May 2010 the program had served about 63,314 beneficiaries, 95 percent of whom are women. Most beneficiaries are from vulnerable segments of society. The cost per beneficiary was DH 2,042 DH ($253) in 2008 and slightly less in 2009.

Promotion Nationale

These public works programs aim to promote direct employment creation. Most are in rural areas and are intended to address seasonal underemployment in certain sectors, such as agriculture. Works include drilling wells, soil restoration, reforestation, and construction projects. Three categories of job seekers are admitted: unskilled laborers receive DH 41.00 per day ($5.07); semiskilled laborers, DH 48.75 per day ($6.03); and skilled laborers, DH 53.75 per day ($6.65). Around 20 percent of beneficiaries are women (Ministry of Economy and Finance 2009, 22–23).

Business Nurseries

This self-employment project is the result of a partnership between local authorities and chambers of commerce. The purpose of the program is to provide large buildings where young entrepreneurs can gather to incubate their businesses. University graduates who are between the ages of 20 and 45 and who present a feasible project can rent space at an attractive rate and use it as an office or production site. The nurseries are generally developed in industrial or rural areas, and once built, they become the property of local partners. Each nursery can host about 60 small enterprises (Ministry of Economy and Finance 2009, 62).

Construction of an envisioned 34 nurseries is forecast to cost DH 620 million ($73 million). These nurseries are expected to create 12,400 jobs, so the unit cost per job would be DH 45,900 ($5,681). Budgetary support for the program is provided by the Young Persons Employment Promotion Fund and by the Hassan II Fund for Economic and Social Development. The project started 15 years ago, and to date, only 10 nurseries have been developed. The main implementation challenge faced by this initiative is the lack of coordination between various players at the local and national levels.

Lessons Learned and Policy Recommendations

The urgent need to find solutions to Morocco's unemployment problem has given rise to a profusion of initiatives, programs, and institutions for employment promotion. An array of entities are involved in different areas of employment promotion: intermediation, training for employment, direct job creation, support for business start-ups, as well as provision of incentives through measures aimed at reducing labor costs. Active labor market programs in Morocco cover different categories of job seekers and employees, including those with high and low levels of education, and those in the formal or informal economy. This chapter suggests three directions for reforming the ALMP package.

First, targeting and allocation of funding should be made more specific and relevant to needs. The priority given to reducing unemployment among graduates in the early 2000s is beginning to bear fruit. Trends show that unemployment among workers with higher education is decreasing more rapidly than unemployment among less-educated workers. However, government allocations are not equitable across sectors. Only the manufacturing industries and high-level services are benefiting from the Idmaj and Taehil programs, while other sectors like agriculture, building, transport, and nonprofit activities provided by NGOs do not benefit from these programs. There is room to develop and expand existing ALMPs to integrate new activities and give incentives to recruit university graduates into activities currently characterized by a lack of skilled workers. Closer cooperation with the private sector would improve training relevance and effectiveness.

Second, greater consultation, coordination, efficiency, and integration should be promoted among the wide range of players involved in employment promotion at the national, provincial, and local levels. Consultative bodies include the Economic and Social Council; the Higher, Regional, and Provincial Councils for Employment Promotion; and the Committee for Human Development. The activation and capacity building of these employment consultation committees could help improve the conception and implementation of employment policies at all levels.

There is also a need to integrate existing programs to avoid fragmentation. Some programs overlap across institutions. Entraide Nationale's main focus, for instance, is to help vulnerable sectors of the population (namely school dropouts) acquire a profession. ANAPEC, an institution that has traditionally targeted university graduates, is now starting to target the same population served by Entraide Nationale. These public actors interact with similar local NGOs and deliver similar programs, mainly through the Local Committees for Human Development established after the launch of the National Initiative for Human Development.

Finally, an integrated monitoring and evaluation framework is needed to assess the impact and efficiency of ALMPs. Available labor market information systems are not integrated. Data from surveys collected by the Planning Department (Haut Commissariat au Plan) are not disseminated to users as raw data. The diverse institutions involved in the provision of ALMPs do not share their monitoring indicators; there is no harmonization, nor are there formal dissemination mechanisms. Currently, only ad hoc evaluation studies of existing programs are conducted by the Ministry of Employment and Professional Training. A relevant identification of employment policy priorities requires an integrated evaluation process, with strongly coordinated data collection and dissemination mechanisms, and an effective, formal, and regular dialogue across institutions involved.

Notes

1. The Moroccan Labor Code, in the latest reform of May 6, 2004, established the Higher Council for Employment Promotion (article 522) as well as Regional and Provincial Councils for Employment Promotion (article 524).

2. In 2009, ANAPEC hired an external firm to conduct an evaluation of the effectiveness of the program. Phone interviews were conducted nationwide, reaching 7,200 job seekers who had benefitted from the program between 2003 and 2008.

3. Information in this paragraph from author interview with Mounia Boucetta, general secretary of the Department of Industry and Trade.

4. Ibid.

5. Information in this paragraph from author interview with Mohamed Talbi, general director of Entraide Nationale.

References

Directorate of Employment. 2011. *Enquête auprès des bénéficiaires du programme Idmaj: Rapport d'analyse*. Ministry of Employment and Professional Training, Department of Employment, Rabat, Morocco.

Haut Commissariat au Plan. 2011. *Enquêtes nationales sur l'emploi 1998 à 2010—Premiers résultats et résultats détaillés*. Rabat, Morocco.

Ministry of Economy and Finance. 2009. *Projet de loi de finances pour l'année budgétaire 2009: Rapport sur les comptes spéciaux du Trésor*. Rabat, Morocco.

CHAPTER 6

Public Employment Programs in Syria

May Wazzan and Diane Zovighian

Introduction

The economy of the Syrian Arab Republic has been growing at an average annual rate of 5.2 percent during the last decade; yet employment growth has been notably shy, averaging 0.7 percent. The state of the labor market has in fact deteriorated considerably. Available data indicate that unemployment has decreased since 2001, but this has been accompanied by a sharp decrease in labor force participation rates from 52.3 to 42.8 percent (table 6.1).

Employment opportunities are particularly constrained for youth and women. School-to-work transition tends to be lengthy and difficult for young Syrians. A 2009 school-to-work transition survey indicates that half of Syrian youth are still without a job a year after leaving school, though the majority of them are actively looking for employment (Gebel 2012). As a result, unemployment rates for youth between the ages of 15 and 24 are higher than for any other age group, with 16.8 percent of youth unemployed (figure 6.1).

These averages mask substantial gender disparities. The school-to-work transition of young women is even longer than that of young men: only 20 percent of young women are employed a year after leaving school, compared to 60 percent of young men. More generally, across age groups, women remain more vulnerable to unemployment and inactivity. Women's unemployment rate is four times that of men, while their labor force participation rate decreased sharply from 21.3 percent in 2001 to 13.3 percent in 2009, one of the lowest female participation rates worldwide (table 6.1).

The Syrian workforce still demonstrates a strong preference for public sector jobs. Young Syrians are queuing for employment in the public sector, often with no positive outcome, in particular among low-skilled workers. The lower quality of jobs in the private sector is certainly one driver of this preference. According to the Labour Force Survey of 2010, 41 percent of private sector workers are in the informal sector and thus have no access to social insurance. In addition, working hours in the public sector are considerably lower than in the private sector, averaging 40 hours per week in the public sector compared to 52 hours in the formal private sector (CBS 2010). Moreover, salaries in the

Table 6.1 Syria Labor Market Indicators, 2001 and 2009
percent

Indicator	2001	2009
Labor force participation rate (age 15+)		
Male	81.4	71.0
Female	21.3	13.3
Youth (ages 15–24)	47.0	29.5
Total	52.3	42.8
Unemployment rate		
Male	7.4	5.8
Female	22.5	23.7
Youth (ages 15–24)	23.5	16.8
Total	10.3	8.1

Sources: CBS 2001, 2009.

Figure 6.1 Unemployment Rate by Age Group in Syria, 2009

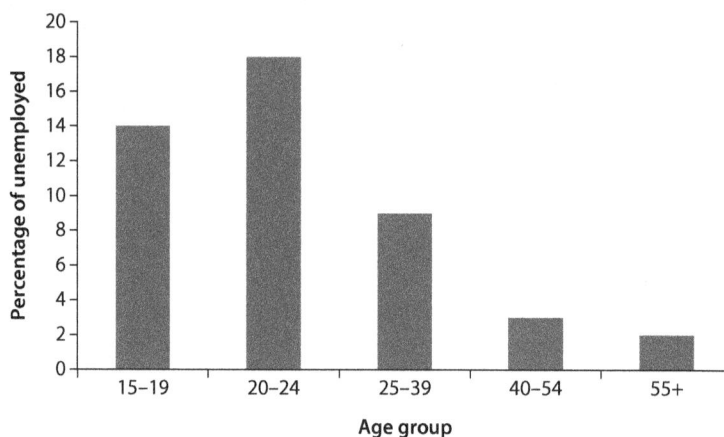

Source: CBS 2009.

public sector are on average 22 percent higher than in the private sector (Kabbani 2009).

Women, particularly those who are educated,, show a particular inclination to work in the public rather than the private sector: some 57 percent of employed women in Syria are government employees, compared to a national average of 28 percent. Most women working in the public sector are teachers. As public sector jobs become less available and there are more female graduates seeking jobs than the public sector can absorb, women may be at a particular disadvantage in finding the jobs they seek.

Evidence from various sources shows that the skills produced by the education and training system are not aligned with the needs of the labor market. Hence, even when jobs are available, a skills mismatch still hinders full and productive employment of the Syrian workforce. In a 2005 survey, 66.3 percent of youth reported that one of the main obstacles to finding a job lies in insufficient or irrelevant education; in comparison, 31.6 percent mentioned the scarcity of jobs in the market (Alissa 2007). Similarly, in the 2009 Investment Climate Assessment survey of Syria, 60 percent of firms rated workers' skills as a major constraint to doing business (World Bank 2009). The quality and relevance of the education and training systems is therefore a major concern in Syria.

Access to employment opportunities, in particular in the private sector, is limited by the predominant role of informal networks in the process of searching for a job. Formal job matching systems and mechanisms are seldom used. Information flows between prospective employers and job seekers, including on job availability, are highly segmented, and access to employment opportunities depends strongly on personal connections. In 2005, 53.6 percent of young Syrians found their job through the help of relatives or friends; only 2.4 and 0.8 percent, respectively, secured a job through public employment offices or the Agency for Combating Unemployment (now the Public Commission for Employment and Enterprise Development, PCEED) (Alissa 2007).

The employment barriers described above call for stronger public intervention through active labor market programs (ALMPs) to help Syrian job seekers, especially youth, in the short term. In the Syrian context, ALMPs have the potential to provide formal and open intermediation channels between prospective employers and job seekers to facilitate information and communication flows, allowing for more efficient job matching. ALMPs can also enhance the skills of unemployed workers and adjust them to the needs of private businesses, and they can stimulate the creation of job opportunities in private businesses.

This chapter examines the public provision of ALMPs in Syria. The main types of ALMPs implemented in Syria include the following:

- Public employment services, particularly services facilitating labor market intermediation
- Training programs, particularly for the unemployed
- Programs supporting micro, small, and medium enterprise (MSME) development

The chapter reviews the institutional framework governing the public delivery of ALMPs and the main stakeholders and examines ALMPs provided by the Syrian government. Finally, recommendations are proposed to strengthen these programs and improve their effectiveness.

Institutional Framework for Employment Services in Syria

The Ministry of Social Affairs and Labor (MoSAL) and its affiliated agency, the PCEED, play a major role in ALMP provision. The MoSAL, through its Central Nomination Unit, provides intermediation services targeted particularly to those seeking jobs in the public sector. The PCEED is an affiliated agency that was set

Figure 6.2 Institutional Framework for Delivery of Public Employment Services and Other Publicly Provided ALMPs in Syria

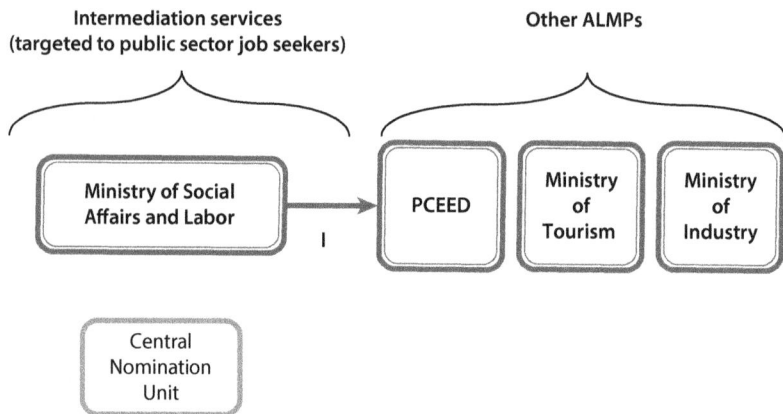

Note: ALMPs = active labor market programs; I = Institutionally affiliated with ministry (chaired by minister); PCEED = Public Commission for Employment and Enterprise Development.

up to improve the prospects of job seekers in the private sector and to support the self-employed and small businesses (figure 6.2).

Other agencies also provide ALMPs, but in an uncoordinated way. A few ministries, such as the Ministry of Tourism and the Ministry of Industry, provide sector-specific training programs. In addition to these ministries and public agencies, some smaller programs or institutions, generally donor-supported, have also been created. They include the Career Management Center at Damascus University, supported by the United Nations Development Programme, and the Business Incubator Program; both are also part of the PCEED portfolio of programs.

Ministry of Social Affairs and Labor

The MoSAL is responsible for setting the labor policy agenda, as well as providing employment services. The Central Nomination Unit at the Directorate of Labor is charged with coordinating and supervising the operations of 15 regional employment offices, set up in 2001 and located in all governorates. Every unemployed person in Syria must register with the public employment agency in his or her governorate.

The Central Nomination Unit within the MoSAL has so far focused on providing intermediation services for persons seeking public sector jobs. The number of registered job seekers at the Central Nomination Unit was as high as 1.7 million in 2009, though this may be an inflated number due to shortcomings in information management. The main function of the unit is to manage the queue for public sector jobs: it operates as a clearinghouse that receives job applications from all job seekers, screens and matches them with announced vacancies from ministries and other government agencies, and forwards them to the concerned employment offices for referral. In contrast, cooperation with the private sector is almost nonexistent, and the unit plays no role in labor intermediation between private businesses and job seekers. The PCEED was created to carry out this function (see below).

Since 2010, the regulation of private providers of employment services has also been part of the mandate of the MoSAL. Until that year, private employment agencies were illegal in Syria, with the exception of those recruiting foreign workers. The 2010 Labor Law reform legalized private employment agencies, allowing them to act as intermediaries between job seekers and private businesses, and mandated the MoSAL to license them and regulate their activities. Private providers of employment services are required to implement the employment policy devised by the ministry and to report to the MoSAL's local employment offices. This includes submitting a monthly statement to the local public employment agency that lists the names of registered unemployed. Those job seekers then receive a registration card from the public employment office, without which they cannot be recruited. The private agencies must also provide details on the placement of job seekers.

The legalization of private employment services is an opportunity to improve the availability and quality of employment services, especially given the lack of publicly supported labor intermediation for private sector jobs. However, this opportunity will only be fully tapped if government plays an appropriate regulatory role. Government intervention should be aimed at improving the quality (for example, by setting quality standards) and equitable targeting of privately provided ALMPs, rather than hindering the work of private intermediation.

Public Commission for Employment and Enterprise Development

The PCEED is the main public agency mandated to support employment in the private sector. Its overarching objective is to help job seekers get a private sector job or set up their own business. Toward this end, it carries out two principal functions: training and retraining of job seekers and employees, and support to self-employment and MSME development. The PCEED accesses the job seekers database maintained by the MoSAL and attempts to influence the preferences of Syrians queuing for public sector jobs. The PCEED also provides recommendations to the MoSAL in relation to its general employment policies.

The PCEED faces a number of organizational and structural challenges. It is a financially and administratively independent institution under the authority of the MoSAL, created pursuant to Legislative Decree 39 of 2006 to replace the previous Agency for Combating Unemployment established in 2001. The PCEED employs a total of 240 staff and has 13 branches. The agency is managed by a director general and overseen by an 11-member board chaired by the minister of social affairs and labor. The PCEED and the MoSAL cooperate in some operational and policy-making areas. However, the official staff allocation of the PCEED has not yet been finalized, and there is no clear assignment of responsibilities to all staff. In addition, legislative and bureaucratic hurdles are affecting the agency's capacity to provide services in a flexible manner.

Public Employment Services and Other Publicly Provided ALMPs

Employment Services

The main function of MoSAL's Central Nomination Unit and its 15 employment offices is to manage the lengthy queue for public sector jobs. While the PCEED accesses this queue to improve job seekers' prospects in the private sector, the Central Nomination Unit gathers requests from ministries and government agencies looking for workers and transfers these requests to the relevant employment offices for referral. After the matched job seekers take the competitive entry tests for specific ministries and agencies, the employment offices send the results to the Nomination Unit, which then sends the names of the candidates to the agencies requesting employees. Since the creation of the employment offices, the ratio of newly registered job seekers to candidates appointed has averaged 10:1. In 2009, for example, 132,000 people registered while fewer than 12,000 were appointed.

There is a strong case for diversifying public employment services in Syria, although this is already happening to a limited extent through the activities of the PCEED. Public employment services provided by the MoSAL focus almost exclusively on public sector employment and play no role in matching labor supply and demand in the private sector. As a result, they are ill adapted to a rapidly transforming labor market, where the private sector employs about 71.5 percent of the workforce (World Bank 2013). The main objective of reform would be to engineer a shift from a traditional focus on managing job matching in the bloated public sector to facilitating job intermediation in the private sector. A first step would be to develop dialogue and partnerships with private businesses, which are currently neither consulted nor engaged. The activities of the PCEED have been geared to fulfill such objectives, though it does not provide employment services per se.

Within both the Central Nomination Unit and the PCEED, there is considerable space to enhance the quality of employment services. Processes are not fully transparent or automated. Neither of the agencies provides an electronic job matching platform, which likely leads to suboptimal matches. Nor is there any systematic monitoring or evaluation of the employment services provided.

The Career Management Center is an experiment in providing integrated employment services oriented to the private sector job market in Syria. Located at Damascus University, the center targets young graduates. It was established in 2007, in close cooperation with the MoSAL and the PCEED. In addition to job intermediation, its functions include labor data gathering, career guidance, and counseling. The center reaches out to employers to collect information on vacancies and hosts lectures by employers from different economic sectors, offering students opportunities to interact with these representatives; it also offers courses in communication skills, career planning, and curriculum vitae (CV) writing. Though it provides an interesting pilot example of the provision of integrated employment services to job seekers, the center's scope and outreach remain limited. Its total budget is approximately $115,000, and its yearly target is to provide services to 500 beneficiaries.

Training Programs

Training programs are a major component of Syria's strategy to upgrade workers' skills and support private sector employment, but there is no integrated approach to the provision of short-term training programs across public institutions. Training courses are provided by a series of public agencies and ministries, including the PCEED, the Ministry of Industry, and the Ministry of Tourism. However, there is no national vocational education and training strategy, nor is there a common, national vocational qualification framework to set goals, standards, and guidelines for training curricula and accreditation. While training provision remains fragmented and unregulated, some programs make efforts to provide certification to their beneficiaries. Table 6.2 provides a brief overview of publicly provided training programs in Syria.

The PCEED is facing some difficulties in fulfilling its mandate to encourage employment in the private sector. The commission's Training for Guaranteed Employment program, which aims to support the hiring of unemployed Syrians in private businesses, responds to an acute demand from the labor market. Yet the program has considerable limitations: it provides services to only a small number of beneficiaries, and three-quarters of them dropped out of the program or refused job offers in the private sector in 2009. The high dropout and refusal rates illustrate the persistent preference of job seekers for public sector employment and the program's inability to provide adequate incentives to change that preference. This could reflect a mismatch between job seekers' expectations and the reality of private sector employment, that is, the low job quality and relatively low wages offered by businesses participating in the program. At the same time, private businesses have not readily engaged with the PCEED: in addition to limited awareness of the programs offered, private businesses have few incentives, financial and otherwise, to make use of the programs. The partial failure of Training for Guaranteed Employment therefore points to the need to develop partnerships with the private sector and to adjust the incentive schemes for both job seekers and private businesses in order to successfully encourage private sector employment.

All training programs face issues of quality and relevance. The absence of a national vocational qualification framework results in the lack of harmonized curricula and certification systems. This absence of quality standards can generate distrust toward the quality of the training system and its graduates. At the very least, it prevents the effective signaling of skills, making it difficult for private businesses to value candidates' profiles and skills. Moreover, the quality of training programs is undermined by the fact that programs tend to be supply-driven. Efforts are made to provide training programs that respond to the needs of the labor market: the design of some training programs is informed by labor market needs assessments (such as the PCEED Training and Retraining Program). Yet private businesses are seldom consulted regarding program design and content,

Table 6.2 Summary of Public Employment Training Programs in Syria

Agency	Program	Type of program	Description	Targeting	Beneficiaries (2009)	Average cost or budget (2009)
Public Commission for Employment and Enterprise Development (PCEED)	Training for Guaranteed Employment Program	On-the-job training	The PCEED establishes contracts with private businesses to place job seekers in on-the-job training for three months, during which salaries are paid by the PCEED. External training can also be financed if requested by the firm. During the first month, the firm or the trainee can opt out. Once the training period is completed, both have to commit to sign a regular contract of one to three years.	95% of beneficiaries are 20–30 years old.	110 completed training period and were hired (out of 439 identified vacancies). High dropout rates and refusals of job offers limit program's impact.	Approximately Syrian pounds (SYP) 4 million ($69 thousand)
PCEED	Training and Retraining Program	Training for the unemployed	Trains job seekers on skills required by the labor market, based on internal labor market needs assessments.	—	—	—
Ministry of Industry	Rapid Training Program	Training for the unemployed	Aims at helping semiskilled workers improve their chances of employment through free six-month vocational trainings on subjects including car mechanics, textiles and spinning, industrial drawing, and electronics. Training is based on market needs determined through outreach to companies.	Applicants undergo testing (general and mathematics) that determines admission.	3,000 graduates. Program is absorbing over seven times its capacity, which is affecting its quality.	Approximately SYP 100 million ($1,7 million)

table continues next page

Table 6.2 Summary of Public Employment Training Programs in Syria *(continued)*

Agency	Program	Type of program	Description	Targeting	Beneficiaries (2009)	Average cost or budget (2009)
Ministry of Tourism	Hotel Courses Program	Training for the unemployed	Upgrades the quality of tourism services in all governorates by offering fee-based (around $150) courses to build skills in hotel management, tourist offices, and guide services. Graduates receive certificates that give them priority to work in tourist offices (they jump the queue at the Ministry of Social Affairs and Labor and the PCEED).	—	—	—

Source: Based on administrative data collected through World Bank interviews with Syrian government officials.

Note: — = not available.

and the responsiveness of most programs to labor market needs remains questionable. With respect to job seekers' incentives, employment subsidies could be used to bridge the gap between job seekers' reservation wage and wages offered by private businesses.

Data collection, whether to inform, monitor, or evaluate training programs, is weak. Information systems that could inform the design of programs, including assessments of firms' needs and of job seekers' skills, are lacking. Similarly, monitoring and evaluation frameworks are weak or nonexistent. Almost none of the programs track the employment or wage status of beneficiaries after program completion.

Entrepreneurship and MSME Development Programs

The PCEED plays a major role in supporting entrepreneurship and the development of MSMEs, particularly by providing entrepreneurship training and support for access to finance. This support is one of the main axes of the Syrian government's strategy to support private sector employment. Table 6.3 provides an overview of the PCEED entrepreneurship and MSME development programs.

There is considerable scope to scale up entrepreneurship and MSME development programs in Syria and enhance their impact. The government's initiatives to train entrepreneurs and facilitate their access to loans and business services have the potential to stimulate the formalization and development of private businesses and generate much-needed private sector jobs. Yet the coverage of entrepreneurship and MSME development programs remains extremely low, especially in contrast with the size of the inactive and unemployed labor force. Arguably, this low coverage is a result of both a low supply of programs and a low demand for the programs. Limited access to credit for the self-employed and small businesses through the formal banking system and the still quite immature microcredit market seems to be a particularly strong barrier.

Entrepreneurship and MSME development programs in Syria suffer from the weakness or absence of monitoring and evaluation systems. Data on program outputs are scarce: some programs provide data on the number of program beneficiaries, but available data do not necessarily reflect all program outputs. In addition, data on program quality, such as beneficiaries' satisfaction and loan repayment rates, and impact, whether on job creation or wages, are virtually nonexistent.

Broader financial, administrative, and regulatory reforms are needed to allow entrepreneurship and MSME development programs to reach their full potential. The business environment, including access to finance, remains unfavorable for the development of MSMEs. The Micro, Small and Medium Enterprise Development Program illustrates this need for systemic reform: the limited accessibility of banking and financial institutions to micro, small, and medium entrepreneurs in Syria hinders the access to credit of the program's beneficiaries.

Table 6.3 Summary of Entrepreneurship and MSME Development Programs Provided by the PCEED in Syria, 2009

Program	Type of program	Description	Targeting	Number of beneficiaries (2009)	Average budget (2009)
Training of Entrepreneurs	Entrepreneurship training and support for access to finance	Screens and trains entrepreneurs and nominates them to financial institutions to obtain funding. Training courses are usually short (15 hours), and topics revolve around creating businesses. Applicants take personality and written examinations to assess their entrepreneurial qualifications.	Priority is given to youth (25–35) and unemployed.	506 entrepreneurs trained.	Approximately Syrian Pounds (SYP) 8 million ($140 thousand)
Micro, Small and Medium Enterprise Development	Loan guarantee scheme	Intermediates and guarantees loans taken up by small and medium enterprises (30% of loan guaranteed) and microenterprises (up to 70% guaranteed) at third-party financial institutions. Firms must have a minimum number of workers according to size of capital. Beneficiaries must establish the project inside the governorate in which they live, complete the Entrepreneurship Training Course, submit a business plan, hold a business license, and contribute a certain percentage of the enterprise capital.	—	From 2008 to mid-2010, 229 small and medium enterprises were referred to cooperating banks, 40 of which were funded; 31 microenterprise projects were referred to nonbanking funding institutions, 10 of which were funded.	—

table continues next page

Table 6.3 Summary of Entrepreneurship and MSME Development Programs Provided by the PCEED in Syria, 2009 *(continued)*

Program	Type of program	Description	Targeting	Number of beneficiaries (2009)	Average budget (2009)
Women Empowerment and Poverty Alleviation	Social services, training, and loan scheme	Provides lending services, social development services, and economic opportunities to women in poor villages. The main component is the provision of loans of SYP 25,000–200,000 ($435–3,500). Lending adheres to Murabaha Islamic principles (profit-free and transparent transactions). The interest rate is 6%, with an exemption rate of 2% that is returned to the female borrower in case of commitment to repayment.	Target group is unemployed women in poor villages. Selected villages must have low living standards and high female unemployment and illiteracy rates. Beneficiaries must be unemployed and hold a literacy certificate at a minimum. If women have children, none should have dropped out of compulsory education and all should be enrolled in the national vaccination program.	1,839 women trained in entrepreneurship. The number of women obtaining a loan is unknown.	—
Business Incubator	Business support services	Aims to help entrepreneurs establish and manage new enterprises by providing them with space, business services, and consultations during the incubation period.	—	Since 2006, two incubators have been launched, assisting 25 projects in total.	—

Note: — = not available.

Lessons Learned and Policy Recommendations

The development of thoughtful regulatory frameworks can positively affect the quality of ALMP provision in Syria. The existence of regulatory frameworks and need for reform varies from one category of ALMP to another. In particular, while the private provision of employment services is regulated, the provision of other ALMPs, such as training programs, lacks coherent nationwide regulations. Hence, in the case of employment services, the major challenge lies in ensuring that the government's regulatory role is oriented toward improving the quality and equitable targeting of services provided by private agencies rather than hindering their work. As for training, priority should be given to developing vocational qualification frameworks that set standards for the delivery of training programs with respect to curricula, skills acquisition, and certification. Ensuring better quality of the services provided to job seekers and providing clearer signals to employers on the skills and capacities of job seekers is crucial.

Sustained and strengthened policy and budgetary commitment to ALMPs will be key to the success of efforts to support private sector employment. The potential of ALMPs as short-term tools to leverage labor demand, supply, and intermediation in the private sector is not fully exploited. The PCEED, which was created to facilitate private sector employment, faces difficulties in fulfilling its mandate: its financial resources and its human and technical capacities remain extremely limited, resulting in few programs with limited coverage. Also, job seekers remain reluctant to participate in its programs, partly as a result of their preference for public sector employment. Syria should prioritize private sector employment and increase public investment to enable the PCEED and other public agencies to fulfill their mandate.

Toward this end, substantial investment should be made in reorienting public employment services toward the private sector labor market. Public employment services are currently geared toward facilitating job matching in the public sector; no public agency facilitates private sector employment, whether through labor market intermediation services or career counseling to job seekers. Syria could consider providing diversified employment services for private sector jobs through the PCEED, possibly building on the experiment of the Career Management Center piloted at Damascus University. The legalizing of private employment agencies is a promising development, calling for the right enabling and regulatory environment.

Scaling up of services provided by public agencies involved in ALMP provision would create more opportunities to support job seekers. Most of the employment services, training and entrepreneurship, and MSME development programs provide a limited number of services to a small pool of beneficiaries.

Innovative financial and career incentives for job seekers are needed to encourage them to cease waiting for a public sector job and actively engage in job search or employment in the private sector. The use of employment subsidies could be explored as a means to bridge the gap between market wages and job seekers' reservation wages.

Also crucial are efforts to strengthen the targeting of youth and women in ALMP provision to ensure their equitable access to the programs. Women and youth form the bulk of Syria's unemployed and inactive, but they are not systematically targeted by publicly provided ALMPs. A categorical targeting of these groups, coupled with a means test, would ensure that programs reach more of those most in need.

Enhanced data collection to inform, monitor, and evaluate ALMPs provides opportunities to improve the quality of service provision. In particular, strengthened labor data and information systems would facilitate the design of evidence-based ALMPs. Labor data and information in Syria are weak, and the use of existing data by policy makers is low. There is an opportunity for the MoSAL, in particular the PCEED, to engage in the development of labor market data and studies to inform the design of ALMPs and ensure their relevance to labor market needs.

Stronger monitoring and evaluation systems would allow policy makers to track the impact of publicly provided ALMPs in Syria. Most of the programs are neither regularly monitored nor properly evaluated: few or no data are available to track implementation, and the short-, medium-, and long-term impacts on employment or wage outcomes remain largely unassessed.

Partnerships with private businesses could help leverage resources and enhance the quality and impact of ALMPs. At present, there is almost no involvement of the private sector in guiding and motivating ALMP design and content. In addition, awareness within the private sector of programs offered by public agencies is limited, and there are no incentives to encourage use of the programs. Building stronger partnerships between public providers of ALMPs and private businesses would enhance the quality of services provided and their relevance to the actual needs of the labor market. It would also help build trust in the programs on the part of private businesses and thus potentially increase their engagement with program beneficiaries.

References

Alissa, S. 2007. "The School-to-Work Transition of Young People in Syria." Employment Policy Paper 2007/3, International Labour Organization, Geneva, Switzerland.

CBS (Central Bureau of Statistics). 2001. *Labour Force Survey 2001*. Damascus.

———. 2009. *Labour Force Survey 2009*. Damascus.

———. 2010. *Labour Force Survey 2010*. Damascus.

Gebel, M. 2012. "The Transition from Education to Work in Syria: Results of the Syrian Youth Transition Survey 2009." Working Paper, European Training Foundation, Turin, Italy.

Kabbani, N. 2009. *Why Young Syrians Prefer Public Sector Jobs*. Middle East Youth Initiative Policy Outlook 2. Washington, DC: Wolfensohn Center for Development at Brookings; United Arab Emirates: Dubai School of Government.

World Bank. 2009. *Syria Investment Climate Update: Accelerating Private-Led Growth and Employment*. World Bank, Washington, DC.

———. 2013. *Jobs for Shared Prosperity: Time for Action in the Middle East and North Africa*. Washington, DC: World Bank.

CHAPTER 7

Public Employment Programs in Tunisia

Diego F. Angel-Urdinola, Anne Hilger, and Rene Leon-Solano

Introduction

Coping with a large population of educated, unemployed youth is one of the most serious challenges facing Tunisia. Despite solid economic growth prior to the Jasmine Revolution of 2011, unemployment in Tunisia was high and increasing (Belghazi 2012). Overall unemployment rose from 13.0 percent in 2010 to 18.9 percent in 2011, accounting for about 739,000 jobless individuals. Unemployment among highly skilled young people between 15 and 29 years of age was even higher, as much as 44.3 percent in 2010 (INS 2011).

Unemployment rates among this group, the most vocal during the Jasmine Revolution, will probably continue to worsen in the near future as new labor market entrants outpace employment creation. Indeed, between 2010 and 2011, the labor force with university education displayed a net increase of 8.6 percent while net employment among this category decreased by 0.2 percent. An important factor in recent labor market trends is that Tunisia is at the peak of its demographic transition, with a median age of 29. Youth between the ages of 15 and 25 account for about 20 percent of the overall population, and young adults between 25 and 34 make up half of new labor market entrants.

Nonetheless, while unemployment rates are highest among educated youth, the majority of the unemployed in Tunisia (67 percent) are workers with no university education (World Bank and INS, forthcoming). Moreover, approximately 40 percent of the low-skilled unemployed have been unemployed for at least 12 months. This is important because long-term unemployment reduces an individual's chance of securing employment in the future. At the same time, the labor market in Tunisia faces important structural problems, such as regulatory rigidities, skills mismatches, a large public sector that distorts incentives, and sluggish labor demand (World Bank and INS, forthcoming).

Active labor market programs (ALMPs) have long been at the core of Tunisian labor market policy. ALMPs were first launched in 1981 to address employment challenges faced by graduates of vocational training institutes. In 1987, paid internships were introduced to facilitate job insertion among first-time job seekers. ALMPs began to offer wage subsidies and exemptions from social security to employers in 2000 as a way to encourage them to hire unemployed university graduates. The system of ALMPs in Tunisia is one of the largest in the Middle East and North Africa, with expenditures on ALMPs surpassing 0.8 percent of gross domestic product (GDP) in 2011 and covering more than 400,000 beneficiaries. The most common ALMPs in Tunisia are wage subsidies to promote on-the-job training among high-skilled first-time job seekers, entrepreneurship support, and regional employment programs, mainly public works.

This chapter presents a brief overview of the main institutions providing public employment services and ALMPs in Tunisia. They include the National Employment Fund (Fund 21-21), the main source of financing for ALMPs; the National Agency for Employment and Independent Work (ANETI), the agency in charge of implementing employment programs and services in the country; and the regional councils, public bodies comprising representatives of regional and local authorities, each council headed by the region's governor. The chapter first sets forth a rationale for the provision of public employment services and ALMPs, then outlines the institutional framework governing employment services. The main ALMPs are described, including regional and entrepreneurship programs. Finally, the chapter identifies the main challenges hindering the effective and efficient delivery of employment services and offers some policy recommendations.

Rationale for Public Employment Services and ALMPs in Tunisia

Labor Market Outlook

The Tunisian labor market faces substantial challenges in providing sufficient jobs of adequate quality for its fast-growing labor force. From 2005 through 2010, labor force participation grew by only about 1 percent in the North Africa region as a whole, more slowly than in the rest of the world (ILO 2011). However, in Tunisia labor force participation grew by 3.4 percent in the same period (table 7.1). This increase is due in part to the country's demographic transition, with a large youth bulge that will continue to put pressure on the labor market. In fact, the labor force participation rate is expected to grow at over 2 percent annually until 2015.

Unemployment rates are especially high among youth, women, and university graduates, but the stock of the unemployed population is mainly composed of nongraduates. Unemployment has been rising fastest among university graduates and women, as well as rural residents. In addition, unemployment affects regions differently, with interior regions facing substantially higher rates than coastal regions.

Long-term unemployment is widespread and increasing rapidly. About 34 percent have been searching for longer than 12 months, and 13 percent have been searching for longer than 24 months. Long-term unemployment rates are particularly high among university graduates, at 44 percent. Not only are jobs

Table 7.1 Tunisia Labor Market Indicators, 2005 and 2010

percent

Indicator	2005	2010
Labor force participation rate (ages 15–64)		
Male	72.78	74.74
Female	25.65	27.03
Youth (ages 15–24)	31.66	31.22
Total	48.93	50.56
Unemployment rate		
Male	12.40	11.09
Female	15.36	19.12
Youth (ages 15–24)	28.19	29.39
Total	13.19	13.27

Source: Based on Tunisia's Labor Force Survey, years 2005 and 2010.

scarce, but the quality of employment is low. Informality is widespread: 40 percent of the employed in urban areas work without a contract.

This evidence suggests that unemployment in Tunisia is structural. In addition to the youth bulge, several other supply and demand factors are constraining employment growth. They include the prevalence of skills mismatches, inefficient systems for private intermediation, rigid labor market institutions, the low quality of education, and low levels of private investment.

Profile of Registered Unemployed Graduates

In 2011, ANETI's database included 802,353 registered individuals, of which 281,218 (about 35 percent) were active registered job seekers. The majority of active job seekers were university graduates (73 percent), first-time job-seekers (95 percent), and women (60 percent). In this section we provide a brief overview of job seekers who are university graduates—a group that constitutes a priority target of labor policy in the country. This profile is based on administrative data for the year 2010.

Data for the period show that 67 percent of graduates registered with ANETI are female. Rising educational levels among women and the rising labor force participation of educated women have been accompanied by an increase in their unemployment rates: between 2005 and 2010, unemployment rates among women with tertiary education doubled. The distribution of the registered unemployed by age (averaging 26 to 27 years old) is very similar for men and women (figure 7.1, panel a). However, a significant gap exists with respect to field of study (figure 7.1, panel b). Unemployed men are most likely to have graduated from sciences and technology, and unemployed women from economics and law.

Registered unemployed graduates tend to be concentrated in few regions (map 7.1). This could be the result of several factors. One is the existence of universities in those areas. Tunis, Sfax, Gafsa, Gabès, and Jendouba are all regions where large public universities operate. After graduating from university in

Figure 7.1 Registered Unemployed Graduates by Age and Field of Study in Tunisia, 2010

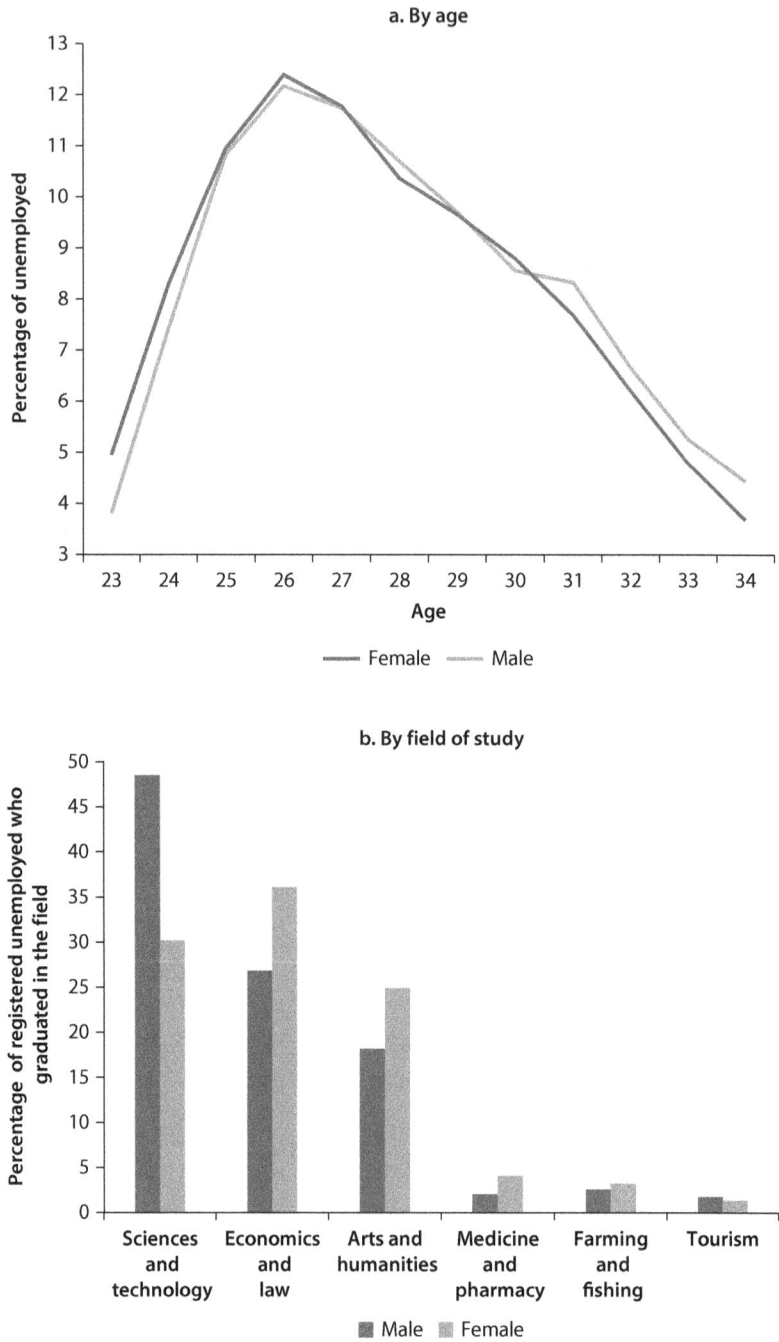

a. By age

b. By field of study

Source: Based on ANETI administrative data.

Map 7.1 Regional Distribution of Registered Unemployed Graduates, Tunisia, 2010

Percentage of registered
unemployed who live
in the governorate

- 5.45–8.37
- 3.94–5.45
- 2.63–3.94
- 0.97–2.63

Source: Based on ANETI administrative data.

a specific governorate, graduates may start to search for work there. A second factor is the availability of employment offices: ANETI has 91 employment offices distributed over the 24 governorates, with an average of 3.8 offices per governorate (see map 7.1). Third, some regions have lower economic performance and a generally higher rate of unemployment than others. For instance, in Gafsa and Jendouba, interior regions without large economic sectors other than agriculture, overall unemployment rates in 2010 were 28.5 and 18.4 percent, respectively—while the national average was at 13.27 percent in the same year.

More than 90 percent of registered job seekers have been unemployed for at least a year, and more than 70 percent for more than two years (average registration duration is 3.18 years). Landlocked regions are particularly exposed to high rates of long-term unemployment among graduates.

Building Effective Employment Programs for Unemployed Youth in the Middle East and North Africa •
http://dx.doi.org/10.1596/978-0-8213-9904-0

Institutional Framework for Employment Programs in Tunisia

The MVTE is the government agency in charge of employment policy in Tunisia, which includes overseeing the delivery of employment services. The MVTE manages the National Employment Fund (Fund 21-21), which finances: (a) regional programs managed by the Regional Councils, notably public works and other social programs (Employment Solidarity Contract, CES); (b) employment programs managed by ANETI; and (c) some micro-credits managed by the Tunisian Solidarity Bank (TSB). Most micro-credits, however, are financed through the National Fund for the Promotion of Handicrafts and Small Trades (FONAPRAM), a fund that was created in 1982 to support the development of micro and small enterprises in the handicraft industry in the country. The Central Bank of Tunisia oversees the FONAPRAM (figure 7.2). Other entities that are involved in overseeing and/or delivering employment services in Tunisia include the Ministry of Regional Development and Planning and the Tunisian National Agency of Vocational Training.

The National Employment Fund (Fund 21-21)

Financing for ANETI's ALMPs comes mainly through the National Employment Fund, known as Fund 21-21. The Fund 21-21 was established in 1999 (Law 99-101) and is financed through a special account of the Treasury. Its budget is

Figure 7.2 Institutional Framework for Employment Programs In Tunisia

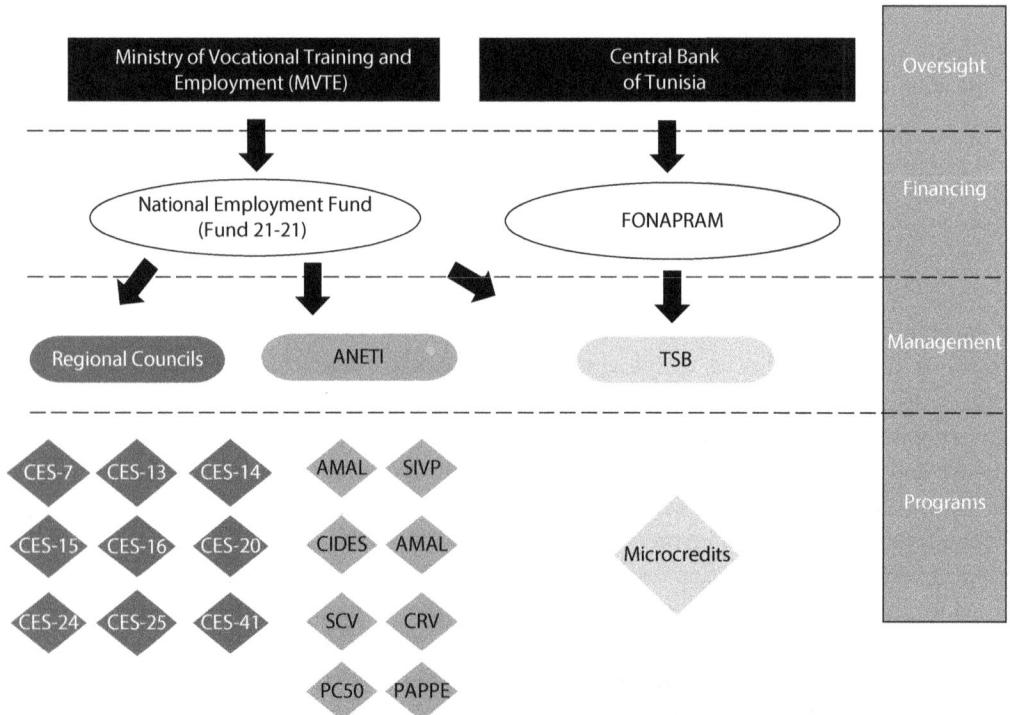

financed through general tax revenues, individual contributions, as well as from earnings from privatization operations. Since 2009, the fund finances ALMPs delivered by ANETI.

The resources of the Fund 21-21 are significant at approximately 460 million Tunisian Dinars (TD) in 2011 ($285 million) (about 0.8 percent of GDP) financing primarily: (a) *regional employment programs, such as public works* (about 10 percent of total fund allocations in 2010/11); (b) *micro-credits* provided by the *Tunisian Solidarity Bank* (TSB) (about 10 percent of total fund allocations in 2010); and (c) ALMPs delivered by ANETI (about 80 percent of total fund allocations in 2010).

National Agency for Employment and Independent Work (ANETI)

The National Agency for Employment and Independent Work (Agence Nationale pour l'Emploi et le Travail Indépendant, ANETI) is responsible for implementing publicly provided ALMPs (Law 93-11 of 1993 and Decree 2003-564 of 2003). It is especially charged with providing employment services to the unemployed through its regional offices, implementing employment promotion and microenterprise programs, and providing placement services to Tunisians who want to work abroad. The MVTE oversees the agency's financial arrangements (approval of budgets, financial statements, creation/abolition of offices, etc.) as well as its administrative organization (management, operations). All procedures related to ANETI's human resources, such as remuneration and classification of jobs, require approval by the MVTE and must be presented to the Ministry of Planning and International Cooperation for review.

ANETI's main mandate is to offer a series of Active Labor Market Programs to job seekers and to disseminate information about employment and job qualifications to firms and job seekers.

- Facilitate employment insertion of job seekers
- Support the promotion of small enterprises and self-employment
- Provide information and training to job seekers to facilitate their insertion into the labor market
- Organize and monitor placement of Tunisian workers abroad
- Facilitate the reinsertion of returning emigrants into the Tunisian labor market

ANETI is headed by a director general (Decree 97-1938 of 1997), who is nominated by the minister of vocational training and employment. The director general oversees the administrative, technical, and financial aspects of the agency and is also the president of the Enterprise Council.[1] Figure 7.3 provides an overview of ANETI's organizational setup.

ANETI runs a network of regional employment and self-employment offices (Decree 2003-564 of 2003). These include three types of offices: multiservice employment offices, sector-related employment offices, and specialized employment offices. Multiservice employment offices carry out a range of tasks such as

Figure 7.3 Organizational Setup of the National Agency for Employment and Independent Work (ANETI), Tunisia

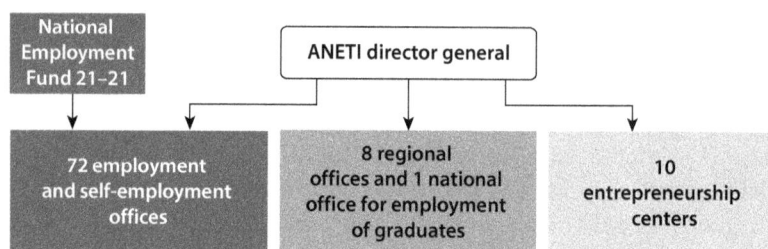

Table 7.2 Possible Regional Employment Office Units and Their Tasks, Tunisia

Information and vocational guidance	Placement and insertion	Microenterprise promotion	Labor market analysis	Administration and financing
Receive persons seeking employment or training. Provide information on employment and training opportunities in private or public sector. Orient training seekers according to their capabilities.	Monitor unemployed. Gather/update firm data to monitor employment. Implement employment promotion programs. Oversee placement of Tunisians abroad and reinsertion of returning emigrants.	Disseminate information. Identify, implement, and monitor projects. Hold training sessions. Create/update list of microenterprises in the region.	Set up/update database on regional labor market. Analyze employment data.	Manage human, financial, and material resources.

providing information and vocational guidance, placement and insertion, and the promotion of microenterprises and self-employment. Sector-related employment offices carry out functions related to one specific economic sector that is of central importance in the region where the office is located. Specialized employment offices cater to job seekers with different qualifications and needs.

As shown in table 7.2, each employment office may have one or more units; the structure depends on the nature and volume of each office. Units are created by decision of the director general of ANETI with the approval of the minister of vocational training and employment (Decree 2003-564 of 2003).

Regional Councils

The regional councils financed by Fund 21-21 are in charge of implementing regional employment programs, notably labor-intensive public works. Each regional council is chaired by the governor and includes representatives of public agencies and local authorities. In each governorate, there is a Fund 21-21 delegate who works closely with the mayor of each municipality in the selection of subprojects and beneficiaries.

Tunisia's Solidarity Bank

The Tunisia Solidarity Bank (TSB) was created in 1997 to facilitate access to microcredit for entrepreneurs (skilled or unskilled) who lack sufficient collateral and/or a steady income to secure a loan from a commercial bank. Its total budget is approximately TD 40 million ($32 million). While the TSB is not involved in the provision of employment services in Tunisia, it is a key player in the promotion of self-employment, as it provides both financing and training (through and in partnership with ANETI) for aspiring entrepreneurs.

Public Employment Services and ALMPs Delivered by ANETI

ALMPs have long been at the core of Tunisian labor market policy. Formal ALMP provision was initiated in 1981 in response to employment challenges facing vocational training graduates. In 1987, program content moved away from the exclusive provision of technical training toward programs aimed at developing professional skills among university graduates. Wage subsidies and exemptions from social security were introduced for university graduates in 2004.

Up to 2009, ANETI managed over 20 programs. Access was virtually unconditional for all categories of job seekers and employers, with little or no targeting of specific groups. Between 1981 and 2009, ALMPs served an estimated 320,000 beneficiaries. In 2009 the MVTE undertook a reform of the ALMP portfolio, consolidating ALMPs into six programs to facilitate their management and financial control. All wage insertion programs consist primarily of on-the-job training and include a small monthly stipend and subsidize social security contributions of participants. The number of beneficiaries of wage insertion programs has increased markedly in recent years, from 85,889 (2008) to 95,415 (2009) to 138,674 (2010). The most important programs are profiled below, with more detailed descriptions provided in table 7.5 at the end of the chapter.

Intermediation Services and Placement

ANETI provides job seekers in Tunisia with a range of labor intermediation services through its Department of Information and Vocational Guidance. The intermediation services provided by ANETI include: (a) counseling and orientation, to assist job seekers to identify and develop their employment action plans; (b) job search assistance, which includes job search strategy development, job readiness training, and job clubs; and (c) matching and placement support through a job registry listing current job offers that are either directly uploaded by the employers or collected through monthly visits to enterprises.

In 2011, ANETI's database included 281,218 active registered job seekers, of which 73 percent were university graduates and 95 percent were first-time job seekers. In 2011, ANETI had approximately 1,271 staff members, of which 1,052 are counselors who are in direct contact with job seekers (a caseload of 267 councilors per job seeker). ANETI is very proactive visiting enterprises. Between years 2006 and 2010, ANETI staff recorded that they had conducted about 95,000 enterprise visits on a yearly basis (table 7.3). As a result of its outreach to enterprises, ANETI registers between 150,000 and 180,000 vacancies

Table 7.3 Statistics on Labor Intermediation Services in Tunisia

Year	2006	2007	2008	2009	2010	2011
Number of visits to enterprises	98,897	98,757	93,597	99,148	94,429	—
Number of registered vacancies	138,177	142,042	147,466	159,893	176,196	100,356
Number of placements	123,366	124,572	134,224	131,403	123,421	46,468
Ratio of placements to vacancies (%)	89	88	91	82	70	46

Source: ANETI's administrative data.
Note: — = not available.

on a yearly basis. In recent years, probably due to economic and political factors arising after the Jasmine revolution, the number of vacancies filled by ANETI decreased significantly. In particular, the ratio of total placements to available vacancies decreased from 82 percent in 2009 to 46 percent in 2011. Furthermore, the decrease in the number of vacancies filled coincided with the introduction of the AMAL program in 2011 (more information about this program is provided below). After the program was introduced, many counselors became burdened with administrative processes related to the registration and payments of AMAL beneficiaries, which clearly undermined ANETI's labor intermediation capacity. Given the fact that vacancies still exist, reinforcing labor intermediation capacity in Tunisia seems a quick win. This could be done by allowing the entry of private intermediation services, expanding the number of ANETI counselors in direct contact with enterprises and job seekers, and simplifying ANETI's cumbersome administrative processes of registry and payment (see Belghazi 2012). According to Tunisian law, ANETI has monopoly status, being the only institution providing labor intermediation services in the country. However, the needs of job seekers in Tunisia make it practically impossible for ANETI to deliver the services required for the diverse group of job seekers, inactive groups, and employers. Enabling private intermediation would require revising Tunisia's Labor Code (Article 285).

Stage d'Initiation à la Vie Professionnelle

The Stage d'Initiation à la Vie Professionnelle (SIVP) seeks to introduce educated first-time job seekers to the labor market by placing them in internships, with a stipend, that usually run for a year. The program gives beneficiaries a stipend of TD 150/month ($102/month) and covers social security contributions as well as up to 200 hours of training cost. The program is targeted at university graduates who remain as job seekers six months after graduation. SIVP is the largest of the Tunisian ALMPs, with almost 47,000 beneficiaries in 2011. In 2010 most beneficiaries were women (61 percent). In terms of qualifications, most beneficiaries graduated with degrees in sciences and technologies, economics, management, or law (69 percent), followed by arts and humanities (16 percent). Employers participating in these programs are mainly in the service sector (42 percent), followed by manufacturing (22 percent) and trade (18 percent). SIVP beneficiaries are heavily concentrated in coastal/industrial

Figure 7.4 SIVP Proxy Placement Ratio in Tunisia by Governorate, January–November 2010

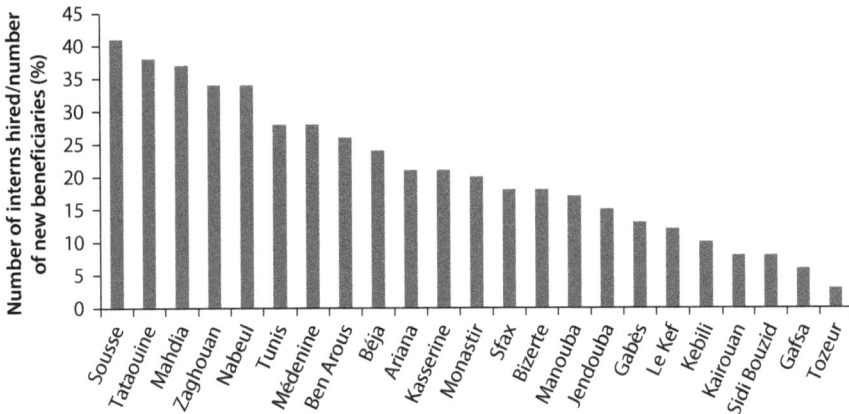

Source: Based on ANETI administrative data.

regions. Most SIVP contracts are signed in Tunis (25 percent), followed by Ariana and Sfax (10 percent each).

An evaluation of SIVP's performance reveals that program beneficiaries have very low rates of job insertion after program completion (at 23.7 percent in 2010) (figure 7.4).

Contrat d'Insertion des Diplômés de l'Enseignement Supérieur (CIDES)

The CIDES program is targeted at higher education graduates who have been unemployed for over three years (revised to two years in 2011). The Program seeks to provide beneficiaries with professional qualifications through an internship in a private firm along with up to 400 hours of training, either in the firm or in a public or private training institution. The program allocates to beneficiaries a stipend of TD 150/month ($102/month) and covers a share of the employer's contribution to social security for seven years (100 percent in years 1 and 2; 85 percent in year 3; 70 percent in year 4; 55 percent in year 5; 40 percent in year 6; and 25 percent in year 7) for those recruited in 2009 and 2010. In 2011, about 3,000 beneficiaries participated in the CIDES program. Like the SIVP, most beneficiaries of the CIDES program are women (61 percent). Beneficiaries are mainly economics and law graduates (42 percent) as well as graduates from science and technology (29 percent). The majority of employers that participate in the program are in the services sector (77 percent). In theory, firms are required to hire beneficiaries after program completion. In practice, placement rates are surprisingly low (at 20.7 percent in 2010). Overall, only 11 percent of all eligible registered unemployed benefit from the CIDES program. This figure indicates that program coverage is rather low, partly due to a general lack of internship opportunities in the private sector.

Contrat d'Adaptation et d'Insertion Professionnelle

The Contrat d'Adaptation et d'Insertion Professionnelle (CAIP) is targeted at nongraduates, those without higher education. In 2011, about 40,000 individuals participated in this program, making it the second largest ALMP provided by ANETI. The program aims to equip each job seeker with skills that fit an open position in a private enterprise. The program provides a small stipend of TD 100/month ($68/month) in 2010 and social security coverage. In theory, firms need to provide 400 hours of training to beneficiaries, but this is largely unenforced and rarely happens. Participating enterprises are predominantly in the manufacturing sector (57 percent) and in the services sector (15 percent). In 2009, 90 percent of new beneficiaries did not have any degree, and 9 percent had only a high school diploma. In 2010, the job insertion rates of beneficiaries after program completion were rather low, at 18 percent.

Contrat de Réinsertion dans la Vie Active

The Contrat de Réinsertion dans la Vie Active (CRVA) targets previously employed workers who lost their job for economic or technical reasons. The program allows workers to gain new skills that match the requirements of a previously identified open position. The program provides beneficiaries with a stipend of TD 200/month ($136/month) and social security coverage. The program also covers 200 hours of training costs and up to 30 percent of all transportation costs incurred by beneficiaries in order to participate in training activities. The large majority of individuals benefiting from this program do not hold tertiary education diplomas (90 percent). The CRVA is small in absolute terms, covering only 1,000 interns in 2011, and basically operates only in Monastir and Tunis (59 and 20 percent of participants, respectively). The weak take-up might be due to a lack of interest from potential employers and the program's interference with the social insurance system in place: participation in the program prevents potential beneficiaries from benefiting from, for example, an early retirement pension (Mani 2011).

Service Civil Volontaire

The Service Civil Volontaire (SCV) is a subsidized part-time internship of up to one year, intended for first-time job seekers with university degrees who have not enrolled in the SIVP.[2] The program mainly serves job seekers who have been unemployed for more than a year (64 percent of all program participants). The program places beneficiaries in professional organizations and associations, where they engage in an activity of benefit to society in order to gain work experience and soft skills. Program beneficiaries receive a stipend of TD 200/month ($136/month) and social security coverage. Placement is not expected to result in permanent hiring. The SCV is a small program, with 8,000 participants in 2011. Associations do not have to meet any quality criteria to participate in the program. Indeed, most that participate are very small, often with low capacity, which reduces the attractiveness of the program.

Prise en charge par l'Etat de 50 pourcent des salaires verses (PC50)

The PC 50 program (Prise en charge par l'Etat d'une part des salaires versés) aims to encourage private companies to hire first-time job seekers with a university degree by paying half of their wage for the first 12 months of the contract, up to TD 250/month ($170/month). The PC50 program exists only in regional development zones (which are defined by the Investment Code) and only applies to firms that are active in high-value added activities with a strong knowledge component. Beneficiary firms are new firms—those that have been in the market for less than 3 years. Due to its very specific target group, the program remains small: in 2011, only 500 graduates benefited from this program for a total cost of about TD 500,000 ($300,000).

The Programme d'accompagnement des promoteurs des petites entreprises (PAPPE)

The PAPPE targets potential entrepreneurs. The program includes coaching, support in conceptualizing a business plan, as well as support after the creation of the enterprise. For supporting start-ups, the program finances up to TD 100,000 ($62,000) per project. On the training side, ANETI offers PAPPE beneficiaries two main entrepreneurship courses: (a) The Méthode Originale de Recherche Active d'Idées Nouvelles pour Entreprendre (MORAINE) is a two-day course that seeks to foster the creativity of participants and encourage them to become entrepreneurs; and (b) Création d'Entreprises et Formation d'Entrepreneurs (CEFE) is a four-week course that trains aspiring entrepreneurs to create a viable business plan. PAPPE beneficiaries can also benefit from coaching services, as well as other technical and management advice and support. ANETI supported 17,000 projects in 2011 for a total cost of DR 4.2 million ($2.9 million).

The AMAL Program

After the Jasmine Revolution, Tunisia's interim government launched the Active Employment Search Program for Higher Education Graduates (Programme de Recherche Active d'Emploi au Profit des Diplômés de l'Enseignement Supérieur) in February 2011. This employment program, known as AMAL ("hope" in Arabic), provides unemployed university degree holders with employment services for up to 12 months. The program offers beneficiaries career coaching, training and retraining in hard and soft skills, on-the-job training, and a monthly stipend of TD 200 (equivalent to $136) to encourage them to actively search for a job.

While conceived as an activation program, AMAL in practice is mainly providing cash assistance to unemployed graduates. This has important implications for the country's budget. Part of the problem is that AMAL is in essence a social response to the Jasmine Revolution, an effort by government to appease unemployed university graduates and achieve social peace. In 2011, the program benefited 155,000 individuals, far more than the original projection of about 30,000 per year.[3] Given the number of beneficiaries, there are clear capacity constraints, in terms of both staff and resources, that make it difficult to implement the activation components of the program as specified in its operations manual (mainly coaching and internships in the private sector). There are also institutional challenges, such as a lack of operational leadership at the central and local levels and a lack of coordination between the implementing agency (ANETI) and the MVTE.

Other Employment Programs Financed by the Fund 21-21

Regional Programs Under the Employment Solidarity Contract (CES)

The Employment Solidarity Contract (Contrat Emploi-Solidarité, CES) is a series of instruments that are also financed by Fund 21-21. In contrast to ANETI's programs described above, however, CES does not target one specific group of unemployed individuals. Instead, it aims to integrate unemployed people within the framework of regional and local employment promotion initiatives. In addition, CES instruments are more socially oriented, focus on specific sectors, and provide governorates and other regional public entities with flexibility in the design of projects and selection of beneficiaries.

CES instruments that target the unskilled include public works, internships in small and medium enterprises (SMEs) and craft workshops, and job-readiness training for the disabled. Each of these programs provides a stipend to both the employer and the beneficiaries. The public works program has by far the most beneficiaries, approximately 14,000 in 2010. Table 7.4 shows the CES instruments that were operational in 2010–11.

Table 7.4 Instruments and Beneficiaries of CES in Tunisia, 2010–11

Number and name of instrument	Year created	Responsible ministry	Number of beneficiaries
7. Employment for Graduates in Adult Literacy	2000	Social Affairs	Total: 20,500 2010: 2,080
13. Vocational Training for National Defense Construction Sites	2000	National Defense	—
14. Internships in SMEs and Craft Workshops	2000	Commerce and Industry	Total: 165,888 2010: 3,878
15. Internships in National Defense Construction Sites	2000	National Defense	—
16. Public Works	2000	Interior and Regional Development	Total: 143,525 2010: 14,391
20. Employment of Graduates in NGOs	2001	Interior and Regional Development	Total: 8,409 2010: 379
24. Foreign Language Training	2001	ANETI	Total: 892 2010: 63
25. Job-Readiness Training for the Disabled	2001	Social Affairs	Total: 12,064 2010: 1,348
41. Public Sector Entrepreneurship	2005	All	Total: 547 2010: 26

Source: Belghazi 2012.
Note: — = not available.

Microcredit and Entrepreneurship Programs

Fund 21-21 also finances some of the Tunisia Solidarity Bank's activities. With the resources obtained through Fund 21-21, the TSB provides concessional loans, either directly to entrepreneurs whose projects exceed TD 10,000 ($6,802) or indirectly through microcredit associations, which must ensure a minimum recovery rate of 80 percent. The TSB provides loans for either the creation or the expansion of small enterprises. Individuals seeking financing from TSB must have a viable business plan and contribute at least 10 percent of the project's total cost. Unskilled youth have access to a line of credit of up to TD 10,000 ($6,802), while high-skilled youth can access loans of up to TD 100,000 ($68,027). In 2010, a total of 82,598 projects were financed, directly or indirectly, by the TSB with funds obtained through Fund 21-21. Of the projects financed, 76,599 had budgets under TD 10,000.

Challenges and Policy Options

ANETI's insufficient human resources constitute a critical challenge to the efficient and effective delivery of employment services in Tunisia. As mentioned before, in 2011, each ANETI counselor served on average 267 job seekers, which is significantly above international standards.[4] The Jasmine Revolution exacerbated the problem, as hordes of unemployed youth registered with ANETI in order to receive unemployment assistance through AMAL. This placed an unexpected additional burden on ANETI's counselors, who had to take on many administrative tasks such as processing applications and payments to AMAL beneficiaries, thus hindering their capacity to provide employment services.

Insufficient and poor delivery of employment services is also explained by the fact that the Labor Code (articles 280–285) gives ANETI a monopoly in the provision of placement services in Tunisia. Private providers of domestic placement services, whether free or fee-based, are forbidden by law. While some private organizations provide placement services to the unemployed in Tunisia, they are mainly temporary agencies and executive search firms ("headhunters"). As temporary labor is not regulated or forbidden by the Labor Code, temporary agencies have the reputation of placing workers in low-quality, low-paying jobs and are thus highly unpopular among labor unions.

ANETI's limited capacity has a marked impact on its outreach and intermediation services. The agency has a special unit in charge of reaching out to potential employers (Unité d'Information et d'Orientation Professionnelle). In 2011, staff from this unit were able to identify 100,356 vacancies (internships and permanent positions), but they filled only about 46 percent of these vacancies. Vacancies are entered in a database open to job seekers, and most are filled by individuals who contact the enterprise directly and then inform ANETI of the match. There is no systematic way for ANETI to match the registered unemployed to available vacancies, which partly explains why a large share of all available vacancies were not filled in 2011.

Building Effective Employment Programs for Unemployed Youth in the Middle East and North Africa •
http://dx.doi.org/10.1596/978-0-8213-9904-0

Table 7.5 Summary of Public Employment Programs Provided by ANETI in Tunisia, 2011

Program	Objectives	Targeting and duration	Stipend and other benefits provided by state	Other requirements	Budget and number of beneficiaries
AMAL: Programme de Recherche Active d'Emploi au Profit des Diplômés de l'Enseignement Supérieur (or contrat SyRAE)	Support active job search through information, coaching, stipend, and internships.	Tunisian first-time job seekers who are university graduates or holders of an advanced vocational diploma or certified vocational training diploma (FP homologué). Must be registered with ANETI and unemployed > six months. May be former interns of SIVP, CIDES, or SCV. Duration: 12 months, including one or two 3-month internships in different firms.	Stipend of Tunisian dinars (TD) 200/month ($136/month). Medical insurance. Right to benefit is lost if registration is not renewed for three consecutive months, if beneficiary is a student, or if employment or self-employment is obtained.	Beneficiary must attend meetings at the employment office, renew registration each month, and update personal information for employment search on ANETI website.	Program launched in March 2011. Budget 2011: TD 252.6 million ($172 million). Beneficiaries: 155,000.
SIVP: Stage d'Initiation à la Vie Professionnelle	Help beneficiaries acquire professional skills to facilitate their integration into the workforce in the private or public sector.	Tunisian first-time job seekers, university graduates or equivalent. Duration: up to 24 months, including one or two 12-month internships in different firms.	Stipend of TD 150/month ($102/month). Social security coverage. Training costs (200 hours maximum).	Firm must provide additional stipend of at least TD 150/month ($102/month). Firm cannot take new interns if it fails to hire 50 percent of previous interns after internship.	Budget 2011: TD 57 million ($38.9 million). Beneficiaries: 46,000.
CIDES: Contrat d'Insertion des Diplômés de l'Enseignement Supérieur	Help beneficiaries obtain professional skills by alternating between a private firm and a public or private training program agreed to by the beneficiary, the firm, and ANETI.	Graduates of higher education who have been unemployed for > two years since obtaining diploma. Duration: 12 months.	Stipend of TD 150/month ($102/month). Additional training (300 hours maximum). A share of employer's contribution to social security for seven years (100% in years 1 and 2; 85% in year 3; 70% in year 4; 55% in year 5; 40% in year 6; 25% in year 7) for those recruited in 2009 and 2010, and for three years (100%, 75%, 50%) for those recruited in 2011.	Firm commits to hire beneficiary at end of internship. Firm pays additional stipend of TD 150/ month ($102/month). Firm receives bonus of TD 1,000 ($680) after hiring.	Budget 2011: TD 5 million ($3.4 million). Beneficiaries: 3,000.

table continues next page

Table 7.5 Summary of Public Employment Programs Provided by ANETI in Tunisia, 2011 *(continued)*

Program	Objectives	Targeting and duration	Stipend and other benefits provided by state	Other requirements	Budget and number of beneficiaries
CAIP: Contrat d'Adaptation et d'Insertion Professionnelle	Help beneficiaries obtain professional skills to meet requirements of a job offer from a private firm for a job that cannot be filled due to unavailability of suitable workers in the labor market.	Unemployed persons without higher education. Duration: 12-month internship.	Stipend TD 100/month ($68/month). Social security coverage. Training (400 hours maximum).	Firms pays stipend of TD 50/month ($34/month) to beneficiary.	Budget 2011: TD 28 million ($19.1 million). Beneficiaries: 40,000.
SCV: Service Civil Volontaire	Improve beneficiaries' employability and facilitate insertion into the workforce through voluntary internships and part-time work in community services.	First-time job seekers who are higher education graduates. Duration: 12 months.	Stipend of TD 200/month ($136/month). Social security coverage.	Association that receives worker pays an additional stipend. This obligation was removed in 2010.	Budget 2011: TD 11 million ($7.5 million). Beneficiaries: 8,000.
CRVA: Contrat de Réinsertion dans la Vie Active	Allow workers who lost their jobs to obtain new skills, meeting the requirements of a job offer previously identified in a private firm.	Permanent or temporary workers, with at least three years' experience in the same firm, who lost their job for economic or technical reasons or as a result of the sudden, final, and illegal closing of the firm they worked for.	Stipend of TD 200/month ($136/month). Social security coverage. Training costs (200 hours maximum). Up to 30% of transportation costs.	Firm provides an additional stipend to beneficiary.	Budget 2011: TD 1 million ($0.7 million). Beneficiaries: 1,000.
PC50: Prise en Charge par l'Etat d'une Part des Salaires Versés (PC50)	Encourage private firms to hire higher education graduates by paying half the wage for 12 months.	First-time job seekers with higher education and recently created firms located in regional development zones, operating in high-value-added activities with a strong knowledge component. Duration: first three years after business entry.	50% of wages of newly hired employees for a year, up to TD 250/month ($170/month). Possibility of training programs provided by ANETI.	Firm must file request with ANETI for review by interdepartmental commission to ensure compliance with active labor market policy priorities.	Budget 2011: TD 500,000 ($300,000). Beneficiaries: 500.

table continues next page

Table 7.5 Summary of Public Employment Programs Provided by ANETI in Tunisia, 2011 *(continued)*

Program	Objectives	Targeting and duration	Stipend and other benefits provided by state	Other requirements	Budget and number of beneficiaries
PAPPE: Programme d'Accompagnement des Promoteurs des Petites Entreprises	Promote entrepreneurship through coaching and support in conceptualizing a project and developing a business plan. Practical internship in a firm for a maximum duration of one year, with technical assistance.	Potential creators of small firms (< TD 100,000) (< $68,027), including small farmers and fishers who make investments in category A under Article 28 of the investment incentives code, and higher education graduates (Article 27 of the incentive code).	Management course (12 hours maximum). Development of business plan (200 hours maximum). Technical assistance (12 days maximum). TD 200/month ($136/month) stipend for higher education graduates and TD 100/month ($68/month) for nongraduates, for 12 months.	For some activities, Fund 21-21 and public entities pay for certain services (year 1, 75% Fund 21-21 and 25% public facility; year 2, 50% Fund 21-21 and 50% public facility; year 3, 25% Fund 21-21 and 75% public facility).	Budget 2011: TD 4.2 million ($2.9 million). Beneficiaries: 17,000.

Source: Belghazi 2012.
Note: The current minimum wage (salaire minimum interprofessionnel garanti, SMIG) in Tunisia is TD 284 ($193) per month for employees on a 48-hour week (Decree 2010-1746 of 17 July 2010).

Beyond these structural challenges, there is a generalized lack of governance, program coherence, and monitoring and evaluation among programs financed by Fund 21-21. In particular, CES programs lack coherence with other programs. Some CES instruments overlap extensively with existing ANETI programs (for example, internship programs for young graduates), while others duplicate similar programs implemented by the Ministry of Regional Development and other donors (for example, public works).[5] Also, there are cases of public works projects (CES instrument 16) that are never completed and/or that pay wages to workers who do not show up for work. In addition, CES programs do not have clear governance frameworks, clear procedures (operation manuals are not applied), or transparent allocation of funds.

The impact of programs financed by Fund 21-21 remains largely unassessed. ANETI's monitoring system is not results-based and only provides data on take-up rates (i.e., outputs). CES programs largely lack monitoring and do not generally cross-reference beneficiaries with ANETI records, allowing some individuals to benefit from various programs simultaneously. There have been some attempts to evaluate ANETI's employment programs, but the results are outdated, sporadic, donor-driven, and lacking in scientific credibility.

The following policy recommendations, grouped around each of the main challenges outlined in the previous section, are critical to improve the effectiveness of employment programs and services in Tunisia.

Improving ANETI's Capacity to Deliver Employment Services

- *Carry out reforms to ANETI.* The government needs to improve the agency's capacity to provide its beneficiaries with modern employment services, including counseling, training in hard and soft skills, and labor intermediation. This implies restructuring the organization at both the national and regional levels, increasing the capacity of training staff, and simplifying the administration and delivery of programs. Also, the government needs to consider adjusting the labor code to allow the operation of private intermediation agencies.
- *Develop public-private partnerships (PPPs) for the provision of employment services.* ANETI should engage in PPPs to (a) deliver entrepreneurship training and awareness programs to high-skilled youth, (b) provide internships and on-the-job training to high-skilled youth, and (c) deliver soft-skills training to all registered unemployed.
- *Improve ANETI's placement services.* ANETI should boost the capacity of its Unité d'Information et d'Orientation Professionnelle to improve outreach to the private sector, better maintain its registry of vacancies, and develop clear mechanisms and incentives to encourage active placements and internships.

Reforming Regional Programs Financed by Fund 21-21

- *Reform the CES.* Fund 21-21 should no longer finance existing CES instruments. Instead, funds should be transferred to the Ministry of Social Affairs

(MoSA) (in the case of social programs) and to the Ministry of Regional Development (in the case of public works).

- *Reform the implementation of the regional employment programs.* There is a need to create implementing units for regional employment programs beyond regional councils. Regional councils lack implementation capacity and accountability and operate on an ad hoc basis.
- *Introduce productive employment programs for regional development.* There is a need to introduce regional programs in close coordination with civil society and the private sector, tailored to regional contexts and needs. These should promote productive regional development (investment and entrepreneurship) and provision of social and community services (health care, elder care, child care, and so on).

Improving the Effectiveness of ALMPs

- *Establish a legal framework to monitor and evaluate ALMPs delivered by ANETI.* ALMPs in Tunisia have been largely unassessed. The establishment of a legal framework, with clear responsibilities, activities, and indicators, will help improve the governance and effectiveness of ALMPs, as well as the use of public funds.
- *Phase out AMAL.* Having such an open-ended system of unemployment assistance discourages active job search, creates dependency, does not lead to employment, and is not fiscally sustainable. The government needs to develop an exit strategy while also designing a communication campaign targeted at current and potential new program beneficiaries.

Notes

1. The Enterprise Council is an interministerial consultative council that includes union representatives.
2. This condition was relaxed in January 2011 (Decree 2011-98).
3. Administrative data from ANETI and ONEQ (Observatoire National de l'Emploi et des Qualifications) indicate that between March and December 2011, 193,920 individuals registered in AMAL, 144,536 benefited from the program's stipend, 6,561 participated in an internship program, 15,422 received three days of life skills training, and 6,708 found a job.
4. Within the European Union (EU), the average staff caseload is around 1:150, while the figure recommended by the International Labour Organization is even lower, at 1:100. This EU average figure hides considerable variation: for example, Germany has a ratio of about 1:200 and the Netherlands 1:60.
5. Instrument 16 of Fund 21-21 and the Programme Régional de Développement (PRD) of the Ministry of Regional Development both consist of labor-intensive public works managed by regional councils. The main differences are the wage rate and the program duration. The PRD pays participants TD 9 per day of work (roughly equivalent to the legal minimum wage) for a period of six months. Instrument 16 pays TD 120 (about half the minimum wage) per month for a period of nine months.

References

Angel-Urdinola, D., and A. Semlali. 2010. "Labor Markets and School-to-Work Transition in Egypt: Diagnostics, Constraints, and Policy Framework." MPRA Paper 27674, Munich Personal RePEc Archive. http://mpra.ub.uni-muenchen.de/27674.

Belghazi, S. 2012. "Evaluation Stratégique du Fonds National pour l'Emploi de la Tunisie." Tunis.

ILO (International Labour Organization). 2011. *Key Indicators of the Labour Market.* 6th ed. Geneva, Switzerland: ILO.

INS (Institut National de la Statistique). 2005. "L'enquête nationale sur l'emploi 2005." Tunis.

———. 2010. "L'enquête nationale sur l'emploi 2010." Tunis.

———. 2011. "Premiers résultats de l'enquête nationale sur l'emploi pour le 3ème trimestre 2011." Tunis.

Mani, M. 2011. "Active Labor Market Programs: Results and Problems" [in Arabic]. Paper presented at the ANETI, Tunis, May.

World Bank and INS (Institut National de la Statistique). Forthcoming. *Recent Labor Market Trends and Main Characteristics of the Labor Market in Tunisia.* World Bank, Washington, DC.

CHAPTER 8

Public Employment Programs in the Republic of Yemen

Diane Zovighian

Introduction

Despite positive economic growth in the past decade, labor force participation in the Republic of Yemen is stagnant at low levels and unemployment remains high. Economic growth is largely led by the oil sector and is not generating enough jobs to absorb the fast-growing labor force. Recent data are not available, but a 2004 labor demand survey indicates that from 1999 to 2004, labor force growth outpaced job growth, with rates of 4.3 and 3.7 percent per year, respectively. As a result, the Republic of Yemen—long the poorest country in the Middle East and North Africa (MENA)—registers among the lowest labor force participation rates in the region, at 42.7 percent in 2008 (CSO 2008). The country also suffers from high unemployment, which increased from 11.5 percent in 1999 to 15 percent in 2008 (CSO 2008; World Bank 2010).

Gender and education gaps deeply segment the labor market in the Republic of Yemen. Female labor force participation is extremely low, at 10.2 percent, compared to 74.7 percent for men (CSO 2008). The unemployment rate for economically active women is as high as 40.9 percent, compared to 11.5 percent for men (CSO 2008). Educated Yemenis face particularly steep barriers to finding jobs: unemployment in 2005 was 44 percent among those with secondary education and 54 percent among university graduates (ILO 2008a).

Employment is dominated by work in the informal and agricultural sectors, raising the issue of poor job quality. Informal employment in the Republic of Yemen, proxied by the share of all employed who do not contribute to social security, is the highest in the region, at 90 percent (Gatti et al. 2012). In addition, agriculture remains the single largest source of employment and job creation: 33.1 percent of employed people are in the agricultural sector (World Bank 2010). Though a shift is occurring from subsistence agriculture to cash cropping, employment in the sector remains vulnerable, with a predominance of low-paying, low-skilled jobs.

With rapid urbanization, the Republic of Yemen has witnessed important transformations in livelihood systems and employment patterns in recent decades. Though 68 percent of Yemenis still live in rural areas (World Bank 2010), a growing share of the population now lives in cities, where employment opportunities are more diverse. While agriculture remains a primary source of employment for rural workers, urban workers have access to public sector jobs and self-employment opportunities in commerce, artisanship, and urban transport. Even so, low-wage informal employment remains the dominant source of income in urban areas, and the low wages and precarious nature of public sector jobs and self-employment often result in workers combining multiple forms of employment.[1]

Although the Republic of Yemen continues to be one of the poorest countries in the region, urbanization and economic growth have resulted in decreasing poverty rates at the national level. The national poverty rate fell from 40.1 percent in 1998 to 34.8 percent in 2005, mainly driven by a rapid decrease in urban poverty. In rural areas, poverty has remained extremely high, with 40.1 percent of the rural population living below the poverty line in 2005, compared to 42.5 percent in 1998 (World Bank 2010).

In a context of insufficient job creation, low job quality, and overall high poverty rates, investments in active labor market programs (ALMPs) in the Republic of Yemen are mainly guided by the twin objectives of job creation and income support. Given the level of need, the Yemeni context calls for strong investments in public works programs and in micro, small, and medium enterprise (MSME) development programs that can address these two objectives in the short term. Due to low labor demand and high informality, investments in other categories of ALMPs, including employment services and training programs, may seem less relevant in the Republic of Yemen than in other MENA countries. Yet along with job creation and income support, increasing the employability of the workforce through training and providing intermediation between labor demand and supply are critical to supporting human development and employability in the Republic of Yemen in the medium term.

The main categories of ALMPs implemented in the Republic of Yemen include employment services, training programs, public works programs, and programs supporting micro and small enterprise (MSE) development. The chapter first outlines the institutional setup for service delivery, then discusses the design and relevance of some of the programs provided. The final section suggests ways to strengthen the relevance, effectiveness, and impact of the country's approach to ALMPs.

Institutional Framework for Employment Services in the Republic of Yemen

Policy and institutional coordination across the ministries and agencies involved in the delivery of ALMPs in the Republic of Yemen is low to nonexistent. There are three main public institutions involved: the Ministry of Social Affairs and Labor (MoSAL), the Ministry of Technical and Vocational Education and Training

(MoTVET), and the Social Fund for Development (SFD). These institutions, however, work in silos with little coordination among them. Mechanisms for institutional coordination between the different ministries and agencies involved in ALMP provision and human resource development more generally—such as an inter-ministerial steering committee—are nonexistent. Policy interventions tend to be piecemeal and are not integrated. This is partly because the Republic of Yemen lacks a national policy framework for labor issues—notably, a national employment strategy—that would set objectives and directions to guide policy interventions by different ministries. Regulatory frameworks, such as a vocational qualification framework for training programs, are also lacking, resulting in weak quality standards for ALMP provision.

In addition, the ministries and agencies involved in ALMP provision face a series of capacity limitations. These include insufficient hard infrastructure, inadequate staffing, low human capacities, and unsustainable funding schemes.

Ministry of Social Affairs and Labor

Established in 1990, the MoSAL has been restructured and renamed repeatedly since its inception, resulting in frequent changes in mandate and responsibilities. Such changes are considered to have had a negative impact on the performance and capacities of the ministry's staff (ILO 2008b). The current mandate of the ministry is twofold:

- Social welfare, including implementation of social protection programs (e.g., cash transfers) for poor people and vulnerable groups
- Labor issues, including implementation of labor regulations (with a focus on occupational safety and health programs), provision of employment services, and maintenance of labor market information systems

There is considerable scope to strengthen the human and financial capacities of the MoSAL to fulfill its mandate, in particular in the area of employment services and labor market information systems. Though the MoSAL has employment offices in all major cities, these offices have limited staffing and capacities to provide employment services. Of 1,647 staff at the MoSAL in 2008, only 60 were in contact with job seekers. Basic infrastructure for labor intermediation is lacking: employment offices do not provide walk-in centers for job seekers or electronic labor exchange platforms. Limited resources and capacities also hamper the MoSAL's role as provider of labor market information: the Republic of Yemen lacks a functioning labor market information system that could inform the delivery of employment services.

Ministry of Technical and Vocational Education and Training

Established in 2001, the MoTVET is the main public provider of training programs in the Republic of Yemen. The ministry has an annual budget of about $88 million, of which approximately 50 percent is made up of contributions from donor agencies. In 2008 it had 386 staff, covered 20 governorates and

Sana'a, and oversaw a total of 78 public centers, including 41 institutes for technical education, 27 vocational training institutes, and 10 training centers providing short courses. In addition, 177 private training institutes are registered under the ministry (MoTVET 2008). Yet given the absence of a vocational qualification framework as well as audit mechanisms, the provision of training by these private institutes is poorly regulated.

In light of its capacity gap, efforts have been made to strengthen and reform the MoTVET in the past decade, with a strong emphasis on hardware. With respect to institutional capacity, the MoTVET faces multiple challenges, including understaffing and insufficient equipment, that negatively affect its capacity to respond to both job seekers' and employers' demands. One of the main responses to the ministry's low capacities has been the building or rehabilitation of hard infrastructure. The government of the Republic of Yemen has financed the construction, enhancement, or upgrading of a large number of training centers over the past decade. In 2008 alone, it invested about $48 million in 75 projects. Foreign donors have also financed the development of hard infrastructure. The Saudi Development Fund provided about $12 million to support 18 projects in 2008 (MoTVET 2008). The ministry's strategy to develop the capacities and autonomy of these training centers is unclear, but a major impediment to their efficient functioning lies in the centralized nature of the centers' management and financing. Similarly, the ministry's approach to building the skills of its staff remains ill defined. Despite the provision of training for some staff, important capacity limitations persist.

The MoTVET has faced challenges in engaging the private sector in the funding and design of its programs. The establishment of the Skills Development Fund in 1995, with support from the World Bank, aimed to broaden revenue collection to include contributions from the private sector. It also sought to create a platform for collaboration between the ministry and the private sector, including in the provision of training courses for employees of private companies. The Skills Development Fund has experienced a series of difficulties in fulfilling its mandate, partly due to the lack of clarity on its objectives, governance, and functioning. However, recent revisions of its legal status have created space to revitalize the institution and further its use as a vehicle for cooperation with the private sector.

Social Fund for Development

Established in 1997, the SFD focuses on supporting poverty alleviation through the creation of job opportunities and the delivery of basic services to poor communities. It is an administratively and financially autonomous agency, supervised by a board of directors chaired by the prime minister and including members of the government as well as private sector and civil society representatives. In 2008, its total budget was $125 million. This budget finances a variety of services and programs, including two major types of ALMPs: the SFD is the major public provider of MSME development programs and a core provider of public works programs in the Republic of Yemen.[2] Nongovernmental organizations and microfinance institutions play a key role in the delivery of services.

Foreign donors contribute substantially to financing and building the capacities of the SFD. The World Bank played a critical advisory and financing role in the establishment of the fund in 1997. In the third planning phase of the fund (2004–10), 14 donors were involved, including the World Bank, the Arab Fund for Economic and Social Development, the European Union, the International Fund for Agricultural Development, the government of the Netherlands, the Islamic Development Bank, the German Agency for International Cooperation (GIZ) and Kreditanstalt für Wiederaufbau (KfW), the Kuwaiti Fund for Development, the Organization of Petroleum Exporting Countries (OPEC) Fund, and the Saudi Fund for Development. Taking into account all contributions, the total budget of the SFD for phase three exceeded $1 billion. In addition to funding, foreign donors have also provided capacity building to the fund in community mobilization, monitoring and evaluation, and other areas.

Public Employment Services and Other Publicly Provided ALMPs

ALMP provision in the Republic of Yemen is essentially geared toward supporting job creation for poor and disadvantaged people. MSME development programs and public works programs form the bulk of the programs implemented. Other categories of public interventions in the labor market, including training programs and employment services, have considerably smaller budgets and lower coverage and face substantial quality challenges.

Small and Micro Enterprises Development Program

The Small and Micro Enterprises Development (SMED), financed by the SFD, aims to create jobs for poor people by providing financial services to MSEs. Established in 1997, the SMED program is a key component of the Republic of Yemen's poverty reduction efforts.

To deliver financial services, SMED provides technical, financial, and institutional support to micro and small finance institutions, which in turn provide financing to micro and small businesses. By 2010, 12 finance institutions had benefited from the program, with total funding of $5.5 million. In that year these finance institutions made loans to 66,000 borrowers, a 50 percent increase over 2009. The average loan is $200. Since the beginning of the program, more than 370,000 loans have been provided through SFD-supported micro and small finance institutions (SFD 2010a).

The Small and Micro Enterprise Promotion Services (SMEPS), also under SFD, coordinates the provision of nonfinancial services, including business services, to micro and small entrepreneurs. SMEPS also engages in training provision, policy development, and market studies. In 2010, the SFD funded six projects through SMEPS at an estimated total cost of $952,000. Youth and women are key target groups of these projects (see box 8.1).

Building Effective Employment Programs for Unemployed Youth in the Middle East and North Africa •
http://dx.doi.org/10.1596/978-0-8213-9904-0

Box 8.1 Provision of Nonfinancial Services to Small and Micro Entrepreneurs by SMEPS, the Republic of Yemen

The following projects were carried out by the Republic of Yemen's SMEPS, with funding from the SFD, in 2010.

Know About Business. This is a general instructional program offered by the International Labour Organization (ILO). The program aims to create an "entrepreneurship culture" among young people to help them develop entrepreneurial skills. Through this pilot program, which was conducted in the Republic of Yemen in cooperation with the MoTVET, the SFD has trained more than 3,500 students in vocational and technical training institutes. The students, 16–22 years of age, were able to develop 3,000 business plans by the end of their training.

Business Edge management training. This project, in cooperation with the International Finance Corporation (IFC), trains existing MSMEs in business management skills such as marketing, accounting, and leadership. In its first phase, more than 30,000 entrepreneurs were trained using the Business Edge curriculum in eight private sector training institutions.

Gender business development. In cooperation with the IFC, SMEPS organized a workshop for 36 female entrepreneurs in the informal private sector. The workshop discussed the difficulties women face in registering their small businesses with the relevant authorities.

Fish marketing study. SMEPS supported the Yemeni Seafood Exporters Association by conducting a joint marketing study on the possibility of exporting Yemeni fish to Gulf markets. The study focused on the United Arab Emirates and Saudi Arabia and identified new market channels, such as the Emirates airline supply chain.

Khadija training program. Under an agreement with SMEPS, the Youth Development Institution has adopted the Khadija training program with a view to promoting creative and pioneering ideas for youth. Two hundred trainees, both girls and boys, were trained to develop an entrepreneurship culture through Know About Business. Management courses using the Business Edge curriculum and personal productivity skills courses were also conducted.

Tomoohi Program. The program aims to support youth access to training and finance. So far, 1,800 young men and women have been trained in a mix of SMEPS training tools including Know About Business, Business Edge, and various skills enhancement courses. The program has also supported a number of microfinance institutions in development-related youth finance projects. SMEPS is also involved in upgrading the capacities of training providers in reaching out to youth with training products.

Considerable efforts are made to promote equity in the design and delivery of financial and nonfinancial services to micro and small entrepreneurs. SMED targets poor people who are economically active in urban and semiurban areas. The targeting of services by the SFD is informed by poverty-related indicators, including those from the 2004 census and the 2005–06 Household Budget Survey. In addition, selected SMED program components provide tailored services to specific categories of the urban and semiurban poor, in particular youth and women. Youth are the exclusive target group of half of the projects supporting the provision of nonfinancial services (box 8.1). The SFD places strong emphasis on ensuring that women have equitable access to financial and nonfinancial services and on monitoring their access (the SFD's management information system tracks gender indicators). Such efforts have resulted in the design of projects tailored to women's needs—for example, the Gender Business Development project—and women make up the vast majority of loan borrowers, 70 percent in 2010.

Available data indicate high levels of efficiency of the SMED program. Its cost-efficiency is increasing. The growth of the SFD micro and small finance sector and the related increase in the number of beneficiaries per project have resulted in decreased cost per beneficiary: it is estimated that in 2010, this cost was almost one-fifth of the cost for 2003. In addition, four of the microfinance institutions supported by the SFD had become operationally self-sufficient by 2010. High levels of loan repayment rates also illustrate the program's internal efficiency. According to the loan officers of the SFD-supported micro and small finance institutions, 98.5 percent of borrowers repay their loan on schedule (Recovery and Development Consortium 2010).

Available monitoring and evaluation studies indicate positive impacts on beneficiaries' economic activities and income. Though detailed data on the program's impact on job creation are not readily available, results from a 2010 evaluation indicate that 85 percent of recipients of income-generating loans claimed that the loan had increased their economic activity; 65 percent said the loan allowed them to take up new economic activities; and 90 percent reported an increase in income (Recovery and Development Consortium 2010).

Public Works Programs

Started in 2006, the Labor-Intensive Work Program (LIWP) implemented by the SFD creates temporary employment for unskilled and semiskilled workers through construction and rehabilitation of basic infrastructure. The program focused initially on poor people in urban areas. However, in the aftermath of the food crisis in 2008, a Food Crisis Response Program was developed under the LIWP with the twin goals of income generation and protection of productive assets for poor rural communities negatively affected by the crisis. This cash-for-work program creates temporary employment in crisis-affected areas and supports the development or protection of productive assets such as agricultural land, water harvesting, and watershed management systems. In addition, the LIWP has a Rural Roads Program that supports employment creation through the building or rehabilitation of rural roads. Road projects are also intended to link urban communities with remote areas around the country, facilitating access to basic services for people living in isolated settlements.

LIWP has had a considerable impact on both temporary job creation and access to services. In 2010, the Food Crisis Response Program and the Rural Roads Program together generated approximately 2.8 million working days (table 8.1). Available data indicate that LIWP has high labor intensity: in 2009, the accrual sums paid out in wages were 81 percent of total contractual project costs (SFD 2010b).

Table 8.1 Size, Coverage, and Impact of SFD-Funded Public Works Programs in the Republic of Yemen, 2010

Program	Number of projects approved	Amount invested (US$, millions)	Number of direct beneficiaries	Temporary job opportunities (working days)
Food crisis response	166	19.9	277,980	1,986,000
Rural roads	81	23.9	296,000	776,000

Sources: SFD 2010a, 2010c.

Efforts are made to mainstream equity concerns in the design of LIWP. Targeting of the poorest communities and households is informed by existing data and qualitative information, including levels of unemployment and poverty in the different governorates (using data from the 2004 Census and Labor Force Survey). In order to simplify and refine targeting, LIWP also relies on local governments and communities to identify the poorest and most crisis-stricken subdistricts, communities, and households for the Food Crisis Response Program. With regard to the mainstreaming of gender concerns, available data indicate that women have lower access than men to LIWP, accounting for only 27 percent of beneficiaries (SFD 2008). Yet the gender gap remains smaller than in the broader labor market.

Data on the long-term impact of LIWP, in terms of employment and earnings, are not available. However, LIWP is designed to be a short-term safety net measure, rather than a bridge to employment; thus the impact on long-term employment and earnings is probably limited. LIWP is not associated with any training program to build workers' skills, nor does it provide employment services such as career guidance or counseling to support temporary workers in their search for permanent employment. International experience shows that cash-for-work programs designed in this way tend to have scant long-term effects on workers' employability or labor market outcomes.

Training Programs

Enhancing the efficiency and relevance of training programs and making their outcomes more equitable is at the core of the MoTVET's strategic plans. In its "Technical Education and Vocational Training Strategic Development Plan" for 2005–14, the ministry emphasizes the need for increased coverage of and equitable access to training programs and stronger engagement with the private sector to ensure that programs are demand-driven (MoTVET 2004). Table 8.2 provides a brief overview of the main categories of training programs provided by the MoTVET in the Republic of Yemen.

The overview illustrates the pronounced gender gap in access to training programs in the Republic of Yemen. Men make up almost 90 percent of the beneficiaries of formal technical education and vocational training programs. Most of the specializations offered by these programs are oriented toward economic activities dominated by men, such as mechanical or electrical engineering. Other categories of programs, such as the short-term courses of the continuing education and training program, provide more opportunities to women; yet gender imbalances remain strong.

Table 8.2 Summary of Main Public Employment Training Programs Provided by the MoTVET in the Republic of Yemen, 2008

Program	Description	Number of beneficiaries	Budget	Performance indicators
Formal technical education and vocational training	Includes different subtechnical training systems (2- or 3-year programs for persons who have completed primary school, and 2- or 3-year programs for those who have completed secondary school). The programs offer more than 40 different types of training (for example, in the fields of electrical and mechanical engineering), mostly in classrooms.	5,975 including 5,334 men and 641 women	—	91% of beneficiaries who start the training program complete it.
Continuing education and training in short-term courses	Short-term vocational training in different technical areas for workers and job seekers. In 2008, 125 courses in 32 subjects were offered in 30 centers across 12 governorates.	2,886 including 1,949 men and 937 women	—	—
Skills Development Fund training	Training courses financed through the Skills Development Fund cater to employees of selected private businesses. In 2008, 2,020 programs were provided. Subjects include language and computer skills.	13,221 from 275 establishments	Yemeni rial (YRI) 51,688,304 (approximately $240,400)	—
Cooperative training	Equivalent to an on-the-job training program. Programs are implemented in collaboration with the private sector. Trainees are offered both in-classroom training and practical skills training at the factories and other work sites.	2,864 including 2,541 men and 323 women, from 612 establishments	—	—

Source: Based on administrative data collected through World Bank interviews with Yemeni government officials from the Ministry of Technical and Vocational Education and Training in 2008.
Note: — = not available.

There is considerable space to enhance the quality and relevance of training programs in the Republic of Yemen. These remain strongly supply-driven, as the programs, including their curricula, are designed with little input from the private sector. Formal mechanisms to facilitate the engagement of private businesses need to be developed. In addition, the design of training programs tends not to be informed by data on labor market needs. The lack of functioning labor market information systems and needs assessment studies means that data are not available on the types of skills in demand in the labor market; this in turn hampers the design of market-responsive training programs. Quality control is also limited: the Republic of Yemen lacks a vocational qualification framework that would set norms and quality standards for training curricula and certification and ensure a more effective signaling of skills.

Monitoring and evaluation systems are poor. The MoTVET keeps records of program outputs in terms of the number of beneficiaries, but data on the outcomes of training programs in the short, medium, or long term are unavailable. The ministry does not implement tracer studies to track the employment or earnings status of program beneficiaries. The effectiveness and impact of training programs are therefore largely unassessed.

Employment Services

Employment services in the Republic of Yemen are largely underdeveloped. Though the MoSAL has employment offices across the country, the services they offer are of poor quality and have extremely limited outreach. Job matching seems to be essentially paper-based and informal; employment offices do not provide any electronic labor exchange platform, nor do they have automated job-matching systems or provide counseling or guidance services to job seekers. Also, unlike most countries in the MENA region, the MoSAL has no labor market information system and is therefore unable to gather information on labor market needs and trends. As a result of these multiple deficiencies and limitations, employment services cater to an extremely small share of job seekers: it is estimated that 2.4 percent of employees found their job through public employment offices in 2006 (ILO 2009).

Lessons Learned and Policy Recommendations

The development of national-level policy and regulatory frameworks, backed by enhanced institutional coordination across public agencies and ministries, would enhance the relevance and quality of ALMPs in the Republic of Yemen. In particular, there is a need to develop and implement an integrated labor strategy that would (a) set policy directions and milestones for the effort to develop full and productive employment in the Republic of Yemen; (b) distribute roles and responsibilities among public agencies and ministries for the provision of ALMPs; (c) set up mechanisms for institutional coordination (e.g., steering committees) and the integration of different categories of ALMPs; and (d) identify sustainable financing mechanisms.

Steps should be taken to develop and implement regulations for the delivery of ALMPs. In particular, the quality of training programs, whether offered by public or private training institutes, would strongly benefit from a national vocational qualification framework, setting standards with respect to curricula, skills acquisition, and certification. Strengthened regulation would ensure better quality standards for the services provided to job seekers. It would also provide clearer signals to employers regarding the skills and capacities of job seekers.

While support for job creation and income generation will remain a critical aspect of ALMP provision in the Republic of Yemen, more needs to be done to enhance employability of the labor force. Given high poverty rates and the prevalence of low-quality, low-paying jobs, short-term measures to create jobs and provide income support through public works and entrepreneurship programs need to be sustained. These programs serve as important, albeit temporary, safety nets. Yet in the medium to long term, a stronger focus needs to be placed on investing in the skills of the Yemeni labor force and providing labor intermediation to boost access to private sector employment. This calls for increased investments in training and employment services. These can be provided as stand-alone programs, but they can also be associated with public works and small enterprise programs, so that the latter serve not only as safety nets but also as bridges to employment.

Expanding the scope and coverage of ALMPs, with particular attention to equity issues, would allow public agencies to cater to more job seekers and better respond to their needs. Employment and training programs in the Republic of Yemen are limited in scope and in the types of services they provide. There is considerable room to offer more integrated and diversified employment services that combine job matching and screening, career guidance and counseling, and skills training. In particular, the needs of private businesses and job seekers could be better served by diversifying the types of training programs provided, with more specializations and more on-the-job training. The scaling up and diversification of services would help broaden the coverage of ALMPs. Any enhancement of coverage should take into account equity issues, as some groups, in particular women, tend be underserved.

Strengthening and scaling up the human, technical, and financial capacities and resources of public agencies in charge of ALMP provision would allow them to provide more and better services. The delivery of employment services and training programs is strongly hindered by the insufficient capacity and resources of the MoSAL and the MoTVET. Though some investments in hard infrastructure might be needed, the major impediment to delivery of ALMPs lies in the limited soft infrastructure of these public agencies. Enhancing efficiency and equity in the delivery of ALMPs requires efforts to (a) reform governance systems to be less centralized and develop coordination mechanisms with other public and nonpublic actors; (b) define sustainable financing schemes for institutions and their programs; and (c) build up human capacity and provide financial and career incentives to staff.

Upgraded data systems would allow policy makers to better design, monitor, and evaluate ALMPs. First, the establishment of labor market information systems would facilitate the design of evidence-based ALMPs. Currently, the provision of employment services is not informed by labor market needs. ALMPs provided under the Social Development Fund make somewhat more use of data, though policy makers rely on census and household surveys and do not have access to regularly updated labor market information. Second, data systems to track program implementation and impact need to be put in place. Available data focus on program outputs, mainly numbers of beneficiaries. Data on employment and earning outcomes are needed to assess the impact and relevance of ALMPs in the Republic of Yemen.

Finally, building partnerships with private businesses would provide opportunities to leverage their resources and expertise and ensure more demand-driven ALMPs. The involvement of the private sector in the design and delivery of ALMPs in the Republic of Yemen remains very low, and awareness within the private sector of programs offered by public agencies (in particular, employment services) is limited. Building stronger partnerships between public providers of ALMPs and private businesses would help enhance the quality of services provided and their relevance to the actual needs of the labor market. Equally important, it would build trust in the programs on the part of private businesses and thus potentially increase their engagement with program beneficiaries.

Notes

1. For more details on livelihood strategies in urban and rural areas in the Republic of Yemen, see World Bank (2007).
2. Its programs also include community development programs to facilitate access to basic social and economic services, as well as capacity-building programs to support community mobilization.

References

CSO (Central Statistical Organization). 2008. *2008 Statistical Yearbook*. Sana'a: CSO.

Gatti, R., D. F. Angel-Urdinola, J. Silva, and A. Bodor. 2012. *Striving for Better Jobs: The Challenge of Informality in the Middle East and North Africa*. Washington, DC: World Bank.

ILO (International Labour Organization). 2008a. *Promoting Decent Work and Gender Equality in Yemen*. Country Brief 3. Beirut: ILO Regional Office for Arab States.

———. 2008b. *Republic of Yemen: Decent Work Country Programme 2008–2010*. Beirut: ILO Regional Office for Arab States.

———. 2009. *Women in Technical and Vocational Education and Training in Yemen*. Policy Brief 5. Beirut: ILO Regional Office for Arab States.

MoTVET (Ministry of Technical and Vocational Education and Training). 2004. *Technical Education and Vocational Training Strategic Development Plan*. Sana'a.

———. 2008. *Annual Report*. Sana'a.

Recovery and Development Consortium. 2010. *DFID Yemen Social Fund for Development: Impact Evaluation*. Maxwell Stamp PLC, COWI A/S, and Interaction in Development. http://sfd.sfd-yemen.org/uploads/issues/2010%20Impact%20Evaluation%20 Report-20120924-113801.pdf.

SFD (Social Fund for Development, Republic of Yemen). 2008. *2008 Annual Report*. Sana'a.

———. 2010a. *2010 Annual Report*. Sana'a.

———. 2010b. *Social Fund for Development Newsletter, no. 49 (January–March)*. Sana'a.

———. 2010c. *Social Fund for Development Newsletter, no. 52 (October–December)*. Sana'a.

World Bank. 2007. *Republic of Yemen: Country Social Analysis*. Washington, DC: World Bank.

———. 2010. *World Development Indicators 2010*. Washington, DC: World Bank.

Environmental Benefits Statement

The World Bank is committed to reducing its environmental footprint. In support of this commitment, the Office of the Publisher leverages electronic publishing options and print-on-demand technology, which is located in regional hubs worldwide. Together, these initiatives enable print runs to be lowered and shipping distances decreased, resulting in reduced paper consumption, chemical use, greenhouse gas emissions, and waste.

The Office of the Publisher follows the recommended standards for paper use set by the Green Press Initiative. Whenever possible, books are printed on 50% to 100% postconsumer recycled paper, and at least 50% of the fiber in our book paper is either unbleached or bleached using Totally Chlorine Free (TCF), Processed Chlorine Free (PCF), or Enhanced Elemental Chlorine Free (EECF) processes.

More information about the Bank's environmental philosophy can be found at http://crinfo.worldbank.org/crinfo/environmental_responsibility/index.html.

green press
INITIATIVE